Outside, the Sky is Blue

By Christina Patterson

The Art of Not Falling Apart
Outside, the Sky is Blue

Christina
Patterson

Outside, the Sky is Blue

A family memoir

TINDER
PRESS

First published in Great Britain in 2022 by Tinder Press
An imprint of HEADLINE PUBLISHING GROUP

1

Cataloguing in Publication Data is available from the British Library

Hardback ISBN 978 1 4722 8262 0
Trade paperback ISBN 978 1 4722 8263 7

Typeset in Scala by CC Book Production

Printed and bound in Great Britain by Clays Ltd, Elcograf S.p.A.

FSC
www.fsc.org
MIX
Paper from
responsible sources
FSC® C104740

Headline's policy is to use papers that are natural, renewable and
recyclable products and made from wood grown in well-managed forests
and other controlled sources. The logging and manufacturing processes
are expected to conform to the environmental regulations
of the country of origin.

HEADLINE PUBLISHING GROUP
An Hachette UK Company
Carmelite House
50 Victoria Embankment
London EC4Y 0DZ

www.tinderpress.co.uk
www.headline.co.uk
www.hachette.co.uk

Contents

Part III

Part IV

This is a work of non-fiction,
but some names and details have been changed.

Prologue

I'd forgotten about the baboons. But I never forgot the lions and that feeling when the last metal gate behind us slid shut. My father refused to wind the windows up until the very last moment. He said we needed the fresh air. I thought the smell of our flesh might float through the gate and they would be ready to pounce, ready to smash the glass of our Morris Marina and sink their teeth into my too plump thighs. When I glimpse the first lion, on the screen in front of me, it all comes flooding back. It's not a lion, in fact, but a lioness. The camera wobbles as she lopes up to the car. In the corner of the windscreen, you can see the sticker with the dolphin. Windsor Safari Park. A fun day out for all the family. Press your nose against the glass and gaze into the eyes of a creature that could tear your limbs from your torso in the time it takes to let out a scream.

It's lucky I didn't know about the crunching. I've always

loved crunchy foods. Crisps. Nuts. The skin of a roast chicken. The crackling on a joint of pork. It's pretty clear from the figure on the screen, now eating candyfloss in front of a monkey cage, that I like my food. But the crunching of a carcass by a lion is almost enough to put you off it. I heard it in Zambia, almost forty years after that first glimpse of a lion. We were summoned to a grassy bank to watch a lion with its prey. It was eating a gazelle. Every crack and crunch of bone seemed to echo round the bush and bounce off the sky.

It's the monkey cage that reminds me of the baboons. Caroline and I are standing in front of it, in matching pink capes. My mother hated sewing, but she'd learnt to make her own clothes as a teenager and would whip up matching outfits for her daughters, after a day's teaching and an evening's cooking, marking and washing up. Caroline's matchstick legs poke down from the pink tartan. Mine are sturdy in white tights that show off my red shoes. Tom's smart in a navy raincoat, over a navy shirt and navy shorts. Navy is the default colour in our family. My mother is wearing a navy jacket and navy trousers. We are a pink and navy family. Two pink girls, a navy boy and a navy wife. The candyfloss my father has treated us to is also pink. We're licking and nibbling as we watch the monkeys swing from tree to tree.

Caroline's eyes are wide as she turns to our mother and then back to the creatures with eyes even bigger than hers. We're all fascinated by the monkeys, but not as fascinated as we were by the baboons. We couldn't help giggling when we saw their bright red bottoms. They looked so bare! They looked so rude. We loved the way they lolloped across the grass, buttocks stuck in the air. We didn't know that the red bottoms were a trick to attract a mate, like red lipstick or skin-tight jeans. Caroline was twelve, but young for her age. Tom was nine. I was seven. We didn't know anything about attracting a mate. My parents made it look easy, as if love was something that just happened to you, like growing out of your clothes and shoes, something that turned you into a grown-up.

We were shocked to see some of the baboons on top of each other, their red bottoms pumping as they let out loud yelps. We were even more shocked to see some of them ambling towards us and shrieked when they started leaping and bouncing on the car. We gasped as a skinny, hairy arm reached down, grabbed a windscreen wiper and snapped it off. My father froze. The next moment, the engine roared as he tried to steer his car away from tiny, sneaky fingers. 'John,' said my mother in the tone she saved for emergencies. 'Daddy!' we squealed, half scared, half thrilled that the naughty baboons had cheeked him. He drove in silence until the gates clanged shut. 'Well,' he said, when we were finally free. 'Let's just hope it doesn't rain.'

And it didn't. Not that day, when my father's old brown cine camera captured the lions and the monkeys, and the children, but not the baboons. It captured the elephants, too. Here's Caroline, rapt in concentration as she strokes an elephant. Here's Tom, grinning as he waves handfuls of grass in front of its trunk. Here am I, skipping in front of the elephant, bunches quivering and with a toothy smile. I look happy. I am happy. I'm with my family and we're having a lovely time. To one side, there's my mother, smiling, as always, elegant, as always. My father, as so often, remains behind the camera. He rarely joins the cast of his family, but when he does, he has the air of a captain inspecting his troops.

In the next frame we're having a picnic. The sun is out now and Caroline and I have taken off our pink capes. Behind us, Tom is kicking a ball. You can see that his world has shrunk to that ball. My mother is kneeling on the blue and white plaid picnic rug, handing something round in a Tupperware box. Caroline and I are sitting close to each other. She leans forward to pick a dandelion. The camera jumps and now we're walking together and holding hands. I can't quite believe it now, but my sister and I are actually holding hands.

I can spend hours replaying my childhood. I do spend hours replaying my childhood. It's odd, in a way, because I was the one who was never all that interested in the past. The films I like most are the ones I'm not in, the ones with the beautiful couple in exotic places, a glimpse of a faraway world. They start with my mother in a garden, slender and gorgeous in a dress that could have been designed to show off her tiny waist. Next to her, there's a young Thai woman, carrying a toddler in a yellow dress. Caroline has a topknot. She's wriggling. She's grinning. On their right is a wall of lush vegetation, a tangled mass of bougainvillea and bamboo. My mother reaches up and plucks a pink flower. She hands it to Caroline, who looks at it carefully and then pulls it towards her nose.

A few moments later, she's standing on a mound. There are palm trees and a glimpse of water behind her, and she's fringed by giant glossy leaves. In front of her, with his back towards the camera, is a tall, dark man in loose white trousers and a baggy cotton shirt. He's leaning towards her, holding out his arms. My sister is hopping up and down. She pauses, as if to gather energy, and then hurls herself towards him and my father scoops her up. She giggles. He smiles, a smile that cracks the corners of his eyes.

Now, we're in a different bit of the garden, with a temple in the background and a red bridge over a tiny canal. Caroline's running around in a pink check dress and my mother looks as if she's off to a cocktail party, in one of the Thai silk dresses she had made from a Dior design. The camera pans across the garden, the bridge, the canal, the palm trees, an expanse of water that looks like a lake. In the next frame, in another corner of the garden, my mother is with a group of elegant women. They are sitting on wicker chairs, sipping from tiny cups. My mother's head is tilted. Her smile is regal. She looks as if she was born to preside over this garden, this kingdom, this Eden where everyone smiles.

And now there are paddy fields, mountains, temples with golden gables, a glimpse of my mother and my sister staring out of a window at a view that's jumping up and down. We're on a train. We're on a journey. It's the five-week journey home. There's a train, like the one in *The Railway Children*, shiny black and belting out steam. Perhaps it's the train that takes us to the ocean liner, a gleaming white vessel with the words SS *Chusan* in black letters on its side. Now we're on deck. My mother is holding Caroline's hand as they both gaze out at the shore.

The Post-it note on the video box fills in some of the details. My mother had all the old cine films made into videos and gave us each a full set. 'Jan 61' the note says in her neat primary school teacher handwriting. 'Farewell Bangkok. Padang Besar, Singapore, Chusan, Penang. Feb 61. Leave the East, Ceylon, Bombay, Suez, Marseilles, Cassis and Gibraltar.' From the footage, I can just about work out the stops. The best is Ceylon, or what was then Ceylon. It must be Colombo Zoo. There are monkeys everywhere, but this time they're running free. Caroline is giggling at a monkey gobbling a banana. Now she's stroking an elephant. Now she's chatting to pink pelicans and now staring, frozen, at a man holding a python. And now she's playing with my father in a swimming pool, wearing four rubber rings. It's a shock to see my father's face looming at the camera. He's so young, so athletic, and his slightly crooked smile is so sweet. He's gazing at his daughter with such intensity that I almost feel I shouldn't look. Suddenly, he plunges down into the water and as he surfaces Caroline squeals. He gathers her up, with all four of her rubber rings, and clutches her in his arms.

In all these scenes, my sister looks so happy, and so beautiful, it catches at the back of my throat.

That's the end of the East, the end of the journey, and after a summer of English beaches and lawns, we're in Rome. Caroline's on the Spanish Steps, eating an ice cream. Now she's on a little horse in a park. I recognise it. It's the Villa Borghese, just round the corner from my first home. Now she's with a friend on a swing, in a communal garden that seems to be mostly made up of crazy paving. In that garden, there's an endless stream of visitors: grandmothers, uncles, Auntie Lisbeth and my parents' friends, sipping coffee on the chic, new garden furniture and keeping an eye on babies in prams.

Suddenly, there's another baby, scowling in a christening robe, with plump cheeks, a pug nose and a smooth head dusted with down. Caroline leans over to kiss him in his pram, and the scowl slips into a sloppy smile. Soon, the baby is clapping in a high chair, inching along the crazy paving, grabbing on to some iron bars on a window, and propelling himself around in something that looks like a Zimmer frame. Now this chubby toddler has a shock of blond hair. He's playing in the sandpit, in an apron with a red donkey on it.

Sometimes he's with Caroline, sometimes with his elegant mother, and sometimes with his dashing father, on a beach, in a park, by a fountain, in a forest. Now you see them by the leaning tower in Pisa. Now they're by the fountain in Piazza Navona in Rome.

I'm fascinated by this glamorous couple with their charming, photogenic children and wide circle of friends, all with photogenic children of their own. I'm jealous. There, I've said it. I'm jealous. You're not meant to envy your parents, but I do. Or perhaps I should say that I did. There's been too much envy in my life. Too much of the green-eyed monster that doth mock the meat it feeds on. It poisons. I promise you, it seeps into your veins.

It's strange how you can watch films of your family and have so many different bursts of memory and feeling that it can feel like a whole childhood compressed. Oh yes, I remember that picnic. That's where we had the choc ices. What happened to roast chicken crisps? Mum looks amazing in that suit. Dad has sideburns! And he's in a yellow T-shirt! He never wore T-shirts. Oh yes, where was that abbey? That's the time Mum forgot our swimsuits! And a group of bikers turned up and we all had to take turns to climb out of the lake in her navy cardigan and Tom's Chelsea football shorts. God, look at the collars. Such enormous collars! Mum's wearing such a short dress. My haircut is terrible. I look so fat.

In quite a few of the films, our faces aren't clear. But

suddenly, in Wales, they are. We're on a train, I think it might be the Ffestiniog, a tiny locomotive going up a mountain in Snowdonia. The camera must be quite close to us, because you can almost see into our eyes. Caroline must be thirteen. Tom must be ten. I must be eight. Our skin looks so smooth and clear. Later, we could all have featured in medical textbooks, and I'm not joking. We all have blue eyes, but Caroline's are darker than Tom's and mine. She's dark, like Dad. We're fair, like Mum. Caroline's smile is sweet, so sweet, so sweet. I could honestly say her eyes are shining. Tom's smiling. I'm smiling. Outside, the sky is blue, the sun is high and a lake glitters.

Two years later, and we're on rocks. We're on rocks in Copenhagen, by the statue of the Little Mermaid. I barely look at her, but I should, because it's not all that many years until I feel I *am* the little mermaid, paying for something that hasn't been explained by walking on knives. I'm scrabbling around on the rocks, but trying to get ahead, away from my family, away from Caroline, who's wearing a huge sun hat and my mother's sunglasses and very flared trousers and a long-sleeved shirt. My skinny sister is no longer skinny. Her tummy sticks out. She's walking stiffly. She looks as if she's the one walking on knives. I don't want to look at her. I'm wearing a blue T-shirt with the word 'CHRISTINA' on it. Look at me. I'm here, too. Don't look at her. Please don't look at her. Yes, I'm fine. Honestly, I'm fine. No, that's not my sister.

* * *

I've got to stop looking at the films because there's so much to do. There are piles and piles of forms to fill in. There's a whole house to clear. There's a whole garage full of boxes. It's only two and a half years since we cleared the last house, the family home for more than fifty years. The last time I ate there with Tom was the day we got the news and sat together at the old kitchen table, eating pizza, drinking red wine and learning to talk about our mother in the past tense.

Tom's a whizz with wine. I'll try that again. Tom was a whizz with wine. Was. Was. Was.

There are hundreds of albums. I'm the only one who never put my photos in albums. Mine are just lying around in boxes, waiting to be sorted out. They're waiting for a rainy day. There never is a rainy day. I'm a journalist. I can't do anything without a deadline.

I don't like that word any more.

My mother wrote 'throw out' on many of her box files, but many of them weren't thrown out. My mother documented almost everything. She took photos all the time. She wrote a diary every day. She wrote letters and kept the letters she got.

Tom had my mother's diaries and letters and albums. He had my father's diaries and letters and albums. He had some of Caroline's books and photos and papers. In his house, there are pictures and ornaments and bits of furniture from the family home. Oh, and there are all his own photos and letters and papers and possessions, of course.

In a box in his garage, I find the apron with the red donkey. It's in a box with a tiny vest, a Scout shirt covered in badges, a Chelsea scarf and a Chelsea rosette. It's the donkey that makes me gulp down air and clamp my jaws shut. It's OK, I think, to whimper like a dog, but it's not OK for my brother's neighbours to hear me scream.

I put the apron on the pile to throw out. It feels like committing a sacrilege, but what else can I do with it? I don't know what to do with all this stuff. Who else will want to see it? Who else will want to see mine?

Just me now. I honestly don't think anyone will want to see mine.

I loved my parents, but they were wrong. They were wrong to make it look easy: this love lark, this having a family lark, this combining it all with a brilliant career lark. I thought it was what you had to do to feel like a grown-up. Perhaps it's why I still don't feel like a grown-up now.

I'm sorry, Mum. I failed. I'm sorry, Dad. I didn't manage it. None of us did, but I think you both thought I was the one who should have. I promise you, I can swear on a Bible if you like, it wasn't because I didn't try.

Part I

Chapter 1

Blueberry Soup

When Abba won the Eurovision Song Contest, my mother swallowed a peanut and nearly choked. We had all been eating peanuts, but I had stopped because I wanted Agnetha's outfit so much it was beginning to feel like a stitch. The sparkly bomber jacket! The blue satin knickerbockers, stretched taut across her neat tummy and her perfect, rounded bum! I couldn't quite imagine myself in it. At ten, I was still, as my father said, 'solid', but I could certainly imagine myself in the silver platform boots. I wanted to look like Agnetha, sing like Agnetha, dance like Agnetha. I wanted to flash perfect, white teeth as I sang about the station my father went to twice a day. But it wasn't just me. There were ten people in our sitting room that night. Perhaps Carl Johan didn't count, because he was just a toddler and didn't really know what was going on. The rest of us did and we were grinning and cheering because Sweden had won.

The timing couldn't have been better. My father had gone to Tilbury that morning to pick up Auntie Lisbeth and Uncle Hans, and our white-blond cousins Peter, Anna and little Carl Johan, all in matching blue corduroy suits. It meant there were six Swedes in the house, three half-Swedes and a Brit who liked Swedes so much he'd married one. My parents had given up their bed for Auntie Lisbeth and Uncle Hans. For the next two weeks, they would sleep on the sofa. Anna and Peter had the bunks in the room Tom and I used to share. Carl Johan had a cot next to them. I was back with Tom in his tiny room. Caroline would stay on her own. It was better for Caroline to be on her own.

My mother had planned a packed schedule of trips to National Trust houses, walks at Wisley Gardens, Winkworth Arboretum and the Chantries, outings to museums and trips to tea shops at Gomshall and Shere. She had filled the freezer with casseroles and used up every square inch of the fridge. Mince for spaghetti bolognese. Bacon for corn chowder. Chicken for the curry she served with dried coconut, sliced banana and Uncle Ben's rice. My mother had mapped out every meal and every moment, but even she couldn't have planned this win at this time, this sweet victory that put her country on the map.

It was our country, too, of course, our part-time country, our other home. The only slight hitch was that we didn't speak Swedish. Auntie Berit and Auntie Gun, who had both married Brits and lived nearby, were shocked that we didn't speak Swedish. They weren't real aunts, but we called them aunts, and their children wrote perfect thank-you letters in perfect Swedish. But Caroline had already sometimes mixed up English and Thai and now she and Tom sometimes muddled their English and Italian. When my mother tried adding Swedish, they started to stutter. So she stuck to basics: Swedish prayers at bedtime, which we only vaguely understood, *tack för maten* (thank you for the food) at the end of every meal and *tack så hemskt mycket* (thank you *so* much) in response to any gift from a Swedish relative. Tom and I had brief learning bursts. I still have the battered book: Hugo's *Swedish in Three Months,* pink to match my bell bottoms. Lesson Three: which is his pipe? The knife is mine. The colour of the flower is beautiful.

Nothing marred our love of Sweden. Not the sea sickness that always gripped me almost as soon as we set sail. Not the slimy seaweed that I was scared to brush against. Not even the stinky outdoor toilet, where you had to light a candle to see anything, but tried not to look down at the sludge that rose until it almost hit you, a putrid stew of rust-coloured liquid and sausage-shaped turds. We went there every summer, except the year my parents said we couldn't afford it and stayed in a Forestry Commission cabin in Cornwall where it rained and we rowed. Later, my father admitted that he sometimes resented spending his precious leave making small talk in Swedish to my mother's literal-minded mother and her maiden aunts.

But he wasn't the one who had given up his country. You have to see family. You're lucky to *have* family, whatever their flaws.

I feel like I win when I lose, sang Agnetha, and we certainly felt we had won. We counted the days to Sweden and were unusually obedient when the alarm went off and it was time for my father to pack the car and us to clean the house. Housework was usually quite low on my mother's list of priorities. Like me, she needed a deadline, and would rush around to clear up before guests. But when we were in Sweden Mrs Young would water the plants. Mrs Young lived next door. Her house was a testament to the power of Jif. So my mother issued instructions. I usually got the bathroom and the downstairs loo. For years, it was pale pink and I would rub until my arm was sore to bring on the holiday and bring out the shine. Sometime in the seventies the pink gave way to avocado. I think that was after Abba's victory, when I had their posters all over my walls. That was before *Abba: The Movie*, which I saw on the boat to Sweden and, more appropriately, Abba: The Soap. As in, a bar of soap, shaped like a cassette.

I suppose it was a ship, but we always called it 'the boat'. We'd arrive jammed between tins of Chunky Chicken and packets of cornflakes and Vesta beef curry. Food in Sweden, said my mother, was far, far too expensive, and we'd all look forward to our meatballs at IKEA and our annual hot dog overlooking the beach. When we got to Tilbury, and later Harwich, we'd join a queue. Somehow, our queue was always the slowest. Every few minutes, my father would get out of the car, glare at the cars that were moving and let out a long, deep sigh. We knew then that we couldn't ask for another Spangle or another Black Jack. We knew, in fact, that we should hardly breathe. Finally, a man would signal and the car ahead of us would begin to inch forwards and we'd be clattering our way up the metal ramp, waiting for the clink of chains on our car and then going down, down, deep into the ship until you couldn't go any further down. There we would find our cabin.

Once we'd dumped our bags, we'd find our 'camp': a set of chairs that would be our base for the next two days. My mother would lay out the felt pens and paper and a pile of Agatha Christies. I still can't hear the name Hercule Poirot without thinking of a grey horizon bobbing up and down. If the weather allowed, we'd spend time on deck, shivering on deck chairs and gazing at the waves. When my mother's Thermos flask ran out, we'd go down to the cafeteria and stare at the blond families piling their plates with salmon or meatballs and chips. My mother would queue up for two cups of coffee and then serve up the picnic she had brought: cheese rolls and Penguins. We loved the penguins in the ad. When you p-p-p-pick up a Penguin there's so much more to enjoy. And my mother did enjoy it all. She would sip her coffee and take a tiny bite of her Penguin, or her little cake, and let out a satisfied sigh. She could have lived on bread and cheese and coffee and something sweet. If you add wine and crisps, so could I.

I wish I could recapture that feeling, of sitting in a waiting room on an ocean, ticking off the minutes till the highlight of our year. It's strange I feel this so strongly, because I often felt, and was, sick. In later years, when money was less tight, my father would treat the other three to the ship's smorgasbord and they would gorge on salmon and herring and Jansson's Temptation, the potato dish with onion and anchovy we had on Christmas Eve, while I nibbled dry bread. But the sickness, the waiting, the tossing on the bunk was all worth it for that first glimpse of land. First, a tiny island, just a big rock with a red wooden house. Then a skyline, a mass of buildings, more rocks. It was early morning, six or seven. In my memory, the sun is out and the sky is blue. We're all standing on deck, watching the land approach. My father turns round and smiles.

My father would tell us all to be quiet as he got to grips with driving on the right. We'd sit in silence as he steered us out of the harbour, out of the suburbs and on to the road where the fields with cows stretched down to the sea. We were all waiting for the first glimpse of the little bridge with the steel arches. 'Sydney Bridge!' we'd all yell out, and my parents would turn to each other and smile. Then we were at the café where we always stopped. It was time for coffee for my parents, the strong Swedish coffee my mother missed all year. There was *vetebröd* for all of us, the sweet yeast bread that tasted of cinnamon and was dusted with sugar pearls and almonds. And for each of us, a bottle of *läsk*, the fizzy drink that tasted of berries or blood orange or pear. Hang the expense. We were on holiday.

Our cousins would be waiting at the mailboxes, at the end of the dirt track through the forest. It was the point where it opened out to corn fields, the wheat the colour you would get if silver and gold paint were mixed. The fields were fringed with banks of cornflowers and marguerites. At the end of one of them, you could see the red wooden mill with the pond and the stream where we played Poohsticks. '*Hej, hej!*' we all shrieked as we leapt out to hug and kiss them and then they followed us as we drove past the cream cottage, and the yellow cottage, and then, finally, reached the red wooden cottage that will for ever be the symbol of my other country, my mother country, my other world.

My parents bought it with *Mormor* – literally, 'mother's mother', and with Auntie Lisbeth and Uncle Hans, in 1964. In fact, it turns out that foreigners couldn't part-own Swedish property, so they didn't have a formal stake in it, but they did split the cost, which was 24,000 kronor, then about £1,650. Many Swedes have a *sommarstuga*, a summer cottage, usually a small wooden cabin near a lake or a beach. Ours was two rooms with a galley kitchen, an outside earth closet that was emptied by the council, and a single cold tap. Mormor eventually had a storeroom made into two tiny rooms with bunks. It was basic. It was beautiful. It was paradise.

And so began our golden days. *Filmjölk* for breakfast, the tart yoghurt my mother sent us off with loose change to buy from the woman at the edge of the forest, and sometimes *blåbärssoppa*, a kind of blueberry soup. I would practise the words and then smile politely when I didn't understand the reply. In Sweden, I wanted to be Swedish. In England, I wanted to be the same as everyone else. Once, my friend Lucy asked me about my mother's accent. What do you mean, my mother has an accent? And then I heard it, not an accent, but a song. My mother speaks in song.

Once we had rinsed our bowls, we were released into our kingdom: the garden with the lingonberries and the hammock and the pump where my mother helped us wash our hair and the forest on the other side of the dirt track. We roamed in it and built camps in it, and with Cecilia, whose family had the cottage next door, I had mock tea parties in it, perched on tree trunks that smelled of the moss and pine cones at our feet. In the evenings, when my father took us all for walks, we would search for golf balls among the pine needles. The forest was on the edge of a golf course, but when you were in it, you felt you were in a hidden, secret world.

I suppose each family has its own rituals, for those weeks when they're snatched from their normal lives and suspended in time. I sometimes think I could measure out my childhood in ours. They were holy rites, those sugar-flecked buns, those hot dogs on the rocks, those walks with eyes peeled for the flash of a ball in a nest of moss. They were the warp and weft of something I have made golden, perhaps because I want there to be something golden left.

The beach, of course, *was* golden. It was just a bit too far to walk to, so we'd leave the car at the edge of the sand dunes, near the bikes that were all left unlocked. There was a long line of clogs. Everyone left their clogs before clambering up, up to the top of the dunes and then charging down to freedom and the endless stretch of sand. If the weather allowed, we'd spend all day on it, playing hide-and-seek in the sand dunes, making angels in the sand and running in and out of the waves. One year, my parents said they would pay us 10 *öre* for each jellyfish we could rescue from the sea. That's about half a halfpenny. Don't touch the red ones, said my mother. They can sting and hurt you. Sometimes, we brushed against one in the water and my mother would kiss the red welts and tell us that salt water would heal it, which it did. I toiled for hours, for days, scooping quivering balls of blue blubber and laying them at the water's edge. I can't remember when it hit me that this task could go on for ever, that I could be scooping blubber out of the sea for the rest of my life, and there would still be more.

Sometimes, we'd play mini-golf, hitting balls up ramps,

round metal circles and through tunnels so that the ball plopped on to a small circle of green felt. Sometimes we'd swim at Simlångsgården, the lake my mother used to swim in as a child and where her parents once thought they'd lost her, as they saw that she had taken the boat to row across it, alone. It made me proud to think my mother had crossed that lake alone. That was the last summer she had with her father, the summer he made a secret trail in the forest, with tiny white arrows for her to spot and follow.

Once every summer, we'd go to IKEA. My mother would gaze at sofas, we'd all eat meatballs and we'd travel back to England sitting on cardboard flat-packs. That was the first ever IKEA, in Småland. My mother went there with Tom three years ago. They discovered it's now a museum.

I felt a jolt when Tom told me that. I can't quite believe that a chunk of my childhood is now a museum. And now it feels as if the rest of it is locked, in boxes, in his garage.

We could tell from my father's frozen smile that he dreaded the coffee parties with the elderly relatives, at the cottage and at *Wäster*, the wooden house in the old quarter of Halmstad where Mormor and her five siblings had grown up. *Morbror* Arthur and *Moster* Agnes still lived there. They had never moved or married. *Morbror* Nisse and *Moster* Esther lived in the house next door. Neither had a bathroom, an inside loo, hot water or a fridge. They dressed in their Sunday best for us, the men in suits and ties, the women in their smartest frocks. They couldn't speak a word of English and our few words of Swedish didn't get us far. While my father wrestled his Swedish into polite questions, and racked up the minutes he could have spent on the beach, we focused on the cakes. There would be a whole table of cakes: *vetebröd,* because you always had *vetebröd, pepparkakor,* the ginger biscuits that tasted of spice, *sockerkaka,* the sponge cake with the hole in the middle, and *kringlor,* the bullet-shaped cakes wrapped in marzipan and rolled in coconut. When you thought you couldn't eat any more, they'd bring out a giant *prinsesstårta* slathered in cream.

At the end of the holiday, when we came to say goodbye, they gave us each a paper bag. Inside, there were chocolates shaped like flying saucers and packets of red liquorice, tangled up like spaghetti. My mother once told us that they saved up for these treats all year.

Sweetness and light. That's what Sweden is for me. Cakes and sunshine and coffee and cornflowers and the smell of pine cones. Golden sand and golden wheat fields and a sudden glimpse of land. The first taste of blueberries. The first fizz of *läsk.* A blue sky with puffy clouds like the sky in a child's painting. A world that's unsullied, without shadows or fear.

My mother. That's what Sweden is for me. My sunny mother, who loved coffee and cakes and conversation and sunshine and beauty and flowers. When she was in hospital and I was sleeping at the family home in Nelson Gardens, I went for a run in some woods at the edge of the park. I saw the pine cones and picked one up. I placed it under my nostrils and breathed in the smell of my childhood summers. I took it to her in hospital and thought that if she inhaled it, it would give her life, it would give her strength. I honestly thought it might.

It was my mother who taught me to believe in magic. Every Christmas, when we made *pepparkakor,* or ate the ones she bought from the Christmas market at the Swedish church, she reminded us that you had to take one and place it in the palm of your hand and press it. If it broke into three pieces, you got a wish. Once I asked her if the wish really would come true. She was silent for a moment and then she said that if, for example, you were ill, you would get better.

Years later, when I was ill, I remembered that. It was true. That time, it was true.

In a box in Tom's hall cupboard I find the old Christmas decorations. For years, we moaned because we wanted shiny baubles like the ones on our friends' Christmas trees, and coloured lights and tinsel. We had boring white lights and our decorations were made of wood and straw. There was no fairy at the top of the tree, but a big straw star. There were no big, fat Santas, just the *tomtar,* Santa's little helpers made out of wisps of red wool. In the box I find the *tomtar* and some little wooden stars. At the bottom of the box, I find the old straw star, but its points have nearly all been broken off. And I find some woven hearts. Yes, in my brother's hall cupboard, I really do find a box of hearts.

The candles started at Advent. We always, always lit candles for Advent. I still light candles for Advent. My Christmas decorations are like the ones I grew up with. They are made of straw and felt and wisps of red wool. I could no more swap them for baubles and tinsel than rip out my tendons or change my blood.

But the big day for candles was Sankta Lucia. That was twelve days before Christmas, on 13 December. It was the festival of light, my mother said, when the eldest daughter of the house was meant to wake the family up, in a long white dress and a crown of candles. She had to sing the Lucia song and carry the tray with the coffee and cakes. There were *lussekatter*, the saffron buns my father said were too dry, and *pepparkakor*, ready for us all to snap and eat. In the early years, Caroline and I both wore white nighties and tinsel in our hair and Tom wore a pointy hat with gold stars, like a wizard. One year, Auntie Lisbeth sent us a proper Lucia crown. It didn't have real candles, like the ones my mother had when she was a girl, but the candles looked quite real, and when you twisted each little circle of plastic a glass flame flickered into life.

Caroline didn't want to wear the crown, so I wore it. When I put the flickering circle of light on my head, for a moment I felt like Cinderella when she finds the shoe fits. I never really knew the words of the Lucia song, but I pretended to sing them anyway. The song, in the translation I've found, talks about the 'shadows brooding in our dark house'. Then Sankta Lucia arrives on the doorstep, wearing white and a crown of light. 'Darkness,' the song ends, 'shall take flight soon,' and a 'new day will rise again from the rosy sky.'

I believe that. After everything, I believe that. I really do.

Chapter 2

From Old Fairy Tales

My parents met on a hill in Heidelberg. It was, they always told us, love at first sight. My father was tall, dark and handsome, with a fierce haircut and intense green eyes. My mother was tall, too: six foot from the age of thirteen. In the photos, he looks like a film star, but she looks mousy and shy. It was love that changed the contours of her face, love that gave her the allure she never lost.

My father was twenty-one. He had spent the summer visiting Greek islands on a scholarship, and was in his final year reading classics at Cambridge, on his way to a double first. My mother was eighteen. She had spent the summer working on a mushroom farm and was about to read modern languages at Sweden's Cambridge, Lund. They spoke in German, but my mother's German was much better. She was in the class above my father on their summer course, but he somehow managed to get himself moved up. My father was the kind of man who would never stop on a double yellow line. He would hold up the queue at customs to declare goods he'd bought at IKEA, which no one else ever thought you had to do. He believed in sticking to the rules. It still moves me that he broke them to be with my mother.

For the rest of the three-week course, they went on picnics, bike rides and walks. Some of the time, they were with two skinny Belgians, Henri and Jan. Some of the time, they were alone. It must have been Henri or Jan who took the photos in the old brown album. Here they are, my slightly gawky mother and my dashing father, sitting on a wall. Here they are, standing a bit awkwardly by a fountain. And here they are, having a picnic in a forest, my father in long, baggy shorts, my mother in a full-skirted floral dress. In some of the photos, she's in Swedish national costume: white blouse, laced bodice, stripy apron and long skirt. In some of the photos, she's in her student cap, a kind of pilot's cap with a black peak. It must have been normal to wear it. My mother was self-conscious about her height and never wanted to attract attention. 'Hideous photographs of the teenager Anne' is a typical caption in one of her albums. But she certainly had reason to be proud of her cap. That summer, she had been the best student in her home town of Halmstad. She was carried in the streets by cheering fellow students and had her photo in the local paper. 'I was just pleasantly surprised,' she says (in Swedish, of course) in the article next to the photo. 'I had no idea what grades I would get. It was great fun to get an A in Latin. Latin is my favourite subject.'

Great fun to get an A in Latin. *Mycket roligt.* That's my mum. You can see why she and my father felt they were a match made in heaven.

My mother and her sister had got by on hand-me-downs and free school lunches. The father they adored had died of TB when my mother was twelve and Lisbeth was eight. A local journalist loved for his wit, he was the one who brought the laughter and the fun. My mother was reading Biggles when she got the news. She knew straight away that that life of laughter had gone. After that, she retreated into books. To get away from the tiny room she shared with her sister, she would climb up into the attic of their block of flats, perch on the abandoned pram she used as a seat and read, for hours, by the light of her torch. Their mother, who had left school at twelve to work as a shop assistant, got a job in the local post office. She got up at four to start work at five. The pressure was on. Money was tight. No wonder my mother dreamt of escape.

My father also shone at school. In Tom's study I find a whole shelf of his books. Quite a few have his school's gold crest on the jacket. They are prizes for excellence, in Latin, in history, in Greek. His big, red, gold-embossed *Works of William Shakespeare* has a printed token on the inside cover. It's a prize for 'good conduct', which makes me smile. My father sometimes gave us the impression that he had entered us all in a competition for 'good conduct', one where he made the rules and was the judge. The school motto, underneath a coat of arms with a nasty-looking eagle, makes me smile less. *Deo Non Fortuna*. Not through luck, but by God. My father never talked about his Christian faith, but I think he held on to it all his life. While he was at Cambridge, he went to chapel every day. As children, we all had to go to the local C of E church. It was what you had to do to get your Sunday roast chicken until, as teenagers, we were allowed to give up. But when I read that motto, I feel the old anger rising up.

Not through luck? Are you crazy?

My father had been brought up to believe that you should honour your father and mother. He was shocked when we didn't always 'honour' ours. He certainly honoured his mother, a charismatic Scot who had married another charming Scot, a doctor who was now senior administrative medical officer for the North East. My father and his three brothers all went, on scholarships, to Epsom College, the boarding school for the sons of doctors. They lived, with their sister and parents, in a big house in Newcastle with a maid. Mama May, my fierce but charming grandmother, had high hopes for her brilliant eldest son. They did not include marriage to a hard-up Swede.

But it didn't take long for my father to make his mind up. It never took long for my father to make his mind up, and when he did there wasn't much hope for you if you disagreed. Luckily, my mother didn't. For what was left of those three weeks, they talked, in German, about all the things they loved. They discussed their favourite Schubert songs. They quoted Goethe and Kleist. They wandered round the castle ruins and under the old bridge, by the banks of the Neckar, they kissed.

'I am thinking,' wrote my father in German as soon as he got back to Cambridge, 'of Beethoven's wonderful song cycle, *An die ferne Geliebte* [To the faraway beloved]. Now I understand the inner meaning, the beauty, the tenderness, the melancholy, a pure unsentimental beauty. As you left Cologne, I wanted to say, like Mignon, "*Dahin, dahin, möcht' ich mit dir, O mein Geliebter, ziehn.*" [There, there, to that place would I go with you, beloved.] But the words had to remain unspoken. It is possible to feel so much that one cannot speak.'

As soon as my mother got his letter, she wrote back. It was, she wrote (also in German) 'terrible' to leave him at Cologne. The rails there had 'sung', she told him, '*Ich hab mein Herz in Heidelberg verloren.*' I lost my heart in Heidelberg. It was a popular song and it could have been written for them.

For the next three years, their romance was conducted in daily letters. They wrote about their daily lives. They wrote about their hopes and dreams. Five months after they met, my father sent my mother a telegram. 'Will you marry me?' it said in English. On yellowing paper, I have my mother's reply: 'YES JOHN I WILL'.

On a boat on the Serpentine, he gave her a ring. Together, they planned their wedding, and their future life. In his letters, which are now in English, he tried to teach my mother about English life. She was the one who would have to learn about his world, his life. But he still peppered his letters with the words of the poets he loved. 'Only he who knows longing knows what I suffer,' he wrote, quoting Goethe. 'From old fairy tales it beckons,' he wrote in another letter, quoting the Heine poem that was also a Schubert song, 'a magic land where colourful flowers bloom'.

Very occasionally, they spoke on the phone. My father had to book the call and make it in his landlady's freezing hall. 'How wonderful it was to hear your voice!' wrote my mother straight after one of them. 'To think that I could hear it across the whole of the North Sea!'

'And then you rang,' wrote my father at the end of the same phone call, when he had left his landlady's cold hallway to go back to his room. 'My own sweetest Anne. Never has your voice sounded so beautiful! What a heavy ache as I put the telephone down! But love is like that. Love brings the ache of parting and brings, too, a happiness that those who do not love do not know.'

When I first read that letter, fifteen years ago, I suddenly felt cold. My father was clear. My father was always clear. A happiness that those who do not love do not know.

Later, when the shadows came back, the letter took a fresh twist in my mind. A happiness that those who do not love do not know, cannot know, might die without knowing. Honestly, for a while, the fear of that was worse than the fear of dying.

It was one of the letters my mother translated when I said I wanted to find out more. I've always known about these letters. There are whole boxes of them and it would take months to plough through them, even if I felt entirely comfortable doing it, which I don't. The letters tell a story I'll never be able to match and set a bar I can't reach. A glance, a smile, a faltering conversation, a kiss, a telegram, a ring. Three years of poetic passion, in a language not your own. Love at first sight. Love for nearly fifty years. Love till death do us part.

On a shelf in my study, there's a box file labelled 'MEN!' There are a few emails printed out from dating sites. There are other emails from men I've had short, disastrous relationships with. Actually, 'relationship' is too strong a word. Meetings. Encounters. Liaisons. When my mother studied *Dangerous Liaisons* for her Open University degree on the Enlightenment, she didn't have any personal experience of disastrous liaisons. I do and I don't want anyone reading that file.

My mother was proud of those letters. They didn't get the yellow stickers saying 'THROW OUT'. But still. It's one thing to read your father quoting Heine, quite another to read his suggestion that she see a doctor to talk about 'birth control'. When I find that letter, I feel a bit sick. It reminds me of the time I was looking for nail scissors in my mother's bedside drawer and found a Dutch cap. I left it on their bed with a note saying 'WHY DIDN'T YOU USE THIS TO STOP ME?' I must have been about ten. I was quite a placid child, at least at first, and have no idea what triggered this outburst. Look at me! Don't look at me! Look at the mistake you made!

Sex or no sex (and I know from my mother that there was no sex before they were married because my father said Christian teaching didn't allow it), they were both so desperate to get married that my mother completed her four-year course in a record two and a half years. Once again, she was featured in the local paper. She started teaching languages at a school in Kristiansand, and was earning more than my father was earning at the Foreign Office. Their wedding was delayed when my father's father had a heart attack during a meeting at Sunderland General Hospital. 'MIN FAR ÄR DÖD' wrote my father in his tiny Letts diary. He had taught himself Swedish and was writing his diary in his latest language. I was older when I learnt the weight of those words. Dad is dead. Three words to change a world.

My father's diary entry for 25 June is equally succinct. '*Den stora dagen!*' The big day! They were married in the white church at Söndrum, next to the old barn that was once part of my mother's grandparents' farm. We sometimes used to cycle there. My cousin Carl Johan was christened there. Built from whitewashed stone and with a conical spire, it looks like something in a fairy tale. It's set in a landscape dotted with red wooden farms and at the foot of a hill sprinkled with wild roses. If you clamber up the hill, among the stones my mother always said were from Neolithic villages, you see green fields stretching out to the sea. As a child, I dreamt of getting married there. I wanted to look like my mother in her wedding photos, statuesque in her coronet made out of myrtle, mysterious with her Mona Lisa smile. In the photos my father looks like a matinee idol. On his broad forehead, there's even a kiss-curl.

After a honeymoon in Norway, where it rained for two weeks, they started their new life in a bedsit in Earls Court. My mother tried to make it cosy, with the cushion covers she crocheted on their honeymoon, the rug she had woven and a selection of embroidered mats. In the kitchen they shared with the other tenants, she practised making English puddings. Lemon meringue. Treacle tart. Queen's pud. I don't know what happened to those English puddings. By the time we came along, the answer to the 'what's for pudding?' question was nearly always a slightly tart 'fresh fruit'. I've always wanted to see a photo of that first home, and now, in an album in Tom's sitting room, I've found one. You can't see much. A fireplace. Some armchairs. A coffee table with a coffee pot and two Advent candles. And my parents, who are drinking coffee with one of my mother's Swedish cousins. Their faces light up the room.

My mother gasped when she heard that their first

posting was Bangkok. For six months, she had been working in a cramped attic, doing clerical work at Foyles. It was just after the Suez Crisis – Anthony Eden had resigned the month before. The Suez Canal was still closed, and the journey took six weeks. When they got there, it was worth it. My parents' new home came with five servants and a white grand piano. There was a lake in the garden, with a temple behind it. The garden smelled of the jasmine the gardener watered and trimmed. In the 'New Look' dresses she had made in jewel-coloured Thai silks, my mother helped my father host cocktail parties and dinners. 'I nearly went hysterical,' she wrote (in Swedish) to her mother when, just before one party, the power died. 'The guests' she told her mother, 'had to walk in total darkness and risk treading on snakes. John says I am stupid to worry. The guests had a lovely time. But what would you have done if you had been left in pitch blackness with seventy-five cocktail guests of high rank, when you were twenty-three years old!'

Although diplomats' wives weren't meant to work, my mother answered an ad for an English teacher in the *Bangkok Post*. She was interviewed, on her veranda, by a monk. Soon, she was walking, every morning, through a temple-yard full of wild dogs. In the classroom, she read out the English phrases she wrote on a blackboard and boys in blue shorts and white shirts shouted them back. On Teachers' Worship Day, they knelt in front of her and bowed their heads. When they heard she'd got food poisoning after a Japanese meal to celebrate her first wedding anniversary, they hired three buses and went to all the hospitals in Bangkok. When they found her, they swarmed on to the ward and handed her baskets of orchids and eggs.

I could spend hours gazing at the photos of my glamorous parents with their glamorous guests. Sometimes, they're staying at the 'You and I' cottage, a holiday cottage for diplomatic staff on the beach at Pattaya. The beach is deserted. In her floral swimsuit, my mother looks like Ingrid Bergman.

I don't think many of the beaches look like that now. They didn't when I went to Thailand and that was twenty-six years ago. My trip was with a company called Intrepid. Apart from me and the guide, it was just an Australian girl and two young Kenyan Asian men who were both going home to arranged marriages. I was so desperate for a boyfriend that I felt like begging their mothers to arrange one for me. My main memory of that holiday is of feeling like an adolescent. I was nearly a decade older than my travelling companions, but I still felt like the adolescent. I was worrying about my spots and dreaming about a colleague I was pretty sure wasn't dreaming about me.

We did the things travellers do. We drank beer. We ate fried silkworms. We trekked with mountain tribes, sleeping in wooden longhouses on rush mats. We climbed rope ladders to sleep in tree huts in the jungle but were kept awake by the frogs. Oh, and we smoked opium. In a bamboo hut in the mountains north of Chiang Mai I smoked several pipes. It didn't make me feel any more relaxed.

I had just turned thirty when I went to Thailand, seeking – well, I don't know quite what. I was also in my thirties when I went to a Greek island to do reiki healing and to Goa with a friend who claimed to be a psychic. She stopped at one pretty beach village and told me that, in another life, she had been there before.

I was always, always seeking something I couldn't seem to find.

My mother was twenty-two when she went to Bangkok. My father was twenty-five. They did not consult psychics. They didn't learn about chakras and practise on people in tie-die pantaloons. They hosted cocktail parties for government officials. They dined with ambassadors. Sometimes, my father wore his diplomatic uniform: white with a kind of pith helmet and a diplomatic sword. I was shocked when I found the sword in Tom's wardrobe. It has a gold tassel and a royal crest, but the blade is still sharp. I'm not sure what to do with it. You can't really give a sword to Oxfam, and I don't want to make life easier for any burglar who might break in. For the moment, I've left it in Tom's house, with the ebony elephants, the Buddhas and the temple candlesticks my mother had made into lamps. A little corner of Dorking that is forever Bangkok. Or at least until the house is sold.

My parents never tried opium. They had their own drug: love. And soon they had it in an even stronger dose. 'Anne expecting' is my father's caption next to a photo of my slender mother in a loose dress. His captions were as laconic as his diary entries. 'Pong, our musical gardener.' 'Ford Prefect and Anne at the Friendship Highway.' 'Buffalo – general view.' His diary entries were sometimes just one word. I was hoping his diary might tell me where they actually went on that six-week voyage to Bangkok. But no. 'Porpoises' is the entry for one day. 'Whales' is another. A few days later, 'Albatrosses'. In Bangkok, his diary entries are usually social engagements. 'HE's cocktails.' 'Supper Harlands.' And then, on 12 October 1958: '0800 CAROLINE ANNE'. Followed, a few days later, by 'Powder under chin? Coloured nappies. Nipple jam.'

My mother was more effusive. She didn't start a diary until 1967, but she wrote long, chatty letters, to her mother, her sister, her mother-in-law and, all her life, to her many, many friends. 'Caroline is the best thing that ever happened to me,' she wrote in a letter to my father's mother. I felt a tiny prickle when I read that.

Every night, my father would rush home from work and kiss both his girls and then gaze at the tiny creature with eyes so dark they were almost like sapphires, and at the full head of hair the same colour as his. How do I know? Because there's album after album, documenting every stretch, every yawn, every half-smile.

On the first Sunday in Advent, they lit a candle, 'picked

Caroline from her cot' and played Swedish and English carols as they 'sat and looked at her' by the light of a flickering flame. On 13 December, when my father had to go to the airport to meet an official, they put Caroline between them in their bed at 5 a.m. and sang her the Lucia song. 'We have got a special photograph album for Caroline,' my mother wrote to her mother that Christmas, 'and look at her photographs all the time. They are very nice, but none of them do justice to our little darling. We tickle her under her chins and she really gurgles with laughter. She is so wonderful that it isn't true.'

Chapter 3
Dancing Bears

I was standing outside my first home when Tom called. Or at least I think I was standing outside it. All my life, I have called my mother to check this kind of thing. She held the family archive in her head or, failing that, her house. If any of us ever needed a fact or date about our past, she could check her diary, or a photo album or a file. She always claimed to be clearing out her papers. All her life, she would never watch a TV programme without ironing, or mending something, or writing her diary or, in the later years, sorting out a pile of papers or weeding out an album or a file. We sometimes joked that on her grave we'd put 'she cleared the loft'.

We didn't, of course, and she didn't, in fact, clear the loft, because the filling up more than matched the clearing out. My mother wanted to mark every moment of her life. She took photos of almost every meeting with a relative or friend. Within a few days, she would have had them printed out, put in albums and copies posted to the relative or friend. She was an Instagrammer before her time. She took so many photos you forgot the camera was there. For quite a lot of my life, I've hated the camera, and most photos seem to show that hate is mutual. In my mother's photos of me, that tension seems to have gone.

The last time I'd been in Rome was with my mother, but this time I was with a man. At fifty-three, I was finally on holiday with a man! In scorching heat, we wandered round the Forum and the Piazza Navona, threw coins in the Trevi Fountain and ate ice creams on the Spanish Steps. I felt as if I was showing him my empire. Yes, aren't the statues stunning? It was as if I had sculpted them, I had cooked the saltimbocca, so meltingly delicious it 'leaps into the mouth', and I had invented the fresh, zesty miracle that is Aperol Spritz. I wanted to show him my first home, but I couldn't remember the address. In the end, I emailed Auntie Lisbeth, who looked it up and emailed me back: 54 Viale delle Belle Arti. Avenue of the Fine Arts. You couldn't really ask for a nicer address to start your time on Earth.

I'd been back to my first home twice before. The first time was on a Thomas Cook coach tour of Italy when I was nineteen. It was our first family holiday in a country that wasn't Sweden, the first time we stayed in a hotel for more than a 'bargain break' in Wales. My mother was just thrilled that someone else had done the cooking. My father was thrilled to be back in Rome. I was obsessed by a boy

I'd met at a college party and worried that my fringe was too short. We left the coach party for a couple of hours, to walk the streets where my parents used to push our prams and peer at the place where Tom and I had gurgled and sucked our way into the world, the house with the crazy paving and the grand shutters. I wanted to feel something strong. Look! This is where I first smiled! This is where I first crawled! This is where I started gazing at the world and trying to take it all in! I felt nothing. I can't even remember what it looked like. All I could think about was the boy I'd met and whether I dared send him a postcard.

The second time was with my mother, one Easter, when I was thirty-one. We stayed in a B & B overlooking Piazza Navona. The room was small and dark, with a bathroom that was literally a cupboard. For most of the trip, it rained. We cowered under umbrellas as we dashed from museum to museum. We caught the bus to the Avenue of the Fine Arts and stared at it in the drizzle. Once again, I didn't take it in. I was wet. I wanted coffee. I can never concentrate on anything if I'm uncomfortable. I've sat through so many plays longing for the interval, even when the reviews have given them five stars.

This time, I wanted to get it right. There had been an ending, an ending I'd dreaded all my life, so now it was time to go back to the beginning. Look, darling, this is where it all started!

I was disappointed when we got off the bus in a busy street that didn't seem to have any residential buildings.

It was hard to imagine Keats or Dante having any great epiphanies about beauty, truth or getting lost in dark woods on this street of office blocks and traffic. I wandered up and down it. There didn't seem to be a number 54. Eventually, I stopped outside a yellow building. When my parents lived there, if they lived there, it was pink. I really wanted it to be pink.

A young woman came out, with a tiny dog on a lead. '*Buon giorno!*' I said and then realised I didn't know what to ask. '*Questa è la mia prima casa?*' Is this my first home?

'*Penso che la mia famiglia abbia vissuto qui una volta,*' I said in the end. I think my family once lived here. I wanted to ask if I could go in through the gate and see if I could find the crazy paving, but my Italian wasn't up to it, and the young woman was looking at me as if I was dragging a trolley of old plastic bags and asking for change. As the gate shut, my phone rang. 'We've completed,' said Tom. He had just shut the front door of the house at Nelson Gardens for the last time.

'Well done,' I said, because he had been the one to organise the sale, and to have done nearly all the clearing out. He wanted to, and I was more than happy to let him, but now I could feel that pressure in my nose I always get when I can feel tears brewing. Five Nelson Gardens. Our family home for fifty-two years, the place we always went back to when the crises hit. It was the poet Robert Frost who said, 'Home is the place where, when you have to go there, / they have to take you in.' It's that and a whole universe more, of course. The last time had been seven years before, after my big operation, when my mother had nursed me and brought me breakfast in bed. At seventy-five, she was still the one who got to nurse me when disaster struck. I was mortified by that, to be honest, but someone has to nurse you after an eight-hour operation and there didn't seem to be anyone else to do it.

The thing about grief is that it takes you by surprise. We all die. She was old. She wanted to go, and I had to let her go. It's what happens. It's fine.

It's not fine. It's absolutely not fine. And now the house has gone, too.

I wanted to ask Tom more, but the line went dead. Bloody typical, I thought. Here I am, standing by my first home at the very moment I hear that my lifelong home has gone. How poignant. How poetic. But I'm not really sure if it is my first home, and there isn't anyone I can ask, and the battery on my phone has died.

There's so much I want to ask. There's never going to be anyone I can ask.

Perhaps, in the end, we can't know anything much? Perhaps, in the end, we can only make some guesses.

I can't claim to have vivid memories of my early life in Rome. I don't know if I even got to eat much Italian food. I have no idea when a baby gets to eat real food. I've barely held one, let alone looked after one, but now I've just googled it and discovered that it's usually at four to six months. That might have given me a few months of *spaghetti alla carbonara, prosciutto, pecorino, tiramisu,* or at least the odd mouthful mixed in with Farley's Rusks. All I know is that when I get to Italy I can't get enough of these things. Or enough Vermentino, Vernaccia, Gavi or Montepulciano. There's even a label called Santa Cristina. They do a lovely Orvieto and a lovely Chianti. I don't know how you describe a wine, apart from to say, 'It's delicious!' Tom would be able to, of course. I mean Tom would have been able to.

Damn. I just can't get those tenses right.

My first memories of Italy are from the summer when I was fourteen. My parents packed me off to stay with an Italian family, in the Alban Hills outside Rome. I ended up staying with two families, in fact, a brother and sister and their spouses and children who lived in apartments in the same block. Enrico, the father of Valeria, was more like my father: serious, thoughtful, correct. '*Va bene, Valeria!*' he would say at meals, when she tried to say the more truncated '*Va be!*' the teenagers preferred. Let's preserve the language of Dante, *please.* It was like Dad. Elbows off the table. I said *elbows off the table.* But like my father, he was also kind.

Roberto, the father of Cristina, Carlo and Claudio, was certainly kind. He was also like a pantomime version of an Italian: effusive, generous, flamboyant and with a gargantuan appetite: for food, for laughter, for life. He would whisk us all off for pizzas the size of dustbin lids, or drive us into the mountains, on impulse, for tiny wild strawberries. There was laughter and singing in that crammed Fiat as we snaked our way up and up, gazing down at the lake below, and wondering what today's treat would be. Everything was the best. The best strawberries, the best *gelato*, the thinnest, crispiest pizza and the most succulent lamb. And the conversation never stopped. Since my Italian had stuck at chapter three of *Teach Yourself Italian*, he would take the trouble to tell me long, complicated jokes in slow, careful French. I fell in love with both families and also with Italy. I've been in love with this land of poetry and art and sunshine and laughter, this land of my birth, ever since.

It's a shame I don't remember anything about my early life in Rome because we followed in the footsteps of a Bond girl. 'This is a lovely flat on two storeys with a nice garden for Caroline to play in,' wrote my mother to her mother. 'It has a gate with a lock so she can't escape! Linda Christian, the film actress, used to live here.' Linda Christian played James Bond's love interest in the 1954 TV version of *Casino Royale* and, later, a mermaid in *Tarzan and the Mermaids*. Born in Mexico, she spoke six languages fluently, which was one more than my mother's five. Before she moved to Rome she had an affair with Errol Flynn.

My mother translated scores of letters to her own mother and gave us each a tailored set in a blue lever arch file. Each is focused on our early childhood. Caroline's ends when she is five. Mine seems to end when I'm four months. By this time, a baby arrival is a little more routine. In my father's diary, I'm squeezed in after the church AGM: 'CHRISTINA MARY 4.27 p.m. 47 cm. 2.45 kilos.'

Caroline's early babyhood takes up a whole album. Tom's takes half an album. Mine takes just a couple of pages. In a letter to Mama May, two days after I'm born, my mother spends almost as long writing about the gas strike as the 'poor little shrimp' with 'quite a wrinkly face'. The Italians, she writes, 'are really quite maddening – first we had a milk strike for ages, then a bus strike and now a gas strike. What next?! I've just talked to John and he's managed to buy some sort of highly dangerous and expensive hotplate at the equivalent of Woolworths, so I hope he will be able to boil an egg at least!' If he did, it must have been one of the few times. When he retired, my mother announced firmly that 'I married you for better or worse, but not for lunch' and made it clear that she would not be cooking two hot meals a day.

In Rome, no one had to do much cooking, because my parents had a maid and nanny called Jolanda. Tom loved her so much that he kept on visiting her, in Anzio, until she died. Jolanda lightened the burden, of housework, of childcare, of life. She's there in the photos and the cine films, a tiny matriarchal figure fifteen years older than my mother, a calm, steady presence kissing bruises and holding tiny hands.

The cine films, the letters and the photos build up

a picture of an idyllic life. It looks like one big holiday. There's certainly plenty of sightseeing. My father's camera lingers on medieval buildings and churches, courtyards full of Romanesque arches, Etruscan tombs and Roman ruins. Here's three-year-old Caroline, in a pink plaid dress, balancing on the edge of a fountain. Here she is again, climbing on a statue of Neptune, by a lake. Here she is, with my mother or my father, and often with their friends, in Liguria, Tivoli, Spoleto, Calabria, Venice, Pisa, Capri, Etruria and Rome. Now Caroline's in a frilly swimsuit on the beach in Fregene. Now she's with my mother, who's wearing sunglasses and a headscarf, at a picnic table on a mountain. And oh look, here's my father, lying on his back in a park, jiggling Caroline up and down. She looks as if she's squealing with pleasure. I wish I could bottle the look on his face. Idiotically, I wave at him. 'Hi, Dad!' I'm sitting on the floor of my flat watching the video recorder I've pilfered from my brother's house and I actually wave at my father. He's so handsome, so young, so full of love. I just want to rush into his arms.

He's too young in the film for me to have met him. I'm old enough to be his mother now. He never saw the lines on my forehead or the softening of my jowls. The last time I saw him was eighteen years ago. I don't want to remember him as he was then. I'll have to pick a photo, or a memory, to freeze in my heart.

In the next shot, they're back on the crazy paving at Viale delle Belle Arti. A family friend is holding a baby in a christening robe. Tom! He's so big he's almost bursting out of it. He was three weeks early, but by the time of his christening, nearly five months later, he's turning into the Incredible Hulk. 'Tom's behind is so fat that he doesn't even notice the injection needle!' wrote my mother when he was seven months old. 'I have just got out all Caroline's play-suits, which she wore when she was a year old. Tom can hardly fit into them because he has such a long body. What will become of this child?'

What will become of this child? Oh, my darling mother. I'm just glad you died before I could tell you.

Everyone who saw the chubby, blond baby adored him. 'Caroline thinks he is the biggest joke ever and laughs and laughs every time she looks at him,' wrote my mother when Tom was two weeks old. 'She is not a bit jealous, but thinks he is a funny toy.'

It's clear from the footage that Caroline took one look at Tom and never wanted to let him go. When he starts crawling, on the crazy paving, she, at four, crawls next to him. On the chair swing, she cuddles him. Before he can walk, when he's propelling himself round on that mini Zimmer frame, she walks over and kisses him. In one scene, they're in a meadow, picking flowers. Tom has split his trousers and then tumbles over. Caroline follows him and laughs. They get up, lurch up to the camera and their sweet, sweet faces fill the screen.

Next, they're at a zoo. It must be the zoo at Rome and I

can't believe it because a bear is dancing. 'After lunch we went to the zoo,' wrote my mother. 'Our friend Marcello knew all the animals and got the elephants to kneel down, the bears to dance and the lions to lie on their backs and the chimpanzee to ride a bike. It was marvellous fun to go with him.' Well, yes, it would be, but I was slightly sceptical when I read about this friend. Who is he, Francis of Assisi? Well, here he is, in a cap and tartan trousers. I only wish we'd seen the chimpanzee.

'We are all well and think that life is wonderful,' wrote my mother in another letter. Their social life certainly seemed to be. Perhaps it was too dark to film inside the Bond-girl flat, but in the footage there's a constant stream of visitors on that chic, mid-century furniture on the crazy paving, many of them dandling babies and jiggling toddlers. And this is on top of the cocktail parties and dinners, the nights at the embassy, the nights at the opera, the skiing trips in Terminillo. I didn't even know my father could ski! But here he is, on skis, and here are my rosy-cheeked siblings on a sledge, in matching Norwegian-style jumpers and hats. My mother knitted them. I can't begin to imagine the effort that goes into knitting a hat, let alone a jumper. I can't begin to imagine the effort that goes into feeding and bathing and nursing and nurturing a baby, let alone a child. I thought I would. I pretended to do these things as a child. Caroline and I both had lots of dolls. She and her friend Rosalind were so keen to wash their dolls that they flooded my mother's friend Celia's flat.

'The whole floor was like a big lake,' wrote my mother, 'in which all Rosalind's toys were swimming. They have marble floors, so it didn't matter.'

Marble floors. Dancing bears. Babies. Toddlers. Family life. It's another world to me. It's a zoo. Watching this is like going to a zoo. I'm watching a species I have never felt a part of. It's strange. It's exotic. It's bursting with youth and life. Let's call it *felix duobus cum pueris*. It wasn't just my mother who was an ace at Latin. I got an A in Latin A level, too. *Vivamus mea Lesbia, atque amemus*. Let us live, my Lesbia, and let us love.

Yes, Catullus, let us all live and love. I have learnt that you can live and love very happily without being part of the species we can roughly translate as happy young couples with small children. But learning that lesson took far, far, far too long.

And what you can't see in the footage is the tears. Who wants to film tears? But my mother wrote about them, to her mother. 'Caroline was terribly difficult yesterday,' she confessed, two weeks after they had arrived in Rome. 'Both John and I were worn out by her fits of rage.' A few months later, she went further. 'Sometimes,' she said, 'Caroline does depress me.' My mother had gone to visit a friend and Caroline had 'started yelling' as soon as she saw the other children, and cried until they left. 'Yesterday I arranged a birthday party for her. I had worked like a horse, made a birthday cake, baked other cakes, made sandwiches and had really spent a lot of money and trouble on making the party a success.' Caroline refused to eat and cried all the time. 'Jill and Diana say that I must take her to a doctor.'

It all started on the boat from Bangkok. This time, it was for three and a half weeks. My parents were expected to eat at the captain's table. Children weren't. 'Bye bye, man!' my sister apparently yelled at the waiter who came to drag her away. 'She'll get used to it,' said the English nanny in charge of the ship's nursery. But the screams got louder and she didn't. For every meal of the voyage, Caroline screamed when she was separated from her parents. By the time they docked, there was a hunted look in my sister's beautiful blue eyes.

Chapter 4

Sunshine and Showers

This house has warmth. That's what the brochure says, in a file on Tom's shelf. It's in his spare room, the one I sleep in when I go there to sort things out. It's in a red lever arch file, one of many that used to be in the bookshelf by the door to my old room. My mother has written 'HOUSE' on it and then, underneath it, 'THROW OUT'. But my brother didn't throw it out and I'm glad he didn't, because I've never seen it before. 'BE LIKE MRS 1970 AND ENJOY UP-TO-DATE WARMTH' it says. 'Mrs 1970's heating automatically warms the house before she gets up.'

This was not to be sniffed at in 1964. When my mother lived in London, in 1956, she was shocked that Brits didn't seem to have heard of central heating. The government buildings in Whitehall, where my father worked, were black, their white stucco coated with layers of coal dust and smog. But Boxgrove Park, an 'imposing development of detached houses within easy reach of the centre of the cathedral town of Guildford,' was brand spanking new. 'An attractive feature,' says the turquoise brochure, 'is the plastic finish to all ceilings' and the 'high grade thermoplastic floor tiles.'

The first glimpse, in the cine film, is of Tom, marching out of the front door in a pale blue jumper and grey shorts. He's followed by a stream of seven children, including Caroline, now with short hair. In the next frame, they're all charging around the front garden, a whirling dervish of children, from across the road and next door. In the road, there's a builder, driving a digger. The pavement is unfinished. All the front gardens are just green turf. In the background, where, in a few years, there will be matchbox houses jammed together, there are green fields. And propped in the centre of the lawn, in front of a red-brick house, there's a baby. It's bald. It has huge, pouchy cheeks. It's grinning. It's me.

As the children dance around me, I'm still grinning. Now I'm grinning in my pram in the back garden. The garden seems to back on to open countryside. This isn't suburbia! It's practically *The Hay Wain*! The green field is, in fact, the playing field of a private school which will soon turn into a massive building site, which we will all treat as a giant playground. We will play hide-and-seek among the cement mixers. We will scramble up teetering piles of bricks. We will climb staircases that suddenly stop. But for now, I seem to be very happy just lying in my pram.

Caroline's pushing Tom in a wheelbarrow. Now Tom's standing by my pram. He leans over to kiss me and then picks his nose. He stares at the blob and sticks his finger in his mouth.

And still I smile, a benign Buddha in a blue knitted cap. Perhaps I was just pleased to have made it. Nine months before, I'd turned up six weeks early, and on the way to the hospital my mother thought she had lost me. 'She is absolutely tiny and terribly skinny,' she wrote to Mama May two days after I burst my way out, legs first, 'well shaped though not beautiful with lively dark eyes.' In the photos and cine films, it's clear I've made up for lost time. I can't help smiling when I see the smirking Churchill on a pouffe. Is that me? Is that really me? That egg in a blue knitted dress, that chunky toddler with a mass of white-blond curls, stuck in the fork of a tree, that little girl giggling at the wheel of a racing car, nappy bulging out below her red tartan dress? There's something about the tiny teeth that makes me want to scoop that toddler up. I want to ask her why she laughed so much and also why she stopped. But I don't need to ask anyone why they called her 'the sunshine girl'.

I don't know how my parents felt about swapping the cocktail parties, dinners and sunshine of Rome for tea with the neighbours in suburban Surrey. Before, my father could walk to the embassy, and eat his lunch-time panino in the Villa Borghese. Now, he had a half-hour walk to the station, followed by an hour's train to Waterloo and a Tube to Charing Cross. Often, the trains were cancelled. Often, by the time he got home, his supper was, as my mother said, 'ruined'. Sometimes, she went to pick him up, only to find he wasn't on the train. And this was before the strikes, when my father had to take his pyjamas to the office and we did our homework by candlelight. Now he was working as a civil servant at the Treasury. The hours were long. The commute was gruelling. It wasn't the original plan. The original plan was more of the same. International postings, climbing the ladder to ambassador, more parties, more countries, more dinners. It was many years before I asked why the plan changed. The answer was simple: Caroline. 'We didn't think,' my father told me quietly, 'that she would cope with all the change.'

My mother, on the other hand, set about her new life with zest. Within weeks of arriving, she had a whole new network. She made friends with all the neighbours. She made friends with people in the 'young wives' group at church. She retrained as a primary school teacher, and made friends with her colleagues, too. She had people for coffee, people for tea and people for dinner, for beef stroganoff and Margaretha's almond cake, a recipe supplied by a Danish friend in Bangkok. We were usually in bed by then, but sometimes crept down to listen in. My mother guided the conversation like a maestro waiting for the right moment to bring in the second violin. My father thought his role was to pour half-glasses of Liebfraumilch, which he thought was plenty, and launch monologues on the big issues of the day, explaining carefully, but with an impatient edge to his voice, why he was right and everyone else was wrong. He used the same tone as he did at our meals. '*Don't* speak with your mouth full. Elbows off the table. *What did I just say?*'

My mother's first diary entry, in 1967, gives a flavour of the tone. 'We went to the children's service at Shackleford. Very nice. All three children behaved very well. Afterwards Anne asked us in for a drink and we had a nice chat with her. Saw David, too, before going back to our cooked chicken (pre-set oven). Nice quiet afternoon and tea over *Thunderbirds* as usual.' More Pooter than Pepys, perhaps. What you might expect from a civil servant's wife in Surrey. Later, more wry humour creeps in.

From then on, she wrote her diary every day. It was mostly a breathless list of things she had done: household chores ticked off, lessons prepared, letters written, friends phoned, rooms painted, old ladies visited, meals cooked, clothes made, cakes baked, dinners hosted, evening classes attended, children ferried and bathed. She wrote, often at midnight before collapsing into bed, because she wanted to mark every precious minute of her life. Life was a to-do list, but also an accumulation of lovely moments. A picnic. A snatched coffee in the sunshine. Something one of us had said. 'After discussion about smoking,' she writes one day, 'Christina said: I am going to smoke when I am a Daddy.' Interesting, that. I've sometimes secretly wondered whether I'd rather be a Daddy than a Mummy, because it seems like a lot less work. Sometimes, there are entries that leap out from the lists. 'The children loved the play,' she writes, 'though Caroline felt so sorry for everybody, including the Genie in the bottle, she cried.'

Nelson Gardens gave us all an instant social life. My best friend was Monique, who lived in the house on the corner. Tom's best friends were her brothers, Paul and Mark. Their garage had been converted into a playroom, and all the children in the street piled in. We took Fred, the goldfish, for a ride in a dinky lorry and squealed when he started flapping around. We made mountains of cushions and dive-bombed on them, to the music for *Mission Impossible*. We played Scalextric, spending hours watching the tiny cars whizz round a wiggly plastic track.

We put on magic shows in the front garden. Sometimes, we put on plays, taking all the parts. Monique and I played a game called 'Mary and Marion'. I was Mary and she was Marion and we had to pile up chairs in the garden and cover them with blankets. When we were called inside for our beef burgers or our Findus Crispy Pancakes, we had to yell, 'There's a storm coming, there's a storm coming!' and whip the blankets off. Why? It was just one of the rules of our new world in the sky. We made the world, we made the rules. Why, we thought, should the grown-ups be the only ones to make rules?

In the cine films, we're often parading up and down

Nelson Gardens, as witches with broomsticks, as Mary and Joseph, as cowboys and ugly sisters and nurses clutching sick dolls. I always wanted to see what it was like to be someone different, in a different place. Even as a small child, when I was put to bed for a nap, I would tuck the fringes of the blanket under my head and tuck the other end under my feet and da-da! I was in a car, about to go on a journey. I was in a ship, about to set sail. Sometimes, I would just lie and stare at the lampshade above me and imagine how I would dance around it, in an upside-down world. I knew I was meant to sleep, but I never wanted to sleep. I still never want to go to bed, and not just because my dreams are full of Tom.

Once school started, our freedom shrank, but it was just a five-minute walk away, on the edge of the estate. It was the time of progressive education. We made dinosaurs out of toilet rolls. We did projects on the Romans, making collages of Roman soldiers from crêpe paper and silver foil. We wrote stories and drew pictures and did 'music and movement' in our pants and vest. But the boys still played football and the girls still played netball. For a while, I was on the school team. I can't quite believe that now, because in our house sport was for boys.

When the sport was on telly, you had to keep out of the way. The sitting room was now a holy place, reserved for 'the men'. My father and my brother would drag two armchairs near the TV and hunch on the edge of them. We would hear their anguished cries. 'No!' 'That was

NOT OFFSIDE!' The agony spread through the house. My mother would try to break it, bringing trays of coffee and tiny cakes. My normally polite father would barely nod. 'Shut the door!' he would mutter as she click-clacked out. And then he would sink back into his gloom.

That shared gloom bound them together, my sports-mad brother and my sports-mad dad. Sometimes, it wasn't gloom. Sometimes, the joy that burst out of the room was like the 'Hallelujah' chorus, which was what my father bought my mother, to play 'on the gramophone' in Rome, when I was born. My father went to watch Tom play football. He went to watch him play rugby. Later, he drove him to Twickenham and spent hours stuck in traffic getting back. They played golf. They watched golf. They pored over the sports pages together, swapping figures and details, quoting match reports. At his last birthday lunch, when my father knew he was dying, he said something to each of us round the table. When he got to Tom, he paused. 'I want to thank you,' he said, 'for introducing me to Sky Sports.'

My father was obsessed with the weather. He lived for the gaps between clouds. When the news came on, we knew we had to be quiet, but when the man at the end appeared with the map, we hardly dared breathe. My father would lean forward in his chair. If the man said sunshine, the tension in his face would melt away. 'Sunshine and showers' got a nod. Rain for the flowers and sunshine to cheer you up. If it was 'steady rain', we knew we were in trouble. 'Well, that's it, then,' he would say. And that *was* it. For my father, the weekend was ruined.

If he could, he would have spent his life in the garden. As soon as he got home, if it was still light and the weatherman said he could, he would swap his suit for baggy trousers and an old cardigan, wolf down his food and go out to inspect his plants. The garden was his sanctuary, his canvas, his domain to tend and tame. Until the light faded, he would snip and trim and tweak the precious plants he had sown, from the seeds he bought at Wisley Gardens, or the bulbs he planted, in the hope of bursts of colour in spring. In the front garden, there was a whole bed of red roses, for my mother. In the front garden, too, there were five silver birches. One for each member of the family, to remind my mother of the country she loved and left.

In the back garden, there were marguerites and pink roses, the flowers she had in her wedding bouquet. There was agapanthus, deep blue, like her eyes. When my father died, my mother opted for a softer, wilder look, but there was nothing wild about the garden while he was in charge. Rogue plants were ripped out. Stray branches were hacked off. Earth was mixed with mulch because it was good for it, good like broccoli, good like homework. Sometimes, the whole lawn was measled with brown holes, because a brutal attack with a spiked roller would 'allow it to breathe'. On his brown wooden 'wireless', my father would listen to clipped voices announcing symphonies, sonatas, slow movements, overtures, and then the music would burst out of it, washing over him, washing over the garden, washing over anyone who came near. Sometimes, I would look out at my father, on his knees by his flowers, and think he was praying.

At weekends, he thought you should go for walks: at St Martha's, the hill with the church at the top, or the Chantries, where there were fields and woods and a hill where, in the autumn, you could pick blackberries. Or at Wisley Gardens, where we had a family membership. My father would march us up and down the herbaceous borders, round the lake and down the rockery. He would stop to gaze at a mass of purple bushes in bloom. 'Look at those rhododendrons!' he would say. 'Just *look* at them!' and he would sometimes sound on the edge of tears. In the end, we would get our reward. Honey cakes in the café, flat like pancakes, crisp like the *pepparkakor* we snapped to make a wish. He would carry the tray, as if it was frankincense or myrrh, and set it carefully on the table. 'Right,' he would say, with a sudden smile that was like the sun bursting through grey haze. 'Tuck in!'

If it was raining, he'd swap the walk for a National Trust house. We soon knew all the ones in Surrey almost as well as our friends' houses: Clandon Park, Polesden Lacey, Hatchlands Park. No detour was too long for an ancient building full of tapestries and gloomy furniture, studded with giant knobs and scrolls. My father would gaze at it all, as if each stitch and mark had a secret message from history, a message we would all do well to read, mark and learn. We trudged around, sometimes daring to race up and down a corridor, hoping that at the end of it all there would be a scone or an ice cream. Sometimes there was, sometimes there wasn't. My father's attitude to treats was that you shouldn't expect them. On long car journeys, he would be the keeper of the cherry bon bons or butterscotch swirls. 'When can we have another one?' I'd ask, desperate for another explosion of sugar on my tongue. 'Soon,' he'd say, in a tone that strongly suggested it was best not to get anyone's hopes up.

This made our treats all the sweeter. It made my father's smile when he bestowed it sweeter, too. Sometimes, when we were all gathered around the TV, he would steal a glance at us that was almost shy. 'Are you enjoying it?' he would ask. He wanted to know that the tight ship he was trying to run was also safe and sound. And he enjoyed the treats, and the TV, as much as we did. As my mother ironed or sewed or wrote letters or her diary, the rest of us sank back into the sofa and stared at the screen. We watched the Sunday tea-time serial, costume dramas like *War and Peace* and *The Pallisers*, comedy shows like *Dick Emery* and *Dave Allen*. My father, who would sigh over Jane Austen and whose favourite book was *Anna Karenina*, would howl with laughter over *The Two Ronnies*. I would look over and see his shoulders shaking.

It fascinates me now that whole stretches of my childhood, those days and weeks and months that often seemed so long, are now shrunk to the flash of a crinoline on a TV screen, a mouthful of sweet crumbs, the glimpse of shoulders shaking.

This house has warmth. Yes, it did. It had laughter and games and toys and a dressing-up box and dolls to play with and books to read and felt pens to draw with and roast chicken on a Sunday and, when guests came round or family came to stay, my mother's delicious fruit cake, a bit dry and with the fruit all sunk to the bottom, but still the best cake in the world. It had ham, from the Christmas market at the Swedish church, with red cabbage, and candles, at Advent and Christmas and on special occasions. It had birthdays that started with the sound of singing, as the whole family trooped into your bedroom in nighties and pyjamas, my mother with the tray of presents, my father with a tray of coffee and candles, and, for each of us, a pink shiny bar of Fry's Turkish Delight. It had family games, of Cluedo and Monopoly and Mousetrap and snap, and a game we all called 'Boy Girl' where my father picked a letter and we each had to come up with a boy's name, girl's name, city's name, river's name and on through a long list of names starting with that letter until we saw who got the most, and won.

This house had warmth and love and laughter, but this house could suddenly freeze. It wasn't the heating. 'Mrs 1970's' central heating was fairly reliable and even more reliable when it switched from oil to gas. It was the eggshells. You never knew who would tread on one, or what would happen when they did. It could be something my mother said, or something my father said, or something no one said. It could be anything. Brush against a hairspring trigger and everything changed. 'I didn't have my elbows on the table, Daddy, I didn't, *I didn't!*' And then there would be screaming and shouting and tears and then my skinny, sensitive, beautiful sister would storm upstairs and slam the door.

I want to remember individual incidents, but I can't, because for so many years I have blocked them out. I could tell you about the yellow silk day dress Susan Hampshire wore in *The Pallisers*, or the white lace dress she wore to a ball. Those memories soothe me. But I can't tell you much about what my mother used to call my sister's 'scenes'. There's one still stuck in my head. We were in Wales. My father would sometimes announce on a Thursday night that we were off for a weekend in Wales. He would drive, for hours, with just a stop for a picnic by a view, until we finally reached a village in a valley or on a hill. Then my father would search for a B & B with a sign saying 'Vacancies', and we would take our bags to rooms with candlewick bedspreads and set off in search of fish and chips.

Once, we went to the Brecon Beacons. Another time, we climbed Sugar Loaf Mountain. Once or twice, we went to Snowdon and my father and Tom climbed quite near the top. 'The boys' always forged ahead and my mother and Caroline, in my father's words, 'took up the rear'. I walked on my own in the middle, imagining that I was Laura Ingalls Wilder, striding across a prairie, or Anne of Green Gables, gazing out at the Lake of Shining Waters.

I don't know where we were this time. I know it was raining and we were stuck in the car, looking out at grey clouds and wet sheep. My father stared out from behind the windscreen wipers as if by staring enough he could make the rain stop. 'I think,' he said, as he tried to wipe a hole in the steamed-up windows, 'it's looking brighter ahead.' We all tried to see the patch of lighter sky, but all we could see was grey.

I can't remember what triggered it, but suddenly Caroline was shouting. 'I hate you, Daddy, I hate you!' Her voice went up a tone and then up another tone until it was like the shrieking of a bird of prey. It went on, and on, and on, and on. My father tried to reason with her. My mother's voice sounded as if she was being strangled. I stared out of the window, desperate to escape from this metal box full of screams. 'Stop the car!' my mother yelled. 'Let me out, John! I can't bear this any more.'

'Please,' my father said, and I wasn't sure if he was talking to my mother, or to Caroline, or to God. 'Please. Please, please, please.' I saw his whole body convulse and I knew he was crying. I didn't know men could cry.

Chapter 5

Try Not to Get Worried

When Caroline was fourteen, she went to stay with a Norwegian family. Their eldest daughter, Christine, had stayed with us the summer before and Caroline was keen to make a return visit. 'I am fine and having a super time in Norway,' she wrote in her first letter home. 'The weather's lovely. It was very exciting when the plane lifted off. It went very fast and soon we were up in the clouds. It was exciting to see the clouds arranged like cotton wool!'

She had never been on a plane before. She was thrilled by the 'wooden tables on the back of the seat in front', the 'cold salmon, lettuce and sauce' followed by 'pear in chocolate sauce with whipped cream', the views from the air of 'forests and farms and sea'. The rest of the six-page letter is an account of the drive, the welcome, the house, the food, the family's summer cottage, the strawberries picked and eaten, and her first impressions of each member of the family. Vigdis, the younger sister, is 'very nice'. Nils

Peter, the older boy, is 'very polite'. Eric Andreas, the younger boy, is 'sweet'. The village is 'lovely'. The meals are 'delicious'. The Underlands are 'the nicest family I have ever met'.

I find the letter in a red lever arch file marked 'CAROLINE', on the shelf in Tom's spare room. There are other letters like this one, written on blue Basildon Bond paper. There is, for example, one written to our Scottish grandmother, Mama May, a couple of years before. 'I am absolutely delighted to be seeing you at Christmas,' Caroline writes. 'It doesn't matter if the weather is bad. Seeing each other will be the best part of the visit. At the moment up here the weather is lovely!'

In that letter, as in so many others, she writes about the friends she has seen, the TV programmes she's watching, the books she's reading. 'You know me, I'm such a book worm,' she says. 'I can read for five hours!' In that letter, she also writes about the maths coaching she's having every Sunday, from the daughter of one of our mother's friends. 'Earlier on I thought I understood it, at least the parts she was explaining. But I don't really understand the homework. The girl who is coaching me,' she adds politely, 'is very patient and very nice.' This doesn't really capture the scale of the battle. For Caroline, doing any kind of maths was like trying to take all the jellyfish out of the sea. They would slither out of your hands or sting you, and the struggle to get them all would never stop. But you could try, and she did try. Caroline never stopped trying.

If I shut my eyes, I can just about remember that polite, shy girl, whose letters are so full of joy. In this letter alone, there are so many sources of it: the prospect of snow at Christmas, the Christmas lights in Guildford High Street, watching cine films with the family, Saturday nights in front of the TV. 'It's much nicer when it gets dark early and it's so cosy!' she tells Mama May. 'All the family watch War & Peace together on the colour TV. On Friday while Mummy and Daddy had a dinner party, Tom, Christina and I watched Miss World in black and white on the TV upstairs.'

I want to freeze that image of the three of us, sitting in Caroline's tiny bedroom, watching *Miss World* as my mother served the beef stroganoff and my father honed the debating skills he also practised on his family. It sounds, as Caroline says, so cosy. So safe, so sweet.

'THANK YOU VERY MUCH FOR INVITING ME TO STAY,' she writes at the end of the letter. 'I can't wait to go walking along the beach by the sea at Gullane.' Caroline always had a special bond with Mama May. She often went to stay with her, on the east coast of Scotland, on her own. I don't know if it was that visit to Mama May that inspired the piece of writing I also found in the file, with the heading 'A Seaside Scene'. I'll just quote the last few paragraphs:

I could see the outline of Arthur's Seat in the far distance, a green purple hump. Gradually, it became very hot. I paddled cautiously in the water but the water was cool and calm. Tiny fish bobbed and frolicked.

I ran happily over the rocks. I felt the rough heat of them over my bare feet. I searched for prawns and star-fish. The water between the rocks reeked of the salt sea mingled with the warm sand and the tang of the seaweed.

For hours, I wandered along the silent beach, one solitary figure.

Dusk soon arrived and the evening shadows fell over the sea. The sun, like a ball of red fire, glowed in the sky. Crimson, yellow and purple lights made the sky blaze with colour. Strips of red light shone over the tranquil sea. I walked slowly in the gentle lapping water and the beauty of the scene sank into me as I watched the sunset in the evening sky.

When I read this, in my sister's spidery blue hand-writing, I feel something well up in me and I have to swallow to try to gulp it down. I want to run up to that gangly girl, alone on that deserted beach, dipping a toe in cool water and gazing up at a ball of fire. I want to grab her hand. I want to tell her that I'm sorry and that I had no idea that this was in her head, no idea that she could catch beauty in a web of words.

Caroline failed her eleven-plus. When she went to her secondary modern, she was put in the bottom stream. She was so upset, and worked so hard, that she managed to get herself moved two streams up, but she still had to watch Tom and me rack up top grades while she was lucky to scrape a C. But not this time, not for that beach, not for that walk, not for that sky. At the end of 'A Seaside Scene', there's a big red tick. 'Well done,' a teacher has written in red biro. 'An excellent description.' Next to it, there's a single letter: A.

Later in that red lever arch file, there's another letter from that holiday in Norway. 'Vigdis and I are back from the west coast of Norway where we were staying with her uncle and auntie on an island called Halsnøy,' she writes. 'It was really beautiful there.' The journey, she says, took them past 'lots of lakes and forests' and then through 'masses of snow and mountains and some really long tunnels'. They passed a waterfall that was 'absolutely fantastic' and got a ferry and then a tiny boat. 'Vigdis's auntie and uncle had a lovely house,' she continues. 'It was built of pinewood and stood in the middle of a rocky area facing the lake.'

After that, the tone of the letter changes. 'The family were very nice to me but Mummy and Daddy I must tell you that I was terribly homesick there. I was longing for you and everything I saw reminded me of you. When I woke up in the morning and looked at the lake it was really awful knowing how far away you were.'

Three weeks after Caroline got back from Norway, she disappeared. She was, my mother told us, somewhere called 'the unit'. We didn't know how 'far away' she was.

* * *

Long Grove Hospital was named after an area of local woodland. 'It stands,' according to the leaflet I find in another red lever arch file in Tom's spare room, 'in approximately 80 acres of attractive park-like grounds. Although the hospital was built 60 years ago,' it adds, 'an intensive modernisation programme has provided and extended up-to-date facilities with the wards together with an environment of pleasing décor.'

The leaflet, produced by Kingston and Long Grove Group Hospital Management Committee, is labelled 'Information for Patients, their Relatives & Friends'. It doesn't mention the forty women typhoid carriers who were locked up in the hospital between 1907 and 1992, to stop the spread of the disease. Most were sane when admitted but went mad after decades of being locked up. The leaflet also doesn't mention that Ronnie Kray was committed to the hospital in 1958 but managed to escape by swapping clothes with his equally violent twin.

I never saw the hospital. Nor did Tom. I didn't understand why we couldn't go and see Caroline or why our parents' faces looked so pinched when they got back. I did write her a letter, on a notelet with crocuses on the cover. That's also in the file. 'Dear Caroline,' it says, 'I'm very sorry that you are feeling unwell. On Monday I've got my piano exam and I'm awfuly [sic] nervous. I am getting very worked up and worried as I am sure I am going to fail. Hope you get better quickly and hurry up and come home.'

Tom's note, added underneath mine, is also focused on exams. 'Dear Caroline, I hope you get better very soon. Today it snowed and settled on the ground and in the evening I went skidding on the square at the top of the road. I am revising very hard for the exams which start on Tuesday and am not looking forward to them very much. The first exam is Divinity and the last one is Geography. I hope you will be back by then and get well soon.'

We wanted her to get well, but we didn't know what was wrong. It was only when my mother showed me her diary, thirty years later, that I learnt the full story of what really happened. 'Went to the surgery to get an appointment with Dr Mulcahy this evening,' she wrote on 12 August, 'because I am so worried about Caroline. She does not sleep and her whole personality has changed in the last few days. She smiles at us all the time, says yes to everything and is so peculiar.'

Two days later, she took her to the doctor, who told my mother that Caroline 'was suffering a nervous breakdown'.

The next day, my mother took Caroline and me to Wisley Gardens. 'Caroline,' my mother wrote, 'says everything is her fault and mixes up bombs and security agents and hears children crying in the streets.' The day after that, my mother 'read books about nervous breakdowns' while my father took us all on a rowing boat on the River Wey.

Four days later, Caroline was admitted to Farmstead Villa, the adolescent unit of Long Grove Hospital. My mother's diary for that day is, for the first time ever, blank.

On yellowing paper in the file, I find notes she has typed, a summary with questions for the psychiatrist. 'She keeps wondering what has happened to her and why she is in this place,' she writes. 'I really don't know what answers to give but tend to say that she got into a very worried anxious state, where she felt she couldn't cope any more with her worries. I should be very grateful for advice on this question. It obviously came as a shock to her when she discovered that she was in a mental hospital. She tells me that all the other children are mentally ill – but why is she there, when she isn't?'

In the sleeve next to the typed summary, there are some handwritten notes, more preparation for my mother's meeting with the psychiatrist. 'Caroline' it says at the top, and then underneath: 'extremely kind-hearted, young for her age (likes playing with younger children), not very sociable, hard to make friends and feels left out at school. Often has no one to walk around with during the lunch-break. Started taking sandwiches to school last term so that she wouldn't have to have school dinners by herself.'

That's the phrase that kicks me. School dinners by herself.

Also in the file, I find a note Caroline wrote, at the school at Farmstead Villa:

Reasons for Wanting to Come to School Daily by Caroline Patterson

I think if I came to this school daily I would feel much less homesick. Also I would be able to see my family again. My mother would be quite willing to drive me to school daily if it could be arranged. Here the evenings are very long and I get terribly homesick and I feel like crying all the time.

It would be a very good idea if I could go home for the evenings and come back to the school at about 9.30 p.m. If this could be arranged I would feel so very much happier and Mummy would be quite willing to drive me home and back. I miss my family so much and love them so much.

Six weeks after she was admitted to Long Grove, Caroline's psychiatrist agreed that she could spend the nights at home. My mother would do the two-hour round trip to pick her up after she had finished teaching and my father would do the return journey at 5.30 a.m. before setting off for work. But when my mother went to see Dr Steinberg, armed with 'lots of notes and questions', she found her in his room, 'obviously heavily drugged, absolutely demented and petrified that the people in the unit were going to kill her'.

'The Saturday passed somehow,' she wrote the next day. 'Caroline came into my bed and needed a lot of cuddles. She said the girls at the unit were going to cut her up and make her into sausage meat.' The next morning, she 'was still petrified of being murdered', but managed to sit in the kitchen with my mother and dry some knives and forks.

After a week at home for half-term, Caroline seemed to be getting better. She was allowed to go to the school prize-giving, where she was given a prize for 'outstanding effort' in German. 'Everything went so well,' wrote my mother. 'She received it beautifully and got lots of applause. She seems just like our old Caroline!'

That night, she ran away. She thought my parents were trying to poison her. My father caught her in Collingwood Crescent. My mother's diary entry for that day is written in Swedish, but she translated it for me:

> *I was woken at four by Caroline rushing down from the stairs from John and out into the street. I rushed after her and managed to get hold of her outside the Behards' house, but she was so strong that I couldn't get her back home until John helped me. She said we were not her real parents. We got her into the kitchen and sat and drank a cup of tea, but she thought it was poisoned. We did not dare leave her for a second. At last she said she would like to go back to the unit. We dressed, but couldn't manage to get her into the car. She tried to run to the neighbours to get away. At last we got her into the front seat and I started to push the car. It didn't start until Collingwood Crescent. Caroline disappeared into the dark and mist and I sank down on my bed, shaking. The children came in just before seven. Thank God, they heard nothing.*

The next day, when my mother called Farmstead Villa from a phone booth, the nurse told her that Caroline kept saying she 'didn't have a parent'. For the next few days, Caroline didn't speak. The nurse told my mother that Caroline was now incontinent and that she shouldn't visit her. A few days later, my mother drove over to see her anyway. 'She stared at me in a frightened way,' she wrote, 'and said I was not her real mother. We sat on her bed and I hugged her and tried to convince her. But she didn't believe me.'

The following day, a Sunday, my mother left Tom with some of his friends in front of the football and drove over to Epsom. 'Caroline met me in the corridor. She said I wasn't her real mother. She looked so, so frightened and is still afraid of being killed. I had brought her a box of chocolates, but she didn't open it. She was still saying that I was being acted.'

Three days later, when my mother went back, she found Caroline in only a tank top under her coat. 'I tried to prove that I was not being acted,' she wrote, 'and said it would be very difficult to find someone as tall as me with a Swedish accent and a blue spot on the tongue. She sometimes believed me, but then she would look at me haughtily and say I wasn't.' It's the next sentence that makes me want to wrap my sister in my arms, wrap my mother in my arms, wrap my whole family in my arms and never let them go. 'When I asked Caroline if she wanted anything from home, she answered: love.'

* * *

Sausage meat. Bombs. Other children wanting to chop you up. A mother who isn't your real mother, even though she has the same blue spot on her tongue. Doubly incontinent. All alone in an asylum and you can't control when you shit and when you piss. Parents that try to kill you. Parents who make you cups of tea, but you know the trick they're playing; you mustn't swallow that poison.

What the hell must the world be like when this is what's in your head? And what would I have said to my skinny sister if I'd known?

All I knew was that when Caroline came home, her shoulders were hunched. Her pale, beautiful skin was peppered with red lumps and her flat tummy had swelled to a giant football. Her voice was flat and her mouth kept twitching into a strange smile.

My mother said it was 'the pills' that made Caroline's mouth so dry and turned her skin the colour of a tomato as soon as she went in the sun. It was 'the pills' that caused the weeping pustules on her face and the swollen stomach that made her matchstick arms and legs look even thinner. But my mother also said she had been ill. So how were you meant to know what was caused by the illness and what was caused by 'the pills'?

In a box in Tom's garage, I find the plastic pill dispenser my mother filled and laid out every day. I want to ask her why she kept it. If I'd been the one to measure out my daughter's life in pills, I think I'd have wanted to burn or bury this symbol of my effort, this little Pandora's box of pain. Perhaps she saw it as one of those smashed Japanese bowls, painstakingly reassembled and glinting from shards dipped in gold. I don't know. I can't know. It's empty now, but I can almost see the little mounds of yellow and white pills, carefully counted into each compartment. There are four compartments for each day and in the red lever arch file I find a giant piece of graph paper, neatly folded up. 'Chart of Caroline's medication (Largactil)' my mother has written on the outside. When I open it up, I see it's a huge graph, charting, in different-coloured felt pens, the rise and fall, and rise again, of Caroline's daily dose. Sometimes it soars to 750 mg a day. Sometimes it goes as low as 150 mg. The low dose was when Caroline was relatively stable. The high dose was for when the TV started talking to her or sending out strange smells.

I didn't know then about the TV or the smells. I just had a new feeling in my chest. It was as if someone had dropped a tangled mass of wires inside it and forgotten to take them out. It meant I sometimes felt I had to hold my breath and walk as if I was trying not to trip. And I had to be even politer to my teachers.

In another box in Tom's garage, I find a diary from that time. I only seem to have kept it up for a few weeks. 'Hated school,' is the entry for one day, 'because everyone surrounded me, called me a goody goody and teased me. Felt very unhappy.' A few days later, I'm equally matter-of-fact. 'Watched Generation Game. Caroline made dreadful fuss about hair. Everyone was rather sad and I cried.'

I'm surprised to find this, because I thought I'd always tried so hard to pretend I wasn't upset when Caroline had one of her 'scenes' or when she stormed up to her room and slammed the door. I certainly tried to pretend I didn't mind when she played the same record, over and over again. I grew to hate the piercing tones of the Mother Abbess from *The Sound of Music*, bouncing through the house, telling us all to climb every mountain. There was one song, from *Jesus Christ Superstar*, that became Caroline's anthem. It was meant to soothe her when she couldn't sleep. 'Try not to get worried, try not to turn on to / Problems that upset you, oh' the character playing Mary Magdalene sang. 'Don't you know / Everything's alright, yes, everything's fine. / And we want you to sleep well tonight.'

I've just listened to a recording of the song, for the first time in more than forty years. I had to stop it halfway through. But even all those years ago, when I heard the words through my bedroom wall, I knew they weren't true.

Chapter 6

Boys in Leather Jackets

I never thought God was an old man with a long, white beard. My father said he could see everything, and so I thought he must be like a giant jellybean, stretched out over the world and scooping up the sky. When my mother came to kiss us goodnight and say the prayers in Swedish her grandmother taught her, I would shut my eyes and think of the jellybean's smile.

At Christ Church, I'd play with fluff balls in the pew and listen to the vicar boom his holy words. 'Art in heaven', 'trespass against us', 'only begotten', 'but above all'. I thought they were magic words like Abracadabra, words that would make wishes come true. On Mothering Sunday, we would all troop up to the chancel and the vicar would hand us each a daffodil to take home. On Palm Sunday, we'd get a palm cross. On Christingle, he'd hand out the oranges we'd studded with cloves at Sunday School, and misted with silver spray. The hymns were traditional, but there were special choruses for us. The Reverend Paine would lead us in the actions to 'Do you want a pilot? Signal, then, for Jesus!' and we would all beckon Jesus on our boat as we roared: 'Bid him come aboard!'

By the time I was seven or eight, I was just ticking off the minutes till our roast chicken and apple crumble, or, when my mother got tired of making that, our ice cream and chocolate sauce. My mother had stopped the Swedish prayers and my father never mentioned religion, except when he told us that we should 'honour thy father and mother'. But if we didn't all make it to church, he would still make sure he got there for 8 a.m. communion and he still always had his prayer book on his bedside table, next to Turgenev or Swift.

It was *The Nun's Story* that jolted me out of my apathy. I knew I would never have Audrey Hepburn's cheekbones and that I probably wouldn't live in a hut in the trees where I was visited by monkeys, but I would inspire so many people with my pure heart and pure soul. I cut off my Sindy's long blond hair and asked my mother to make her a black dress and veil. At church I started singing more loudly and gazing up at the rafters, hoping someone would notice my zeal.

No one did, and I got bored with it. Really, I just wanted to be seen. But there were other times when I spoke to God and didn't want anyone to see. When Caroline started shouting or crying, or when she stomped around the house, slamming doors, sometimes I'd shut my eyes and beg God to make things better. *Please* make it go away, *please* make her quiet, *please, please* stop the screams. I'll stop eating Jaffa cakes. I'll tidy my bedroom every day. I'm begging you, God, *please*. When the screams stopped, they soon came back and I decided God couldn't hear me, or if he did he didn't care, or perhaps he simply wasn't there.

At school, now a grammar school where you couldn't just make dinosaurs out of toilet rolls, the French teacher introduced us to Camus and Sartre. Mrs Hudson had short, spiky hair and wore so many bangles they clanked when she talked. It only took a few pages of *L'Etranger* for me to realise I was an existentialist. I was going to sit in cafés in Montmartre and sip tiny cups of coffee and smoke Gauloises. I knew it was important to be authentic, so at church I stopped singing the hymns or saying the prayers. I told my parents that I didn't believe in God and didn't want to be a hypocrite, and that Louise, my new best friend from school, didn't have to go to church and I didn't see why I had to when she didn't. In the end, they sighed and said I could stop.

The problem was boys. The problem for me has so often been boys. There were plenty of boys at primary school when you didn't need them, but when you did, there weren't. Caroline's *Jackie* gave advice on what to wear to attract a boy and even how to kiss one, but what were you meant to do when there weren't any boys to kiss?

Our hope, at first, lay in Tom's school. The Royal

Grammar School, in Guildford High Street, was jam-packed with boys. Twice a year, it had a barn dance in the school hall. At the first one I went to, with Louise, I wore the flowery maxi-dress my mother had made for Uncle William's wedding, which had a strip of nylon lace down the front and a tiny velvet bow. I was still, as my father said, 'solid', and a year in a school without boys had made me scared of them. Louise and I mostly giggled and whispered as we watched shy girls and gawky boys gallop round the room, trying to look as if hands resting on shoulders or flanks was no big deal.

By the next barn dance, I had shed some pounds. *Jackie* had given me clear instructions on how to do it, and I had followed them like a novice fresh to the convent's Rule. No more than 1,000 calories a day. Swap cakes for carrots. No more Dayvilles ice creams – with thirty-two different flavours! – on the way home from school. True, I had a new bible on my bedside table, a lavishly illustrated M&S paperback called *Cakes, Pastries and Bread*. True, I had my lapses. Quite big lapses. My dreams were full of chocolate eclairs I couldn't eat. But the blubber was melting away. And when Louise and I walked into the giant school hall for the second time, I was deathly pale, in my rust-coloured shirt and brown corduroy pinafore, but slim.

A boy with meaty arms and angry eczema asked Louise to dance. A boy with frizzy hair and a sprinkling of pimples asked me to dance. When his fingers rested on my hip I felt something quiver through me. I knew my cheeks were puce as we stripped the willow, turning, spinning, parting and then linking hands and spinning again. So this is what it's like, I thought. This jumping in your chest is what you get when you like a boy and he seems to like you. At the end of the evening, he didn't say goodbye. Oh, I thought, of course. Three days later, on my thirteenth birthday, he called. 'Hello, it's Tim Collins. I wondered if you'd like to meet for a coffee?'

My mother said I was too young to meet a boy. She made me call every Collins in the phone book until I found the one I was not allowed to meet.

That year, grammar schools were abolished. Tom's school went independent and was paired up, for social events, with the local girls' private school. My school turned comprehensive and started admitting boys. The trouble was, the boys were all eleven.

So when a boy called Steve from Tom's class invited him to his youth club and said he could bring me, I asked if Louise could come, too. It was hard to know what to wear. In the end, I went for jeans and the Peruvian jumper I had bought in Carnaby Street after a birthday Big Mac. Louise went for jeans and a powder-blue mohair jumper, with her precious pair of almost-platform shoes. She smiled when she opened the front door and her braces caught the light, but I could see that she was as nervous as me.

The youth club was in the Millmead Centre, a squat block of sand-coloured brick and plate glass with a flat roof that suddenly jerked up and into a giant triangle that looked as if it might topple off. My stomach lurched as we passed a line of motorbikes and a cluster of boys in leather jackets. It lurched again as Tom pushed open the front door. It reminded me of the time in Wales when we had jumped off a wall and on to a strip of sand and seen the tide creeping up it and realised that the only way to escape was to get back up that wall.

As the glass door swung behind us, a stocky teenager in a check shirt came racing up. 'Hi, Tom!' he said, reaching up to pat him on the back. 'Great to see you.' Steve had eager eyes and a firm jaw. He seemed very short beside my giant brother, but then everyone seemed short beside Tom. A girl in a cheesecloth smock was striding towards us. She smiled and stuck out her hand. 'Hello! I'm Jackie.' Jackie led us to a hatch and a counter where a woman with mousy hair was spooning Maxwell House into mugs. She said she was called Cath. She worked in a bank. Her jeans were neatly pressed. Cath asked us where we went to school. Jackie asked us what we were planning to do for O level. Cath asked us about our hobbies. Jackie asked us about our holidays. Cath and Jackie both nodded and smiled as we talked and I tried to smile back and not to look at the boys who were standing a few feet away. One, in an Arran jumper, had glossy dark hair and sparkly blue eyes. One, in a leather jacket, had a cheeky smile that made you want to smile, too. Another one in a leather jacket was thin and blond and looked like one of the Botticelli angels in my father's *History of Italian Art*.

'Right,' said Jackie suddenly. 'We need to sort out the teams.' I felt a sudden twitch of panic. I was nearly always last to be picked for rounders and never understood how you were meant to hit a tiny ball with something that looked like a rolling pin or what was the point of chasing a ball with a wooden hook when your thighs were mottled blue. But if everyone else here was going to be in a team, then I was going to be in one, too.

Jackie led us past the vinyl armchairs and into a big hall with hoops high up at both ends. I heard someone say the words 'volleyball' and then I heard a whistle and then everyone scattered round the room and stood, with knees bent. Suddenly, the ball was in the air and I hoped it wouldn't come anywhere near me. I wasn't sure which side I was on, or who else was on it, or how you could tell. Once, the ball went near Tom, and he tapped it high into the air and through one of the hoops, and I wanted to yell out that he was my brother. Once, it bounced against my shoulder, and I giggled and turned round to try to hit it, and then heard it bounce away. The boy with sparkly blue eyes was standing quite near me, and I could feel my cheeks go hot.

When the game was over, everyone went back to the hatch for more Maxwell House. A man with curly red hair and freckles told me he was called Sam. A man called Barry asked if we were having a good time. A man called

Chris shook our hands and said he was so pleased we had come. Barry and Chris both had beards and wore glasses. They said they were both youth leaders. Sam and Jackie and Cath all said they were youth leaders, too.

I wanted to ask them why so many people here had beards. But when I looked up, I saw my father standing outside the glass door. To one side of the door, I could see the boy in the Arran sweater talking to the Botticelli angel and I wished I could find a way to talk to them.

'Well,' said my father, as we walked to the car. 'How was it?'

For a moment, I didn't know what to say. 'It was great!' said Tom. 'It was lovely!' said Louise. I couldn't seem to find the word for the new feeling I had inside. It reminded me of sitting on the beach in Sweden, the sun washing over me as my ankles and toes were lapped by the tide. 'It was,' I said as I sank into the back seat, 'fantastic.'

On our second trip to the youth club, my father picked us up later, so we were able to stay till the end. As everyone flopped on the vinyl chairs, Barry gave out the notices for the week. He reminded us that Jenny and Bob were getting married on Saturday and that 'everyone's invited'. I was shocked. How could everyone be invited? I was hoping to have my wedding reception at the Clavadel Hotel, wearing an elegant, classic dress like my mother's, and it was certainly not going to be open to any Chris, Sam or Barry who wanted to rock up. Then Barry told us that Folkus would be at Paul and Jan's on Sunday. Folkus? What was Folkus? Who were Paul and Jan? And then Barry closed his eyes and said something that confused me. 'Lord,' he said, 'thank you for this precious time together, thank you for our fellowship. Bless us, Lord, in our witness this week.' I looked around. I thought a witness was someone who took part in a trial, but everyone was nodding and had their eyes closed. Even the boys in leather jackets had their eyes closed. In that moment, I decided that whatever Folkus was, I was going to it, too.

Folkus, it turned out, was the name of the Sunday evening coffee and chat at someone's house, after the evening service. And the evening service was just one of the services that took place in the building on a Sunday, because the Millmead Centre was also a church. It didn't look like any church I'd seen before. It looked, I whispered to Louise, as we walked, two days later, through the double doors on the other side of the coffee bar, more like a theatre. Instead of lines of pews, there was a semi-circle of wooden benches with vinyl cushions and vinyl padded backs. There were no stained-glass windows. There was no pulpit. There wasn't even an altar. There was no decoration, nothing to look at except people, but there were so many people, I prodded Louise and gasped.

It was a relief when Jackie waved and beckoned us over, and told us she had been saving us seats. We had to squeeze past Geoff, Julian and Robert to get to them and I hoped they didn't think my jeans were too tight. I was excited to see that the Botticelli angel and the boy with the Arran jumper were two rows in front. They were, we'd found out, brothers. The blond one was called Pete and the dark one was called Andy. Perhaps tonight would be the night we'd get to speak to them? Perhaps they, too, were going to Folkus at Paul and Jan's? Then I looked around and realised that everyone else looked excited, too. It reminded me of the gig I had been to at the Civic Hall, my first proper gig, with the Boomtown Rats. As everyone waited for them to come on, it was like waiting for a gun to go off. When they bounced on the stage, it felt as if a tiger had been released and people were jumping, waving, screaming, shouting, electric with the thrill.

The music stopped. I hadn't noticed the man at the piano until the music stopped. The silence felt heavy. And then a man in a grey suit with a neat beard walked up to a microphone. His eyes were so bright I couldn't look away. 'Welcome,' he said, 'to the Lord's house.' His voice was like the dark chocolate my mother hid at the back of the larder that I sometimes crept down and stole. 'We are here to celebrate and praise the Lord. Let us begin by singing of his greatness. Let us stand and worship him!'

We all stood up. The people around us grabbed the book from the pouch on the back of the bench in front of them. It had the words 'Living Waters' on the front, hovering over a rainbow and a dove. The piano struck up, a tinkling harmony that sounded more like a pop song than anything we ever heard in Christ Church, and then every voice in that hall burst into song. I had a strange feeling in my stomach as I heard the swell of voices in a single cry, 'Father, I adore you.' It rose up, up to a crescendo: '. . . lay my life before you.' And then the crash, like an ocean wave: 'How I lo-ove you.' The words were so simple, but they didn't sound like any hymn I'd heard. They sounded, I thought, like a cry, like a plea, like a moan of something that might be pain or joy.

All around us, people were gazing up at the ceiling. Some raised their arms as if they were trying to touch something they couldn't quite reach. As the music faded, the man in the grey suit looked out at us, and this time I almost felt I couldn't look at him because I thought something might happen if he caught my gaze, something I couldn't stop. 'Lord,' he said, 'we ask you to bless your children. *Open* our ears, Lord. *Send* your Holy Spirit to move in our hearts.'

Then a man in a check shirt walked towards the piano and a woman in a flowery dress started shaking a tambourine. I didn't know the words they were singing, but I suddenly felt as if they'd been written for me. 'Jesus, take me as I am,' they sang, 'I can come no other way./ Take me deeper into you. / Make my flesh life melt away.' I thought of all the efforts Louise and I had made to make sure our flesh had melted away, and I thought of all the delicious cakes in *Cakes, Pastries and Bread* that I still wanted to bake and eat. I still wanted them, but I suddenly felt that they would never be sweet enough.

The music finished and the man in the grey suit went back to the microphone. 'Today,' he said, 'I want to talk to you about God's love.' Afterwards, I couldn't remember what he said. I could only remember that it felt like the most gripping book I had ever read, and the shock when I realised that he had talked for an hour.

At Folkus, at Paul and Jan's, I still kept my eyes fixed on Pete and Andy, but I couldn't shake off the feeling that I'd had a sip of champagne that someone had snatched away. I wanted to go back to that wooden bench, be back in that hall with the bare white walls. I wanted to feel that music washing over me. I wanted to hear that voice like dark chocolate, talking about love.

Three weeks later, when the man in the grey suit stood at the microphone, his voice was quiet. 'The Lord has spoken to you,' he said. 'He wants you to accept him as your Lord and saviour. The Lord sees you. The Lord loves you. He is the way, the truth, the life. If you have heard his voice tonight, then now is the time to invite him into your heart.'

Now is the time. My mouth felt dry. I could hardly swallow because something was pounding in my chest. When the service ended, and the last chords of 'He is Lord' faded away, I whispered to Louise that I was now a Christian, and she whispered back that she was, too.

Part II

Chapter 7

Blue Butterflies

The first time I spoke in tongues was on a green velvet pouffe. It was in the sitting room of Louise's bungalow. She was sitting opposite me on the sofa and we were gripping each other's hands. When I started to speak, in words she didn't recognise, she said she felt something electric coursing up her arms.

We had both wanted to speak in tongues since Sam told us about the gifts of the Holy Spirit. We had read about them in the Bible, of course. In my Bible, that passage, about the sudden noise from the sky and the sound like a strong wind blowing, is underlined, and so is the sentence that follows. 'Then they saw what looked like tongues of fire which spread out and touched each person there. They were all filled with the Holy Spirit and began to talk in other languages, as the Spirit enabled them to speak.' I couldn't get my mind off those tongues of fire. It made me think of the Lucia crown and its flickering, battery-powered flames.

My Bible is falling apart now. The spine has come off it. The back is hanging on by a thread. The front is clinging on with three layers of Sellotape, one of them now brown. 'To dearest Christina on your 15th birthday' my mother has written on the first page, 'with much love from Mummy and Daddy'. Underneath it, I've stuck a blue and red sticker. 'JESUS' it says in red capital letters on a blue background. Next to it I've written 'died for ME!' On the inside jacket, there are four more stickers. One says, 'God loves YOU', with the O as a giant smiley. One says, 'HE WAS BORN TO DIE'. Another says, 'Put Christ back in CHRISTMAS'. And the last one says, 'Have a HAPPY NEW LIFE with Jesus'. That's the one that leaps out at me. HAPPY NEW LIFE.

My Good News Bible is falling apart because I read it every day. 'Got up early,' I've written on the first page of a notebook with blue butterflies on the cover, 'to start what I pray will be the beginning of a lifetime of early morning Quiet Times.' A 'quiet time' was spent reading the Bible and praying. Barry made it clear, at Folkus and at Network, which is what I discovered the Friday night youth club was called, and at Extra Time, the new Monday night teaching sessions for young people, that everyone had to start their day with one. You were meant to set your alarm early, so your first moments of the day were with the Lord. During that time, you would ask him to speak to you through his Word. The Bible, we learnt, was his Living Word. As we read and prayed, the Lord would direct us, encourage us and sometimes rebuke us, to live as his children, spreading the good news of his love.

In the notebook with the blue butterflies, which I've labelled 'SPIRITUAL DIARY', I've written lists of people to pray for. They include school friends and people I've met at the youth club. Many have a tick next to them. 'A Christian!' I've written next to the tick. One down, many more to go. Next to Tom's name I've written: 'Had a serious talk with Tom about Christianity this evening, but he's so anti-Christian.' Tom had given up going to the youth club after a youth weekend on a barge, where one of the youth leaders had tried to baptise him in the Holy Spirit. Since then, Louise and I had been going to Millmead on our own.

The rest of the diary is an account of my daily Quiet Times, quotes from the Bible, accounts of trips to the youth club, and notes from talks at Network or Extra Time. The tone is not always positive. 'I'm really cross with the RE teacher,' I write one day, 'who, whatever her private beliefs, tells some pretty non-Christian stories, and frequently says "Oh my God" etc. I find it insulting to Christianity that the RE teacher in a school should not be a Christian!' A few weeks later, I'm angry again. 'One thing that has really made me mad is the newly released *Life of Brian* Monty Python film, which is nothing but a blasphemous mockery of Christ. It's hard,' I add, 'to feel forgiveness for the makers of such a film.'

By now, it's clear that my love of clothes is a sin. Cakes,

too, don't just threaten my zip. 'I must stop being so greedy,' is a frequent theme. 'Gluttony is a sin.' It's also clear that my wages from my Saturday job at Cranks health food shop and café are no longer strictly mine. 'If Christ is going to be Lord of all,' I've written, 'then he's going to have to control money as well, and that means stopping indulging in all these records, clothes, snacks.' Cranks, like school, was an opportunity to be a witness for Christ. Not just an opportunity, but an obligation. 'I had a rather tiring day at work,' is the entry a few days later, 'but I did get the opportunity to tell Robin I'm a Christian and I've also invited Alison to see *The Cross and the Switchblade*.'

The Cross and The Switchblade, based on a book with the same title, was a film about members of a violent gang in New York who had their lives transformed when they met a young pastor who helped them off drugs and showed them God's love. The sequel, *Run Baby Run*, by the gang-leader-turned-preacher, was even more dramatic. I couldn't get enough of these books. At school, I read *Pride and Prejudice* and *Far from the Madding Crowd*. At home, I gulped down *The Hiding Place*, about two Dutch sisters sent to a concentration camp who used hidden Bibles to spread the message of God's love, and *Chasing the Dragon*, about a young English woman who preached the gospel to members of triads in Hong Kong.

The book that thrilled me most was *From Witchcraft to Christ*. It was by a woman who had been a prostitute called Daring Diana, who became a heroin addict and then a witch. In her coven, she and her fellow witches would slit the throats of birds and animals and sometimes Satan would appear, rising up from the scattered feathers, fur and blood. Doreen became queen of the black witches in Britain. When she found the Lord, forty-seven demons came screaming out.

At church and at Extra Time, we learnt more about Satan. He was, Barry told us, trying to keep us away from Jesus. He wanted, in fact, to keep everyone away from the Lord. I thought about all the Halloweens I'd spent with Monique in the Wendy house, in the witches' hats we'd made from cardboard, drinking Cherryade blood. I didn't know how I could have done that, or how my parents could have let me. I knew now that you should never celebrate Halloween. You shouldn't do yoga either, or meditation, or anything that had anything to do with an Eastern religion, because it was 'dabbling in the occult'.

There was an awful lot to think about. 'Sam said that the supernatural should become a natural part of our everyday lives,' I've written in my spiritual diary. 'I know I'm going to learn a lot from this diary and that the Lord is going to bless my Quiet Times by showing me relevant portions of His Word.'

I'd like to learn from this diary, too. I'd like it to tell me how a fifteen-year-old girl can go, in a few weeks, from a passionate atheist to someone praying out loud on a green velvet pouffe in a language with no actual words. I'd like it to tell me what those adults thought they were doing. I stare at that handwriting, which is very clearly mine, but can't find a clue. And when I close my eyes and think of that girl, so desperate to please and so desperate to be liked, and try to find the hairline crack between believing all of this and believing none of it, I realise it was more like a slide. Once I'd climbed the ladder to the top of it and peered around, and then sat down, I didn't even feel the nudge that sent me whooshing down. It's only when I'm sliding that I realise it's not just a slide. It's a flume ride, like the one we went to at Liseberg in Gothenburg, one that twists and turns and sends you upside down, and where you suddenly get drenched and you can't stop.

Sam had said that if we wanted to deepen our relationship with the Lord, we should be baptised in the Holy Spirit. Sometimes, he said, when the Holy Spirit comes, people start to cry or shake. Sometimes, they even fall on the ground. That, he said, was being 'slain in the Spirit'.

I was desperate to be slain in the Spirit. I was trying hard to have a daily Quiet Time and to pray every day for my school friends and family. I was trying not to think about chocolate eclairs or dream about the cheesecloth dress I'd seen at Etam. Most of all, I was trying not to think about Andy Johnson, the brother of the Botticelli angel, whose cheeks cracked into dimples when he smiled. All week I looked forward to Network, church, Folkus and Extra Time. I hoped to catch a glimpse of Andy and I wanted to see my new friends. But I wanted more than that. I wanted to recapture that feeling I'd had when I first shut my eyes and said yes to Jesus.

On the Friday night Barry announced there would be a youth weekend, we all started whispering that this would be the time. On the coach to Sussex, we chatted and giggled, but the coach went quiet when we drew up at a big white house in rambling grounds. Louise and I had already agreed that we would share a room with Cathy, Fiona and Priscilla. We dumped our rucksacks on our beds and then raced out to explore the grounds. That night, we ate lasagne and salad in a giant dining room. Afterwards, Barry called us into a room with beanbags and big, squashy sofas he called 'the Well'. He led us in Prayer and Praise and we sang quite a few of my favourites: 'Jesus, Name Above All Names', 'I Will Enter His Gates' and 'Come, Jesus, Come'. I always felt something in my stomach lurch when we sang 'Come, Jesus, Come.'

That night, I couldn't sleep. I couldn't find a way to shut out the pounding of my heart.

In the morning, we had a talk on 'How to witness to your friends'. I felt bad that I hadn't talked more about Jesus at school. I knew I should have tried harder to invite Linda, Sarah and Karen to youth club, but I hadn't really wanted them to meet Andy Johnson, in case he liked them more than me. I tried not to look at him during talks or 'Prayer and Praise', but once our eyes locked and my cheeks went red. After the break, we had a session on 'How to get more out of your Quiet Times' and I felt bad again, because I wasn't very good at waking up when my alarm went off, and sometimes had Quiet Times that were only fifteen minutes.

In the afternoon, we went canoeing. I wasn't sure how to stop the canoe from rocking, and kept thinking it was about to flip over and that I would be sent plummeting into brown water and tangled weeds. It was a relief to be back on dry land, but I still felt as if the ground wasn't firm. When we got back, I couldn't eat all my chilli con carne before we were called back to 'the Well'.

I knew as soon as the singing started that something was going to happen. I could hear it in the voices, like a wave building to a swell. 'I love you, Lord, and I lift my voice, to worship you, oh my soul rejoice.' I felt as if the words and the notes were rippling through me, almost as if they were lifting my feet from the ground.

'I believe,' said Barry in a voice that seemed deeper than usual, 'that the Lord wants to move powerfully among us tonight. The Lord is here. Let us show him how much we love him!' He prayed for a long time, and then we sang 'Jesus, How Lovely You Are', and then 'Jesus, Take Me as I Am' and 'Our God Reigns'.

'And now,' said Barry, 'we will wait on the Lord. Oh Jes-us! Come and move among us, Lord! Come and show us your power!' He stopped and bowed his head. The silence was like the silence in a storm. From one corner of the room, I could hear sobbing.

I clenched my buttocks, on my beanbag. I shut my eyes as tightly as I could. 'Oh Lord,' I prayed. 'Please, Lord, please, Lord, please, please, please.' I heard Sam praying loudly in a corner. He sounded so fierce that I thought maybe he wasn't talking to God, but to the demons he had told us were trying to keep us from the Lord. At church, we had begged the Lord to halt the army of demons marching through the land, using abortion as their weapon and IRA bombs. I knew you had to use the sword of truth to fight the demons. I couldn't resist opening my eyes and I saw that he and Barry both had their hands on Howard's head. Howard was rocking back and forth and tears were running down his face. It was the first time I had seen any of the boys cry.

I shut my eyes again and suddenly felt something hovering above me. Then I felt hands cupping my head. Before they spoke, I knew it was Barry and Sam, standing on either side of my bean bag. 'Thank you, Lord!' said Barry. 'We *feel* your presence here, Lord!' Sam was talking too, but not in English. He was talking in a language I had never heard before. As he spoke, I felt something surge through me, from my head to my chest to my stomach, legs and toes. After a few minutes, he started speaking in English, as if he was translating the words he'd just said.

'Look at me, my daughter,' he said. 'Look into my eyes. I love you, my daughter. I love your radiance, like the golden hair that I created. You are like a precious flower to me. I have seen the fear and sadness in your heart, and I want you to know that you must not be afraid. I am with you, my daughter. I will always be with you. Trust in me, for I have plans for you.'

I heard someone crying and then realised it was me. I felt as if something that had been tangled up had been unknotted. I felt as if I had plunged into clear, pure water and was now, for the first time, clean.

I carried on crying when Sam and Barry moved over to Louise and then, when someone started playing a guitar and singing, I joined in. 'As the deer pants for the water,' we sang, 'so my soul longs after you. You alone are my heart's desire, and I long to worship you.' When I closed my eyes, I could see Jesus. I felt that his big, soft eyes could see straight into my heart.

The next day, when I got home, I wrote my spiritual diary. 'The Youth Weekend,' I wrote, 'was the most fantastic time of my life!' I wrote down what Sam had said that God had said. 'Lord, I just want to thank you,' I wrote, 'that you were merciful enough to actually speak to me out of all the millions of people in the world. Lord, I love you . . . PRAISE THE LORD!' That night, when I was trying to get to sleep, I suddenly felt colder than I had ever felt. I didn't dare open my eyes, but I knew there was something by my bed. I wanted to scream but I couldn't open my mouth. I buried myself in my blankets and silently begged Jesus to make it go away.

At Extra Time the next day, I told Barry about my

terrifying night. He said it was Satan and that he was there because he was fighting for my soul.

One night, at the end of Extra Time, Barry told us about his vision. The Lord had told him, he said, that the time was right for us to reach out to young people across Guildford. He wanted us to have a week of outreach, with meetings, talks and events. We would turn the games room at Millmead into a kind of café, with tables and chairs and a stage for music and talks. There would be guest speakers, who would share their stories of how they had found the Lord. We wouldn't just invite people to Millmead, he said. We would go out to where the people were.

At a special prayer meeting, we prayed for a logo and a name. The name God gave us, said Barry, was Star Rock. It was 'rock star' transposed, of course, but it was also the star that was the light that was Jesus and the rock that was Jesus that was the church. The logo was a yellow star next to a circle, like the Colgate ring of confidence, around the words 'STAR ROCK' in red blocked letters with a thick black edge. It looked, we thought, like something a rock star would put, in glitter, on his drums. It reminded me of Greenbelt, the rock festival I'd been to with members of the youth club, where all the bands who played were Christians. There were stalls selling Christian T-shirts and spicy bean burgers, and talks on things like 'How to be a more effective witness' and 'Does the Devil have all the good music?'

We'd had to walk miles from our tent to the field with the music. We'd had to wash in buckets and queue for hours for the loo, which was a wooden bench with a hole over a ditch. When a band called After the Fire leapt on to the main stage in their leather trousers, I wanted to yell out that their lead singer sometimes went to our church. As he sang 'Love Will Always Make You Cry', I thought of Andy Johnson as I gazed up at the stars.

I knew it was wrong to think about boys. In the STAR ROCK folder I've found in a box in Tom's garage, there are typed handouts from Extra Time. There's one on predestination. That one lists Bible verses, parables and additional notes to show us that 'ALL are eligible for God's grace' and that God 'did *not* predestine *anyone* to damnation'. There's one on discipline. That one runs to four pages and reminds us of the need to maintain discipline of body and mind. 'The discipline,' it says, 'is to say no to the unloving, fearful, doubting or impure thoughts which come every day.' My handwritten notes, in black biro on foolscap, back up the official handouts. One, headlined 'Relations with Family and Friends', has doodles of stars and flowers among the stern instructions. 'Should be gracious to non-Christian parents,' I've written. 'Don't patronise or condemn your parents. Make time to talk to your family.'

I did make time to talk to my family. Even though my parents still went with Caroline to Christ Church every Sunday, I knew they weren't proper Christians, because they hadn't accepted Jesus as their Lord and Saviour. One day, I tried to explain to my mother why it was important to be baptised in the Holy Spirit. We had both just had a cup of coffee and I had allowed myself a giant slab of her fruit cake. I didn't want to talk to her about the Holy Spirit. I wanted to talk to her about the lovely platform shoes I'd seen at Dolcis and that I'd hoped she might help me buy. But I felt God giving me one of the prompts I knew I shouldn't ignore. When I finished speaking, my mother put down her coffee cup and stared at me. 'Christina,' she said, 'you're beginning to sound like a fanatic.'

I felt a flush of something hot ripple through me, but I managed to gulp my anger down. Honour your father and mother, Barry had said. 'Keep away,' it said in Timothy 2, verse 23, 'from foolish and ignorant arguments: you know that they end up in quarrels. The Lord's servant must not quarrel.' I had to remember this when I talked to my school friends, too. It was the Holy Spirit who brought people to the Lord. Careful arguments could play only a part.

I wish I could ask my mother now what she thought about all of this and how she felt about being lectured on the Holy Spirit by her youngest child. I can't believe I never did. My best guess is that her worry quota was full.

I couldn't tell anyone that I was slightly relieved when Linda, Karen and Sarah all thanked me and Louise for our kind invitation to Star Rock, but said they were busy. I still went there every night. I wore my Star Rock sweatshirt in

Guildford High Street and handed out leaflets as Jackie stood behind a microphone, outside the coffee shop that wafted the smell of roasting coffee into the street, and told passing shoppers how she had found the Lord.

By the end of the week, fifty-seven people had given their lives to Jesus. Barry asked me if I would write about it for the church newsletter. It was the first thing I ever had published.

Chapter 8

Cup of Sorrows

Caroline fell in love with the Romanovs after watching the film *Nicholas and Alexandra*. She fell in love with Janet Suzman, too, who played the Empress Alexandra. In a file marked 'CAROLINE CARDS AND LETTERS', on a shelf in Tom's sitting room, I find a black and white photo of Janet Suzman, with a scrawled signature on the bottom left-hand side. In one of Caroline's albums, I find a photo of her with Caroline, by the stage door at the Yvonne Arnaud Theatre. Suzman looks majestic in a pink satin dressing gown. Caroline looks overwhelmed in a red jacket. The expression on her face makes me think of the verse from the Book of Revelation. 'His face was as bright as the midday sun.'

'At the moment I'm reading a very thick book,' she writes in a letter to Mama May. 'It's called *Nicholas and Alexandra* by R. K. Massie. As I liked the film so much I was dying to read the book. It's very good but I'd like to read more about the actual Royal family rather than the Russian Revolution and politics. I'm very interested in Nicholas II at the moment.'

You can say that again. In Tom's garage, I find a box of books about the Romanovs. It's so heavy I can't lift it. They mostly have rather similar titles – *The Last Tsar, Last of the Tsars, Nicholas II: The Last Tsar* – with the occasional one ringing the changes: *One Day in Russia 1917*. They used to be in the bookcase in my bedroom at Nelson Gardens, which became Caroline's sitting room after I left. When Caroline liked a book, she read it till the pages fell out. When she liked a record, she played it until it got so scratched you could hardly hear the notes. My parents bought her a tape recorder, which helped. They also bought her a Betamax video recorder, which may have been the single gadget in her life that brought the most joy. Now she could record the costume dramas we all watched as a family, shut herself in her room and watch them again and again and again.

In the red lever arch file, I find a whole essay on *Nicholas and Alexandra*. 'The story,' she writes, 'shows Nicholas and Alexandra's fond attachment to each other, their devotion to their son who had an incurable illness and also their agony about his painful illness.' It is, she says, 'an enthralling book, very dramatical [sic] and keeps one in suspense. It is also terribly sad.'

There's no date on the essay, but it looks as if it was written after she left Long Grove Hospital. After four months at the adolescent unit, my mother had begged the psychiatrist to let her come home. The last few weeks there had been grim. Before sending Caroline back to school, she wrote to the headmistress and the school counsellor. 'Great help,' she says, in some notes for her next appointment with the psychiatrist. 'Talked to the girls, who rallied round, sat next to her, talked to her, walked home with her.' At first, every day was a struggle. 'She said they all looked at her at assembly,' she writes. 'Also that the piano teacher didn't like her. Thursday lunch said can't concentrate because of obsessive thoughts. Friday – girls laughed at her tummy. Stepped up dose to 300 mg but too late.'

From now on, Caroline walked a tightrope between medication and alertness. The higher the dose of her Largactil, the worse the side effects: the slower her brain, the bigger her stomach and the more slurred her speech. When she was relatively well, her medication levels could be kept low. Then she could read, do homework and even take an exam. As soon as she had trouble sleeping again, my mother knew it was time to double or even triple her dose. It would take months to get the dose back down. When Caroline was too ill to go to the George Abbot, my mother would sometimes take her to her own school. A kind colleague would let her 'help out' at the nursery school, and my mother would dash back at breaks to check on her. 'Loved my nursery school,' she has written in the same set of notes for the psychiatrist, 'and was very good there. Can't work on 400 mg. Tummy out and complexion bad. Sentences stop halfway. Cramps. Too many pills? No more delusions now.'

I didn't know about the delusions. Or at least I thought I didn't know about the delusions. I've never forgotten the night when Caroline, Tom and I were watching *The Waltons* and Caroline suddenly announced that Olivia Walton, the mother of a wholesome brood on a farm in Depression-era Virginia, was about to commit a murder. I looked at Tom and Tom looked at me and I felt as if someone had kicked me. That was years after she left 'the unit' and I still remember the flash of it: oh my God. My sister's mad. I knew she was mentally ill, of course. We all knew she was mentally ill. But bonkers? Bananas? Barking? Loony-tunes? No one, I wanted to yell, ever told me this!

I don't know why I thought that, because it isn't true. In a diary of my mother's, written three and a half years after Caroline's breakdown, I've found this entry:

> *Caroline said she had been at the George Abbot for 100 years! It broke my heart to see how confused she was. I felt desperate and just didn't know what to do about tomorrow. John has got several meetings on devolution and can't take any time off. We had a family council in our bedroom this evening, all four of us crying and talking and wondering if we can possibly keep her from Brookwood.*

Brookwood was the mental hospital where Caroline was now being treated. She lived in terror of being forced to stay there as an inpatient and, after seeing what happened to her at Long Grove, my mother was determined to keep her out. Two days after that diary entry, my mother wrote that she took Caroline to school with her, but that she had to keep leaving the room 'because she thinks the overhead projector is an electro-convulsive machine'. That night, she gave Caroline two sleeping pills, but they 'did no good'. Caroline, she wrote, 'was utterly confused about the TV programme and thought it was about Nicholas II and her.'

The next day was even worse.

What a terrible day. We thought Caroline had slept all night but perhaps she had just had terrifying visions. She scared the life out of Christina when she saw her in the morning, because she was dressed in three jumpers on top of her nightie and tons of necklaces and a white chiffon scarf around the waist. She said the Bolsheviks were after her. John took her for a long walk at Frensham Pond and tried to get her to talk sense, but she was terribly confused.

Somehow, the storm passed. Somehow, the storm always passed, or at least well enough to keep Caroline out of hospital. That walk at Frensham Pond was one of hundreds my father took her on after she got ill. On these walks, he built a new bond with his eldest child. When they got back, we sometimes glimpsed a gentleness in his face that the rest of us rarely saw. I would hear him explaining things to her, in a slow, patient voice and in a tone that suggested there were things in life you just had to accept. When everything else failed, my father would set off in the car with her, to St Martha's Hill, or the Chantries, and they would trudge together, through autumn leaves or winter mulch or sandy paths sprinkled with pine needles, and often when Caroline came back, there was a sense that something jagged had been smoothed.

It was my father who bought her the book that became her bible. It's called *Tutor to the Tsarevich: An Intimate Portrait of the Last Days of the Russian Imperial Family*, compiled from the papers of Charles Sydney Gibbes. Like my Good News Bible, it has layers of Sellotape holding it together, some of them now brown. Some of the pages have fallen out. The jacket is faded and torn. It's signed by George Gibbes, the adopted son of the tutor to Alexis, only son of the last Tsar. The inscription is by my father. 'To dearest Caroline with many happy returns – a sad but wonderful book for your happiest autumn for a long time.'

On a table in Tom's sitting room, I find a cup. It's the shape of a flower pot, with a geometric pattern in orange, cream and blue and a gilt rim and base. On one side, there's a two-headed eagle with a crown. On the other, there's a crown over two Cyrillic letters and the date: 1896.

It's one of many that were given out to the crowds at the coronation of Nicholas II, along with sausages, beer and commemorative scarves. Half a million people crammed into the Khodynka Field in Moscow, in front of the podium that had been put up for the Tsar. A rumour swept through the crowd that each cup contained a gold coin. In the stampede that followed, 1,400 people died. No wonder the Empress Alexandra later named the coronation cup 'the cup of sorrows'.

The Romanovs knew all about sorrow. For the first ten years of their marriage, Alexandra was under pressure to produce an heir and, after four daughters, there was talk of a curse. When she finally had a son, his illness ruled their life. It's his face that stares out in a portrait on the title page of *Tutor to the Tsarevich*, serious, anxious, a small boy in military uniform carrying a helmet with an Imperial star. Inside the book, there are photos of him sitting on a veranda in a sailor suit, out for a drive in a carriage with his tutor, playing with friends in the hay. The photos were taken at the Alexander Palace in Tsarskoye Selo near St Petersburg, the last home of the Romanovs before they were taken to Ekaterinburg and shot.

The book has photos of all the Romanovs, in the palace, on the terrace, in the grounds. Here are Anastasia and Marie, in white frocks and straw hats, picking flowers in a meadow. Here are Tatiana and Olga looking pensive in military uniform, one dark with gold tassels and a helmet with a huge ostrich feather, one pale with a helmet that's more like a busby, with a gold crest. Here's the Empress, in a lace day dress, reading on a balcony. Oh, and here's

Rasputin, fierce with his beard, her confidant and 'Man of God'.

Caroline took photographs of the photographs and hung them on her bedroom walls. She didn't take a photograph of the photo in the book that makes me gasp. It's a colour photo, of a chandelier. The chandelier is made up of glass tulips with bronze flowers and green and gold leaves, and I gasp because I've seen it before. It is, the caption says, from 'the House of Special Purpose in Ekaterinburg where the Imperial Family was murdered'.

When my mother saw how much Caroline loved *Tutor to the Tsarevich,* and how much time she was spending talking and dreaming about the Romanovs, she wrote to George Gibbes and asked if Caroline could visit St Nicholas House at Oxford, which, according to the epilogue, now housed some of the artefacts in the book. Gibbes's wife, Ruth, wrote back to say that it was a private home, not a museum, but that if she wrote again in the autumn, they could arrange a visit.

St Nicholas House, it turned out, was the Victorian house in Oxford bought by Charles Sydney Gibbes in 1949. He had stayed in Ekaterinburg until January 1919. For a while, he worked as a secretary to the British High Commissioner for Siberia in Omsk, where the White Russians were still just holding on. At one point, he was asked to look after a box with the remains of the Russian royal family, which was later moved to 'a safe place'. He also had some mementos from the royal palace: some photographs, some papers, some exercise books used by the Grand Duchesses, an icon given to him and signed by the Tsarina, a handkerchief, some sleigh bells, a coat of arms.

He took them with him when he left Siberia for Harbin in Manchuria, where he worked as a customs officer. It was there he met George Paveliev, a thirteen-year-old Russian Sea Scout who had lost touch with his parents. Gibbes adopted him and later moved to Oxford, where he was ordained as a Russian Orthodox priest. He chose the name Father Nicholas, after Nicholas II, called his new home St Nicholas House, and converted one room into a Russian Orthodox chapel and another into a library. When he died in 1963, George took over as warden and continued to hold Russian Orthodox services in his memory.

My sister and George Gibbes became friends. I don't think it's overstating things to say that the son of the tutor to the Tsarevich and my sister became friends. In the old bookcases in Tom's sitting room, the teak ones he took from Nelson Gardens, I find a big red album with a gold crest on the front. It's the Russian Imperial coat of arms. In the album are pencil drawings of some of the key photographs from the Gibbes collection. On the inside cover, there's a simple inscription: 'To Caroline from George'.

In the file marked 'CAROLINE LETTERS AND CARDS', I find a thank-you letter from George's wife, Ruth. 'Thank you so much for the Dickens plate,' she says. 'It was my favourite present.' In another letter, George thanks

Caroline, who almost outdid my mother in obsessive snapping, for the latest batch of photos. 'You are,' he writes, 'as qualified as Lord Lichfield. Now I feel you should be visiting St Nicholas House more often and carrying on taking snaps of all the individual items – providing you allow me to buy the films and pay for development of same.'

Caroline first went there, with my parents, in 1975 when she was seventeen. After that, she went at least once a year, until 1986 when it was sold. She was invited to special services George and Ruth held in memory of the Romanovs. She made friends with a girl called Elizabeth who was as interested in the Russian royal family as she was. I don't know when George gave Caroline the cup with the eagle and the crown. There's a photo of her clutching it, with George, in suit and tie, sitting next to her in the sitting room at Nelson Gardens, but there's no date on the back. I do know that that cup remained one of her most cherished possessions.

I only went to St Nicholas House once. I remember the haunting faces of the Grand Duchesses staring out from the walls. I remember the pungency of the incense in the chapel and trying hard not to cough. And I remember the chandelier. I didn't until I saw the photograph in the book, but now I remember the chandelier. Sydney Gibbes brought it all the way from Siberia without breaking a single leaf or flower.

On Tom's teak bookshelves I find another album with

the Imperial coat of arms. Perhaps that, too, was a present from George Gibbes?

I still remember how her eyes shone when she came back from her first visit. The caption in this album, put together some years later, confirms my memory of what she said. 'We have a marvellous feast and meet marvellous people. George Gibbes has invited us to his home since 1976 when I held an exercise book belonging to Anastasia Romanova and one labelled M. Romanof.' It's the other thing she mentions that makes me smile, but also suddenly want to cry. 'I actually touched,' she wrote, 'the Tsar's boots.'

My mother made us each a file of 'important papers', which includes certificates and school reports. I managed to lose my degree certificate a few years ago, after an interview for a job I didn't get. It was the only time in my life I've been asked to show my degree certificate to anyone, but when I got home and opened the file it had gone. My mother would have requested a replacement by now. I need a deadline to do any admin at all and anyway I'm drowning in paper. I think five people's papers is quite enough.

My school reports, like Tom's, are mostly variations on a theme of A. After one of mine, my mother has noted in her diary: 'showed Marie [a close friend] Christina's report and she had never seen anything like it.' But my parents were always careful to moderate praise for our reports, particularly when Caroline was anywhere near. I only remember being congratulated on one. 'Do you know my favourite bit?' my mother said. 'It's "Christina is sensitive to the needs of others." That,' she said, 'made me really proud.'

Caroline's reports tended to focus more on effort than achievement. Her grades at primary school are mostly C+, with the odd B for English. 'Caroline has had mixed successes but I feel some progress has been made,' said the head teacher when she was ten. 'She is helpful and co-operative at school and less timid than she was, and she ventures an opinion, whereas before she rarely did.' Her final report at primary school is one I almost want to frame. 'A thoroughly nice girl who is a very good influence in the school. Shy and diffident – she tries extremely hard.'

After the shock of being put in the bottom stream at her secondary modern, Caroline made huge efforts and some of them paid off. Her grades now were mostly Bs and B+, with the odd C+ or C. For maths, she got Ds. 'Caroline makes an effort, but has very great difficulty with the subject,' pretty much sums it up. After her breakdown, everything changed. It was an effort sometimes just to stay awake, as the Largactil muffled her racing thoughts and blocked the signals in her brain. Some of those thoughts needed blocking. 'Vacillated between thinking and fearing she would be killed,' wrote my mother, after one very bad relapse, 'and thinking she was Jack the Ripper and responsible for all the bombings in London.'

Who wouldn't want a chemical cosh if they thought they had blown off the limbs of people having a pint? But that cosh came at a price. Side effects, according to one medical website, include 'dizziness, feeling unsteady, blank facial expression, restlessness, agitation, weight gain, unusual, slowed or uncontrollable movements of any part of the body, dry mouth, changes in skin colour, shuffling walk'. Caroline had all of these, though not always at the same time. No wonder she struggled with quadratic equations and the fine detail of the Treaty of Versailles.

When she left, at eighteen, with four O levels and two CSEs, the headmistress wrote her a letter. 'We shall miss you, Caroline,' she said. 'In our work we grow much closer to those who have a more difficult passage through school, for whatever reason. I know how courageous you have been and I am sure you will keep up the good fight, for life is truly a very beautiful gift.'

Chapter 9

Into Her Dream

For a while, I kept it on my bedside table. It's not as battered as *Tutor to the Tsarevich*, but it still looks quite well thumbed. It has a green jacket, with sepia photos of stern young men in blazers, earnest young women sitting primly with their hands in their laps and a rakish man in an open-necked shirt showering himself in champagne. It's called *My Oxford* and when I saw it on a bargain table in a bookshop, I had to snap it up. There's a chapter by John Betjeman about his time as an 'aesthete' at Magdalen, one by Antonia Fraser about her 'Vivacious Gypsy' phase at Lady Margaret Hall and one by Martin Amis on his time at Exeter College, girlfriend-hunting in his velvet suit and snakeskin boots.

I knew the Bible should be enough. 'For in our union with Christ, he has blessed us by giving us every spiritual blessing in the heavenly world,' it said in Ephesians 1, verse 3, which I've written out on the inside jacket of my

Good News Bible. I still looked forward to Network, Extra Time and Folkus. I still dreamt about Andy Johnson, even though he had told Jeff that he 'wasn't looking for a serious relationship'. Barry had told us at Extra Time that you shouldn't ask a girl out unless you thought the Lord wanted you to marry her, so it was clear that a 'serious relationship' was the only type you could have. He had also said that 'the joy of marriage is not given to everyone'. To some, he said, 'God grants the special gift of being single.' When he said that, I suddenly felt cold.

Barry and Sam said that God had a plan for my life, but I wasn't sure how that worked. If, for example, you went to a shop that sold bananas and at that shop you met a man and fell in love and married him, did that mean that God had predestined for you to go to the shop that sold bananas? Did God send the man to the shop with the bananas, or did he go of his own free will? What happened if you didn't go to the shop with the bananas, but went to the shop with baked beans? Did that mean you wouldn't get married? And if so, was it God's fault, your fault, or the man's fault, for not listening to God's voice?

If God knew that earthquakes were going to happen, and floods, and hurricanes, then why didn't he warn people? Why was it OK to pray for nice weather on your weekend in Wales, but not OK to ask him not to cause an earthquake that might destroy a whole town? And why was God so horrible to Job? Job said he loved God, but then he lost his camels and sheep and sons and daughters and he was covered with weeping sores and boils. My spots were getting worse and I felt sorry for Job. Why did God allow these terrible things to happen to him when he made sure that Jackie's car passed its MOT and healed Barry's cold?

The answer, said Barry and Sam and Jackie, was faith. I must stop doubting and trust God. I was beginning to feel like one of the heroines in the TV dramas we watched on Saturday nights, laced into a corset that made it hard to breathe. At church and youth club, I was starting to feel that I couldn't speak without being told that my doubt was a sin. At school and at home, I was on red alert for the moment I would have to stand up for Jesus.

One afternoon, when I got back from school, I said hello to Caroline, but she didn't reply. I looked up and saw that her face was contorted and her mouth seemed to have a strange tic. When I spoke, she started twitching. When I tried to approach her, the shape of her mouth made me think of an animal baring its teeth. I told my mother, and saw that her eyes were red and puffy. 'Caroline's not well,' she said, in a strange, tight voice. 'It would be best for you to keep away from her.' It was Louise's eighteenth birthday and I had been looking forward to her birthday dinner, but now I didn't want to go. For most of the meal, I couldn't speak. When my father came to pick me up, Caroline was in the car. As I opened the door and climbed into the back seat, she reared back as if she had been kicked. I knew then that what I'd feared was true.

Caroline had developed a sudden, violent allergy and what she was allergic to was me.

I applied to Jesus. I really did apply to Jesus. Someone told me that it was the college at Oxford with one of the best records for taking students from state schools, unlike the ones in *Brideshead Revisited*, that autumn's lavish TV hit. On Thursday nights, I gorged on Anthony Andrews as Sebastian Flyte, pink and shining in cream linen, and Nickolas Grace as Anthony Blanche, reciting *The Waste Land* in a honey-coloured quad. I wanted to eat quails' eggs and tiny strawberries in wood-panelled rooms! I wanted to be with brilliant, beautiful people, reading poetry and swapping glittering barbs. Linda, Sarah and Karen had already decided that they wanted to apply to Oxford, after spending some exciting weekends at Christ Church with Linda's brother, Mark. My school had stopped doing most Oxbridge tuition when it turned comprehensive. Linda, Sarah and Karen found a private tutor who specialised in supporting people through Oxbridge entrance. I didn't get the private tuition, but everyone said, 'Oh, *you'll* get in.'

When I got the news, from a college secretary on the phone because I could not stand the waiting, I went up to my room and shut the curtains and placed my fingers over my eyes and lay, frozen and could not swallow, because my dream had turned to ashes in my mouth. 'Ask and it shall be given to you,' said the Bible. 'Knock and the door shall be opened to you.' I had asked, and I had knocked, and the door had not been opened. I had begged Jesus for this one thing and Jesus – both Jesuses in fact – had turned me down.

It was my first taste of the kind of grief that feels as if something has sliced off a part of you and you are left looking at the stump, numb before the pain kicks in, and thinking it is not possible to function in the world without the thing that has been lost. Looking back, I'm tempted to sneer. Middle-class girl fails to get into her first choice of university! Hashtag: FirstWorldProblems. But I will not do that, I will not. I've just listened to the theme music of *Brideshead*, for the first time since I was eighteen. It's solemn and sad and beautiful and it has brought it all back: the yearning for something golden, the soul-deep longing for something unsullied. The theme tune is a version of Ave Verum Corpus, a fourteenth-century hymn. My Latin is no longer up to the task of translation, so I've googled it. *Esto nobis praegustatum / Mortis in examine*. May we get a foretaste of the trial of death.

I tried to smile when we pulled up at the squat brick blocks that would be my home for the next few years. There was a central block, of beige brick with black, white and blue geometric panels, and five residential blocks, with zigzagging windows, arranged around an artificial lake. I tried not to think about Linda, Sarah and Karen at Somerville, St Hilda's and Balliol, as I walked past the boys playing football in the corridor outside my room. I jumped when I heard the thwack of their ball against my door, but I carried on smiling as my parents helped me unpack. I had used my Cranks wages to buy a duvet cover, sprinkled with tiny flowers in primary colours, and made cushions to match. I Blu-tacked posters of Impressionist paintings to the wall and got out my new mug tree and my new Habitat mugs. My mother put the kettle on and my father got out the Nescafé and Coffee-Mate. He sat on the vinyl armchair. My mother and I both sat on the single bed. 'Isn't this lovely?' she said. Her tone was brisk.

I have the leaflet in front of me. 'Van Mildert College, University of Durham', it says on the front, above a photo of the sixties blocks. There's a black and white photo of the Junior Common Room, which looks very much like the coffee area at Millmead Baptist Church. There's a section on 'Recreation and Sporting Clubs' and on 'the College Chapel-Quiet Room', which turned out to be a tiny, windowless room with orange plastic chairs and a poster of a forest. Over the next three years, I spent a lot of time in it, taking my turn to lead Bible Study and Prayer and Praise. Keith, a chemist on the next corridor, played the guitar.

In a box in Tom's garage, I find a list of choruses I've written out for Van Mildert Christian Union Prayer and Praise: 'I Will Enter His Gates', 'Rejoice in the Lord Always', 'It's the Presence of Your Spirit, Lord', 'You Are the King of Glory'. I also find a leaflet. 'The Pill: the questions you ask and our answers' it says in big red letters, over a soft-focus photo of a woman with flicked-back hair and soulful eyes. I can't imagine why I kept it. I hadn't even kissed a boy. In Spetse with Louise that summer, an Irish boy had tried to kiss me, but I had pulled away.

During freshers' week, I joined the English Society, the Italian Society, the Durham Union Society, a Christian drama group called The Kings' Men and DICCU, the Durham Intercollegiate Christian Union. For the first time, I met lots of people who had been to private schools. Everyone called them 'rahs', but when *The Sloane Ranger Handbook* came out the following year, we started to call them Sloanes. 'Rahs' were tall and pink. They had nice cheekbones. They had nice clothes. The boys wore Guernseys and cords. The girls wore Guernseys and pearls. After freshers' week, they all found each other and didn't talk to the rest of us unless they needed to. It was long enough for me to find out that Guildford was an embarrassing place to come from. 'Gin and jag belt!' said one young man with strong white teeth. I didn't like to say that my parents hardly drank and we had a Morris Marina.

Beowulf proved quite a challenge after *The Cross and The Switchblade* and *Run Baby Run*. On a camping trip in the Yorkshire moors with friends from the Christian Union, I lugged round my second-hand copy of *The Faerie Queene*, reading snatches by torchlight and hoping they would get me through my essay. I always stayed up all night to do my essays, unable to write the first sentence until the tutorial was just a few hours off. I'd picked Italian as a subsidiary, thinking it would help me on my trips to my friends near Rome. I wasn't expecting to write essays on Dante, in Italian. 'The language essay I've just done,' I've written in a letter to my parents I find in a file marked LETTERS FROM CHRISTINA, 'was a comparison between, and appreciation of, two Italian Renaissance paintings: *L'Orazione nell'orto* by Mantegna and Bellini respectively.' Agony in the garden, in Italian.

I'm amazed now by how much I tell my parents: not just about my struggles with Anglo-Saxon poetry or the Italian subjunctive, or who I've met for coffee, but accounts of my preparation for Bible Study. 'I have,' I write in one letter, 'hit on a method that requires minimum preparation and provokes maximum response. Instead of asking a series of questions, only to be greeted by dull silence, I make them look at the passage for twenty minutes in silence, and then we discuss it. It seems to work fairly well.'

There are several boxes of letters from other people to me, and some of their names barely ring a bell. There are quite a few from someone called Mark who is generous in his advice on running Bible Studies. 'Ideas I have had (I hope from God),' he writes 'suggest we should be looking at "the weapon of praise", spiritual warfare and armour and maybe something on Judgement. Please pray about this.' It's the brackets that make me smile now ('I hope from God'). So confident. So casual. I often lay awake at night, wondering what God wanted and hoping that his plans for me bore some relation to mine.

* * *

I met him at a party. It was a birthday party for Tracey from the Christian Union and he was standing in the corridor outside her room. You couldn't miss him, actually, because he was six foot six. Taller than Dad! Almost as tall as Tom. Unlike Tom, he had big brown eyes. When I looked up and into them, I felt something in my chest flip over.

It was my friend Janine who marched up to him and gestured to me to follow. Janine had had, at the last count, twenty-two boyfriends. Like me, she was fourteen when she went to the youth group at her local Baptist church, seeking boys and finding God. Unlike me, she had managed to go out with most of them. Janine conducted the conversation like someone who thought it was perfectly normal to go up to a tall, handsome man and ask him lots of questions. I gulped down the answers, like delicious sweets. He was called Jonathan. He was in his final year reading chemistry at Castle College. He went to Emmanuel Church. By the end of the conversation, it was clear that we were going there, too.

'Emmanuel: God With Us!' said the banner over the door. It was the entrance to an old carpet factory on an abandoned industrial estate. Inside, there were hundreds of people standing, with their hands raised. 'Come bless the Lord!' was booming out of two giant speakers. I wasn't sure why so many of the women were wearing headscarves. Janine whispered that it was because of the passage in 1 Corinthians 11 that said that 'any woman who prays or proclaims God's message in public worship with nothing on her head disgraces her husband'. I was confused, but I soon forgot about the headscarves because there, in the fourth row from the front, was Jonathan.

I tried to concentrate on the prayers, and on the psalm read, very slowly, over a recording of the music from *The Deer Hunter*, by a woman in a maroon beret and a blue dress. I tried to listen to the sermon, which was given by a man in a shiny suit. It was about how God brought blessings to his children, and not just spiritual blessings, but material and financial blessings, too. I tried hard, but what I was really concentrating on was the way Jonathan turned to whisper things to the boy sitting next to him, and how his shoulders shook when he laughed.

At the end of the service, Janine said we should go up to him, but Jonathan saw us first. He smiled, and his smile made my heart flip again. He walked over to us. He introduced us to his friend. He invited us back for coffee in his room.

On our family trip to Italy that Easter, the Thomas Cook coach tour that was our first foreign holiday in a country that wasn't Sweden, I couldn't think of anything else. Michelangelo's *David* looked, I thought, just like him. The paintings at the Uffizi were full of him. The gondolas in Venice should have had us in them, entwined in each other's arms. After days of worrying whether I should, I forced myself to send him a postcard. As soon as I posted it, I wished I hadn't put three kisses. But when I got back to Guildford, there was a four-page letter waiting on the mat. He was spending the Easter break in Durham, he said, revising with friends. Why didn't I come back early and join them?

We made cheese toasties in the kitchen in his block. We went for coffee in the Undercroft at the cathedral. We walked over Prebends Bridge, where couples kissed. We still hadn't even brushed hands.

I couldn't sleep. I couldn't work. For the first time ever, I couldn't even eat. When I read *Troilus and Criseyde*, and learnt how Troilus couldn't sleep or eat for thinking about Criseyde, I couldn't believe Chaucer knew how I felt. 'Who koude telle aright or ful discryve / His wo, his pleynt, his languor and his pyne?' asked Chaucer, and I wanted to shout that I could. Ask me!

In that box of letters, I've found one that I wrote to Jesus. 'Lord Jesus,' I've written, 'please help me to have control over my emotions. You are the ultimate reality and I will spend Eternity with you, so help me to realise that You are my lover, and to rely on you totally. May you be my heart's desire and may I seek no other.' Above it, I've written some notes. 'It's totally, totally impractical. 1) He's got finals in a few weeks. 2) He'll be leaving soon. 3) He's then going to Canada for at least a year.' Underneath this, I've written, in capital letters and underlined twice: 'I LOVE HIM.'

Two weeks into the summer term, after a day we'd spent

revising in different parts of the library, Jonathan walked with me to the main road and then stopped. He looked as if he wanted to run away. 'Will you,' he said, in a voice that was almost a croak, 'go out with me?' I could hardly swallow. When his lips touched mine, I nearly gasped. I had no idea a boy's lips could be so soft.

When he knocked on the door of my room, later that night, he was carrying a white flower he had picked on the way. We sat on my bed and then leaned back against the wall. I hadn't realised that kissing could make you feel as if there were electrical currents running through your body. I didn't know that a finger brushing against a hip could make something happen inside you that sometimes felt like ripples and sometimes felt like waves. He didn't touch my breasts. He didn't touch me anywhere a Christian boy wasn't supposed to touch a Christian girl. He didn't need to. Every fleeting flick of a finger made me think of Keats's 'Eve of St Agnes', and Porphyro's visit to Madeline. 'Into her dream he melted, / As the rose blendeth its odour with the violet.'

We went, in his old Datsun, on drives through the moors. We lay in the grass at Barnard Castle. We walked in the moonlight at Seaham harbour, gazing up at the stars and smelling the salt from the sea. Sometimes, we prayed together. Once, we went to a baptism in a local village church. The church was full and we had to squeeze on to the balcony. I could feel him standing behind me, and the air between us was like an electric shock.

He was expecting to get a first and planning to do a PhD, in Vancouver or Australia. He said, in a tone that sounded deliberately casual, that I should visit him. I said I'd like to, and tried to sound casual, too. I knew I shouldn't think about the future, but I couldn't help wondering what our wedding might be like, and whether our children would look like him or me.

He invited me to the Castle Ball. It was the nearest Durham got to a ball at Oxford or Cambridge. The night before, I stayed up all night, finishing the blue taffeta ball gown I'd been sweating over for weeks. In the official photo, set on maroon card, and with 'The June Ball' printed on the front in gold letters, Jonathan looks relaxed, but I look pale and tense.

We had cocktails in the courtyard. We had dinner at the Great Hall. We danced to the Pasadena Roof Orchestra, and had Buck's Fizz in a punt on the Wear. When dawn broke, we walked on the riverside and kissed.

Four days later, Jonathan drove me to a country pub. He bought me a half of cider and told me it was over. He was, he said, very sorry.

The next day, he dropped a present round. It was a photo of Durham Cathedral, and there was a note. I have it here. The handwriting is neat. 'Sorry it all had to end this way.' He asked me to think of him and pray for him and not to lose contact with his friends. 'God bless, keep and strengthen you always,' he wrote, and signed it without a kiss.

Chapter 10

Basildon Bond

I can't find the gold pendant. I've looked for it, but in the jewellery box in the chest of drawers in Tom's spare room I've found only some necklaces, earrings and brooches. The pendant is in quite a few of the photos and it was given to Caroline by Mama May for her twenty-first birthday party. 'I am absolutely thrilled with it,' she writes in her thank-you letter, 'and have been wearing it all the time.'

'My twenty-first birthday,' she adds, 'will always be such a happy memory for me. My family gave me a celebration in the morning and in the evening we went to the Thai restaurant in Guildford. We had a delicious meal, really exotic and sat on cushions round low tables. We saw Thai dancing and the whole evening was most exciting.'

We were all excited about the new Thai restaurant at the top of Guildford High Street. We were a bit embarrassed when Mum tried out her Thai on the waitresses, but relieved when they nodded and smiled. We normally went to the Golden Dragon on special occasions, but now discovered that chicken satay was much, much nicer than chicken chow mein. But the best thing about Caroline's birthday was the one she mentions in the next paragraph of her letter: 'I am still loving my work. The girls in my office are terribly nice and friendly and it is so nice to have a new set of friends. The staff, too, are wonderful. They made the day such a joy.'

When Caroline left school, with four O levels (three Cs and a B for Eng Lit) and a couple of CSEs, she went to Guildford Secretarial College. She was not a natural typist. 'Has failed elementary exam twice,' my mother has written in notes for the psychiatrist. 'Perhaps impossible to get enough speed on pills? Will try elementary again in a month. Meantime a kind neighbour is coaching her and grandmother in Edinburgh has bought her a typewriter.'

Underneath that, she has written 'Future' and underlined it. 'Should suspect Largactil or equivalent will always be necessary – at least for next few years. In this case, prospective employer must be told. Am afraid she won't be able to compete on open market. Too slow and also too tired on all these pills. Is it a good idea to have her labelled as handicapped? Employers would be sympathetic. Less stress? Should she be told what is the matter with her? Discouraged, as she thinks she is no better after five years.'

I don't know how much Caroline knew about her illness at this point. I don't even know how much my parents did.

In a letter from Botleys Park Hospital three years later, a psychiatrist told my parents: 'I can truthfully say that, except for the doctor patient I mentioned, I have not met anyone before who has been able to talk about their illness so sensibly and objectively.' Caroline certainly knew she had a mental illness. She knew she was, in many ways, a hostage to 'the pills'. But did she know what her illness was called?

'The word "schizophrenia" is flung about today with flip facility, bobbing up in films, television scripts, literary criticism, even political articles,' it says in a leaflet I've found in yet another red lever arch file. The file has the label 'MENTAL HEALTH' and the heading of the leaflet is 'A Case of Schizophrenia'. The article, it says underneath the heading, was first published in *The Times*. 'Virtually nothing,' it says, 'is established about its aetiology or its genetic, environmental or other predisposing factors, so no means exist for either prevention or permanent cure.'

No means exist. Three words to crush a heart. I hope to God Caroline didn't see them.

In spite of 'the pills', she did eventually pass her elementary typing exam and went on to pass her intermediate exam. She applied for a job as a clerical assistant at the Ministry of Agriculture. She had a typing test in June. She had an interview in July. She had a medical assessment in September. She had to send in a copy of her passport. She waited and waited and waited and then, on 21 November, had a letter saying she was 'unqualified in respect of health to be offered an appointment at this time'.

Two months later, she got a job as a copy typist at Cornhill Insurance. My mother burst into tears when she got the news. Now, when Caroline came home at the end of the day, she talked about Mary and Betty and Debbie and Anne, and who had brought in birthday buns and who she sat next to in the canteen. She did a history evening class. 'It's fascinating,' she writes in that letter to Mama May. 'I'm really glad I made the effort because I've had such fun with it and I do like meeting the people at the class.' She was still devouring books about the Romanovs, the Brontës and her latest obsession, Emperor Claudius. She had a signed photo of Derek Jacobi, who played him in *I, Claudius*, which we all watched together and which she taped and watched again in her room.

Sometimes she worried that she was too slow at work. Sometimes she couldn't sleep for several days in a row and my mother had to increase the dose of her pills. When she wasn't at work, she rushed around seeing friends, and bought records and books with the money she now earned. 'When you next come to Guildford,' she says to Mama May in that letter, 'I'd love to take you to a meal at the Thai restaurant.' She was saving up to go to Norway, to see the Underlands, the family that was there when it all started, the family she loved so much. There was something in her eyes, a glitter, a light, that made it clear to all of us that Caroline was happier than she had ever been.

* * *

Tom's headmaster asked him to be head boy. Tom didn't like the idea of telling other people what to do and turned it down. The headmaster also wanted him to apply for Oxford or Cambridge. Tom decided that he wanted to read French and Marketing at Lancaster instead. He did agree, in the end, to be deputy head boy. 'I am grateful,' wrote his headmaster in his final report, 'for Tom's support as school Vice-Captain and congratulate him on the excellence of this report. His is a record to be proud of.'

From a quick flick through the file labelled 'TOM REPORTS, CERTIFICATES, ETC.', it certainly looks like one. There are photos of him in the *Surrey Advertiser*, in various sports teams, often a head taller than the rest of the team. 'Guildford Grammar School first XV,' is the caption on one of these photos, 'who have made a good start to the season.' There he is in the back row, golden, serious, handsome. There he is again, arms raised high. 'Tom Patterson jumps for the ball' is the caption. That's the one that makes my throat feel tight. Tom Patterson jumps for the ball.

He had fallen in love with French and decided to spend a year in France before he started his course. In the file, there's a letter from the *Ministère de L'Éducation*, offering him a post as an '*assistant de langue anglaise*' in Thuir, near Montpellier. There's a letter from Rugby Football Union, too, giving him permission to play rugby in France, but pointing out that 'it is essential' that 'the Regulations Relating to Amateurism' are 'adhered to at all times'. And there's a card. '*Fédération Française de Rugby*', it says at the top. '*Membre Actif*'. On the other side, there's a black and white passport photo of Tom. He has spots. By this time, we all had spots. But I can see why the girls were beginning to flock.

In the 'TOM LETTERS' file, there's a four-page letter, in his neat, no-nonsense handwriting. 'All is, as ever, wonderful,' he writes. 'Tomorrow I shall see France–Wales at a friend's house, after eating a superb Spanish dish. On Sunday I'm going skiing with a lady and her half Italian/half French daughter! Everything is great, but most of all the job: if I could do it for another year, I would seriously consider it, because I know that I would want to do that as a career. I will almost certainly go to Lancaster next year but I'm not sure, because even you, Dad, would agree that one more year is worth ten years at Lancaster. I know you always told me that England was special, but I can honestly say that I prefer the Midi because I have already been accepted. If you play rugby here, you are treated like a hero. The weather is great, the food too, I adore the people.' He ends the letter by saying 'Anyway, keep well and happy like me.'

My father wrote a six-page letter back. 'We were very glad to get your airmail letter', he writes, and 'glad to hear you speak on the telephone twenty-two days before. We are certainly prepared to read more frequent letters, with more news of your activities.' He will, he adds, bring the form for Lancaster for Tom to sign when he visits him, and then responds to his specific point: 'You certainly cannot give up that place without prejudicing your whole future career and ability to support yourself in the comfort to which you no doubt feel accustomed! The last thing I would agree with is the statement that an extra year at Thuir is worth ten years at Lancaster. You would do best to regard your spell at Thuir as a break in your career of school-university-job, which you are fantastically privileged to have.' He ends the letter by saying 'You are really having a *de luxe* trip at present.' Underneath the 'love Dad', my mother has written: 'Hear, hear, love Mum'.

That's my dad. *De luxe* trip. It's eighteen years since I spoke to him, but when I read his letters he leaps out of the page. Here he is: warm, affectionate, upright, stern. Sometimes, I missed the warmth. Sometimes, he hid it. My father wanted us to do what was right. He wanted us to be clear about our privilege. He wanted us to be good citizens and to pay back what we had been given. My mother wanted that, too, but her letters had more fizz. 'I had a *marvellous* day in London,' she wrote, in her first letter to Tom after seeing him off on the train, 'and enjoyed every minute of it except for the farewell.' The rest of the letter is an account of her activities for the day: trip to Foyles to buy the books for her latest Open University degree, hunt for light bulbs in Goodge Street, bargain-hunting in Heal's sale, coffee at Cranks, a photography exhibition, a shopping trip to Covent Garden, a trip to the French Impressionists at the National Gallery, a trip to the Swedish church and then *The Marriage of Maria Braun* at the Haymarket cinema and *pollo a peperonata* at the Spaghetti House before rushing to the Tube to catch the last train home. My mother rarely took a day off, but when she did she certainly knew how to pack things in.

When Tom went to France, Caroline missed him terribly. 'I can't wait,' she wrote in one letter, 'for you to come home.' In the CAROLINE LETTERS file, she has written several pages, on the blue Basildon Bond we all used, that don't seem to be a letter. I think they're a kind of diary of that Thomas Cook holiday, and in particular the trip to Rome. She writes about a visit to the Roman Forum, to see some of the places that featured in *I, Claudius*, and one to the nursery school she went to as a small child. She writes about a meal out, with Tom. 'He spoke Italian to the waiter so nicely and in such a friendly way,' she says, 'and knew the exact money to pay. It was such fun walking and talking to my wonderful brother in the dark streets of Rome.'

Caroline did save up her money and she did go to Norway. I don't know why my father didn't go to Sweden that year, but she and my mother travelled over to Sweden together on 'the boat'. On lined foolscap, there's an account of the journey. 'Dad drove us to London,' she writes, 'terrible traffic jams all the way and we said goodbye at Victoria station. He wished Mum a lovely holiday in Sweden and me a lovely holiday in Norway. He waved to us on the coach and stayed until it went, even though it meant he was late for work. He kissed us both and smiled. He is a very unselfish, kind man and I love him and wish I was clever like him.'

When I read this, I thought of all the rows. Often, they would start with my father, spelling something out in a voice that made you think of an elastic band that was about to snap. There would be a pause, and then the response was like a machine gun, a volley of hurt and hate. 'I hate you, Daddy, I hate you!' That was always the moment I felt sick, when I tried to block out the calm voice with an edge and the shrieking I thought would never stop. But beneath all that was this. Or perhaps it came out of it. When Caroline came out of Long Grove, my father built something, on those walks at St Martha's and Wisley Gardens and the Chantries, and what he built never broke.

'Earlier,' she continues in the account, 'I started to read *Hard Times* by Dickens. Oh, it is wonderful! Oh, Charles Dickens is revealed as such a compassionate, kind, gentle, sensitive man, with a deep perception of human nature. I love the little circus girl Cecily, who is so humble, yet warm and loving. She was always the one in the school class who couldn't answer questions.'

The one in the school class who couldn't answer questions. The one who struggled to pass her exams, perhaps, when her siblings got straight As.

On the next page, Caroline describes her joy at arriving in Norway and seeing Mrs Underland again. 'My heart swelled with love,' she says, 'as I saw her dear kind face, the gentle eyes and the general sweetness of her.' I shouldn't have been surprised by her comment a few lines later. I shouldn't have, but I was. 'I told Solveig of my problems with Christina.'

Three years after Caroline started at Cornhill Insurance, she phoned my mother from work. She had, she told her, been called in by the personnel officer. He had told her that she was too slow. He said they had tried to help her and looked for other jobs that they thought she might be able to do, but there wasn't an easier job than the one she was doing. They were sorry.

My father was on a work trip when he got the news. 'CAROLINE HAS LOST HER CORNHILL JOB' he has written in his diary. 'Feel sick.' My mother's diary entry is less succinct. As always, she kicked into action. She picked up Caroline from work, spoke to various friends and phoned Caroline's psychiatrist. She also called the personnel officer and tried to plead. It didn't work. Her last sentence is the shortest. 'John rang and cried on the phone.'

They gave her a reference. I have it here now. 'TO WHOM IT MAY CONCERN', it says. 'Miss Patterson was employed as a Typist here at Guildford for the period 15 January 1979 until 9 February 1982 and during that time proved to be a conscientious and loyal employee with a good attendance record.'

Chapter 11

Spaghetti Bolognese

My parents were pleased when I told them I was going to Perugia, but not so pleased when I told them that I was going to tell Muslims about Jesus. 'That sounds extremely unwise,' said my father in the tone I imagined he used in meetings at the Treasury. 'What *exactly* are you hoping to achieve?' My mother started humming in the way she often did when she was keen to ward off a row. 'Coffee?' she said brightly. 'Perhaps we could open Auntie Bell's chocolates?'

I hadn't been sure at first. I was still finding it difficult to hear God's voice. Since Jonathan had told me it was over, I had been trying to focus on the Lord. I'd always suspected there was something about me, a spikiness, perhaps, born out of fear, that put boys off, and Jonathan had shown me I was right. I wrote an essay on *Moll Flanders* and couldn't believe she could tumble straight from one man's arms into another's. I knew Jonathan had left Durham, but I often wondered what I'd do if I bumped into him. Even thinking about it made my stomach lurch. I thought he might gag at the stench of my shame.

I wrote an essay on *Middlemarch*, too. I have it here, in a grey lever arch file, with a jacket that's a picture of a girl in a peasant blouse smelling daisies, above the word 'Reverie'. It seems like the right word for what I felt when I read the book. At times, I almost felt I *was* Dorothea, juggling hopes and dreams and passion and doubt. I underlined the passages that made my whole body tingle. Some made me want to cry out. 'If we had a keen vision and feeling of all ordinary human life,' says the narrator at one point, 'it would be like hearing the grass grow and the squirrel's heart beat, and we should die of that roar which lies on the other side of silence.' Die of that roar. I wanted to roar. But you wouldn't know it from my essay. George Eliot, I wrote, 'was brought up in an evangelical family and for some time her greatest wish was to be a good and pious Christian. But she also possessed one of the greatest minds of the nineteenth century and . . . found herself unable to accept intellectually the dogmas of Christianity.'

George Eliot did not keep going to a church in a carpet factory where people danced and prayed in tongues, even after the person who had introduced her to it had dumped her. I did. I danced and prayed in tongues, too. When I say I danced, I mean I bounced around, waving my arms and raising them up, up to the fluorescent lights above us, up, up to the Lord. When I say I prayed in tongues, I mean that I moved my lips and tapped my tongue against my palate and my teeth, and sounds came out and I hoped they were from God. I thought that the more I bounced and the louder I prayed, the more likely it was that God would reach out to me, the more likely it was that he would show me that I should ditch my doubt and that George Eliot was wrong.

And then, one day, God spoke to me. It was at DICCU, the intercollegiate Christian Union that met in the lecture theatre over the student union. A girl called Sarah, who was on the executive committee, said that the Lord had told her that he wanted DICCU to glorify him by extending our witness throughout the world. Sarah had prayed with other members of the committee and they had decided that the Lord was leading them to Perugia. They asked members of DICCU who spoke Italian to ask if he was calling them to join them in that work.

My mouth went dry. My heart started thumping. I knew God was telling me to go.

Before we went to Perugia, we went to Ilford. Sarah and Jack, who were leading the Perugia witness group, had designed a three-day 'orientation programme' and someone from Sarah's church in Ilford had lent us a flat. There were eight of us in the group: four boys and four girls. We brought our own airbeds and slept on the floor. At 7 a.m., we crawled out of our sleeping bags for our Quiet Times, before group Bible Study, teaching sessions, prayer and worship, drama workshops and spiritual warfare, led by Dave, an elder from Sarah's church. In spiritual warfare, you had to put on the armour of God, to fight the demons who were trying to thwart his work. You had to follow the instructions given in Ephesians, chapter six, by putting on the belt of truth, the breastplate of righteousness, the shield of faith, the helmet of salvation and the sword of the Spirit.

I have the schedule in front of me, together with the Perugia prayer map, on blue card, and the final report. It starts with 'fun & chat' on the Sunday night and ends with 'Evangelism: the aims and tasks of an evangelistic campaign'. I have my notes, too. On the Monday, Jack gave a talk on Islam. He told us that Christians were encouraged to think for themselves, but Muslims weren't. Sarah gave a talk on Roman Catholicism and witness. She told us that Catholics bowed down to statues and candles, which was idolatry and a sin. A boy called Andrew gave a talk on Italian life and culture. He said it focused on the family. I thought of Roberto and Lelle and Cristina and Valeria and Claudio and Carlo and Luciana and Enrico, and the giant pizzas, and the *gelato* we always had before meeting up with the massive group of friends for the *passegiata*, and the beautiful clothes, and the laughter, and the siestas, and the singing in the car, and the games of cards on the beach. I felt as if someone had just told me that Botticelli's *Primavera* was quite a nice picture of some naked women. I thought of my parents' friends, Azra and Fiyaz Hussein, and their string of degrees and their precise and sparkling conversation, and wondered what they would think about Jack's talk on Islam. But Jack had already told me, in a sharing session on our strengths and weaknesses, that he had 'concerns' about my attitude, so I just nodded and smiled.

Jack drove the minibus, first to Dover and then through France and Switzerland. We slept in a youth hostel in Lucerne. When we were about thirty miles from Perugia, a red light started flashing on the dashboard. We all prayed that God would get us there safely, and sang 'Our God Reigns!' until he did.

The boys stayed in a house in Perugia belonging to someone from the local Brethren church. The girls stayed in a flat on the edge of the city, in an apartment block on a suburban street. Jack picked us up in the mornings, before breakfast and after our Quiet Times, and drove us back at night. As I gazed out at the golden stone and the terracotta roofs, I wanted to yell out that he should stop the van, so I could climb out of it and wander those streets and drink in the beauty, and the architecture, and the art, and allow the sun to soak into my veins. But I knew we had a tight schedule and had to stick to it.

On the first morning, Jack led a session called 'Preparation for Witness'. He told us that we should remember that we were in a battle. We should have a blueprint in our mind. We should be warm and friendly and natural. We should avoid a frivolous attitude, but we should use humour. We should be able to give our personal testimony in three minutes. What it came down to, he said, was ABCD: Admit, Believe, Consider, Do.

We should, he said, use a questionnaire to break the ice. I have it here. Which country do you come from? *Da dove vieni?* Would you say you have a faith? *Diresti che hai una fede?* Do you know what Jesus has to say about himself? *Hai gia letto delle cose che Gesu ha detto di se stesso?* Would you like a gospel in your own language? *Ti piacerebbe un vangelo nella tu lingua madre?* Would you like to hear a little more about what Jesus means to me? *Vorrei sentire un po piu di che Gesu vuol dire per me?*

For the next two weeks, we went out in pairs. I went with Frank, who was reading theology at St John's. We stood on the steps of the *Università per Stranieri*, and my heart hammered as we looked for our prey. Frank soon developed a patter and I tried to join in, but I didn't like interrupting people's day. We met a German called Theodore. We met two Nigerians called Philip and Bello. We met Ali from Algeria and Sa'ad from Tunisia and Hafez from Syria and Mahmoud from Iraq. Some people walked off when we started asking questions. Others were far from home and pleased to see a smile. Three young Iranians invited us back to their flat. Their cooker had run out of gas, so they cooked a full Persian meal on a single mini Campinggaz as we all sat on the floor. They told us about the beauty of their country and we told them about Christ.

When a conversation went well, we would invite the other person, or people, for supper. We took it in turns to make it and that was how I learnt I couldn't cook. I'd had a brief frenzy of baking in the time of *Cakes, Pastries and Bread*, when I was meant to be on a diet and went to bed dreaming of chocolate eclairs. Since then, I had barely stretched to a toasted sandwich. Now we had to make dinner for whoever turned up. Some nights, it was twelve. Some nights, it was more than twenty-five. I made a kind of tomato sludge and served it with spaghetti that looked more like semolina. I smiled bravely as I ladled it out.

One night, thirty-two people turned up. That was the night an Italian boy called Luigi, who was going out with a girl from the Brethren church, told everyone at the table that he had something to announce. Over tuna bake cooked by Sharon, he told us that he had asked Jesus into his life. Sarah cried and Jack said 'hallelujah!' We all sang choruses late into the night.

On our last day, when I was talking to a Syrian boy called Ahmed about how I had found the Lord, I felt some drops on my leg. I thought it must be raining. When I looked down, I saw a small dog, with its leg cocked.

I was relieved to get a first. It made me feel better about my decision to put off the earning-a-living question by doing an MA. I had been to see a careers officer and told her I wanted to be a journalist. I couldn't think of anything I'd like more than being paid to ask questions and write. 'Oh dear,' she said. 'That's very competitive. Are you sure?' I thought back to my other dream, of golden spires, and glittering conversation, and epiphanies in wood-panelled rooms, and of the taste of bile that followed. I shuffled in my plastic chair. 'No,' I said.

The careers officer arranged for me to do a multiple-choice test. The results were printed out on lined paper with holes on each side. I should, it told me, become a residential care worker, probation officer or psychiatric social worker. For two years, I had helped out at a local Gateway Club for 'the mentally handicapped' in a hospital on the edge of the city. The day rooms, where people slumped on vinyl armchairs in front of TVs they weren't watching, smelled of cabbage and saliva. In the main hall, where we ran the club, the smell of saliva wasn't so strong. We made animals out of plasticine. We did puzzles and played games. Sometimes, we danced. The grip of some of the patients around my back was so tight it sometimes hurt, but it was the only time anyone ever touched me.

I knew I didn't want to do this for the rest of my life and was relieved when one of my tutors asked me if I'd thought about academia. After flicking through a few brochures, I applied to do an MA in 'The Novel' at the University of East Anglia. The course, said the prospectus, would cover Defoe, Sterne and Robert Louis Stevenson, and people I hadn't heard of like Jacques Derrida and Roland Barthes. I went to Norwich and was interviewed by Lorna Sage. She said the essay I'd written on 'The godgame: intention and achievement in the novels of John Fowles' wasn't 'at all bad' and offered me a place. I asked God if I should take it, and took his silence as yes.

As soon as I met Sean, I liked him. He had curly dark hair. He had smiley blue eyes. After the 'welcome drinks' and the first seminar, he invited me for spaghetti bolognese in his room. He was witty. He was well read. He was older. He was sophisticated. He was urbane. He was charming. He was married.

My father had helped me move into my new room, in a Victorian house belonging to a lecturer in art. I filled it with pictures and objects I'd brought back from Turkey. On the wall, I put prints from the Topkapi Palace. On the windowsill, I put the coffee cups from the market in Istanbul. On the beige carpet, I put the rug I'd bought in Fethiye. And at the 'welcome drinks', I wore the black shalwar kameez I'd bought in Kas. My friend Juliet had bought some, too. We'd spent three weeks wandering around Turkey without a map, a guidebook or plans. We'd had adventures and I wanted more.

At Durham, the lecturers had called me 'Miss Patterson'. I'd met my 'moral tutor' once a year for a cup of tea. At UEA, the lecturers told us to call them by their first names and invited us back to their houses for wine. It was a thrill to be sipping Rioja with 'Angela', who had shocked the literary world with *The Bloody Chamber*, and with 'Malcolm', whose novel *The History Man* had been on TV. 'Lorna' had written a book on Doris Lessing and did book reviews for the *Observer* and the *TLS*. She was married to a man who lived in Florence. You could see that she had once been mesmerisingly beautiful, but she smoked so much that every sentence was interrupted by a rattling cough.

Half the intake was doing the MA in Creative Writing, which Kazuo Ishiguro and Ian McEwan had done a few years before. I was in the other half, which didn't want you to be creative, but did want you to write essays using words like 'problematise', 'interrogate' and 'deconstruct'. You were meant to say 'narrative' instead of 'story' and 'notion' instead of 'idea'. You were meant to use the word 'privilege' as a verb. I thought my essays were beginning to sound as if they were written by a robot, but didn't mind what words I used as long as I could keep going to parties and talking to Sean.

As soon as Sean told me he was married, I knew this was a party that would end. He was, he explained, separated from his wife. He was, in other words, free. I didn't know how to find the words to explain that he might be, but I wasn't. I couldn't even kiss him, and not just because he was technically married. I couldn't go near him, except as a friend, because he didn't know the Lord.

I told my house group leaders in Guildford about him, but I knew what they were going to say. It was a shame, said Ian and Cath, that I had finally found someone I really liked, someone who was charming, witty and excellent company, and who also seemed to like me. But it couldn't be helped. 'Do not be yoked together with unbelievers,' it said in 2 Corinthians, verse 6:14. God was absolutely clear.

When Ian and Cath spelled it out, I felt something inside me drain away. I moved out of the house belonging to the art lecturer. I'd heard a whispered phone call in the hall. 'Oh, you know, boring,' his girlfriend had said, in response to a question on the other end of the line. 'Creeps around. Goes to church.' I'd felt my cheeks burn. I wanted to march down the stairs and yell that I would show them fucking boring. Instead, I moved into the spare room of a maths teacher from my new church, on a seventies estate. The maths teacher was nearly thirty and very upset about being single. I thought if I was nearly thirty and still single, I'd be very upset, too.

On Friday nights, the English department hosted literary events with writers like Martin Amis and Gore Vidal. I longed to go to them, but didn't because they clashed with the young people's fellowship group at church. I did my course work, I met fellow students for coffee, and I made friends at church. I did a dissertation on 'pattern in the novels of Iris Murdoch'. I called it, in a quote from one of her essays, 'Cheering Oneself Up'. I tried not to think about Sean as I wrote about the 'complicated and intertwined sexual relationships' in her work. I quoted what she said about her characters, who 'find the prospect of muddle very deeply disturbing and whose lives are full of the attempts to build meaningful patterns'. I quoted a character from *The Black Prince* who said: 'if I could not build a pattern of at least plausible beliefs to make some just bearable sense of what had happened, I should die.'

Guido Almansi taught on the 'Evolution of the Novel' course. He had written a book on Boccacio's *Decameron* called *The Writer as Liar*. At the end of a tutorial one day, he told me that a friend of his was looking for someone to teach English literature at the University of Arezzo.

Arezzo! That golden city on a Tuscan hillside! Home of Petrarch, Michelangelo and Vasari! And not all that far from Perugia, that other golden city I hadn't had time to explore. I saw myself in a courtyard, surrounded by students, smiling and eager for my words. I saw myself in a café, sipping espresso with a handsome man. I saw myself reading on a balcony and gazing down at olive groves. At last, it was beginning to make sense. I had often felt, like Dante, that I was lost in dark woods, but now I could see that God was leading me back to the land of my birth.

Professor Almansi interviewed me, in Italian. When the interview was over, he shook my hand and told me the job was mine.

Chapter 12

Angels at the Doorway

I didn't go to Arezzo. I went to Tooting Bec. I shared an attic in a suburban street with a friend from church called Priscilla.

For weeks, I had dreamt about sun-drenched piazzas and a new palate for my new life, of rich, warm colours – terracotta the shade of autumn leaves, sandstone the shade of freshly harvested wheat. It would, I thought, make even Oxford look grey. And then I went on a weekend away with my church. It was my home church, Guildford Community Church, a 'house church', like Emmanuel, which had formed when Millmead split. Bev, from the leadership team, had invited me to join them on a retreat for 'future leaders'. I was flattered. I was surprised. Bev had changed quite a lot since she became a leader. As a primary school teacher, she had been big and soft and worn loose, flowery frocks. Now she was slim and sleek and wore smart suits. The weekend, in a Georgian house in Sussex that was now a Christian conference centre, followed the usual format: of teaching sessions, followed by worship, Bible Study and Prayer and Praise. It was in the final Prayer and Praise session that Bev came over and told me that she had had a word of knowledge. The Lord, she said, didn't want me to go to Arezzo. He wanted me to do his work here.

When she said this, I felt as though I was watching a film that had switched, in one moment, from brilliant Technicolor to faded black and white. I had glimpsed a city on a hill, a golden city, but there was a wall around it and the gate through it had been slammed shut. I wanted to yell that it wasn't fair, that Bev could fuck off, they could all fuck off, but I knew I could no more do that than fly off and over that wall. If this was what the Lord wanted, then so be it. It was seven years since I had given my life to him. I had promised to serve him, to follow him and to obey him. 'I have been put to death with Christ on his cross, so that it is no longer I who live but it is Christ who lives in me.' It's there, in blue biro, in my handwriting, on the inside jacket of my Good News Bible. Above it, in capital letters, I've written the reference: 'GALATIANS 2, 20–21.' I kept swallowing as Bev prayed with me, but my tears stung my eyes.

I told my parents that I wasn't going to be teaching in Arezzo and my father wrote one of his letters, on blue Basildon Bond. I have it here. At the top, in blue fountain pen, he has written: 'On Rendering Unto Caesar'. Underneath the heading, which is underlined, he has put five points. 'Most people,' he says in the first one, 'leave school at sixteen and most of them get work – they then start to pay tax at 30% to help to pay for the NHS, schools, student grants etc. and supplementary benefit for those in need.' Many more, he says in point 2, 'leave school at eighteen and point 1) then applies'. The 'privileged', he says in Point 3, 'get three more years of first-degree work' and 'are supported by the rest of the population (including sixteen-year-old taxpayers) many of whom are on quite low incomes'. By Point 4, he is in full senior-civil-servant-briefing-the-minister mode. 'Those even more privileged get a year or more on top of their full-time study and are supported by the rest of the community.' Point 5 is the climax. 'A prime obligation of the citizen is to earn money to pay taxes (Caesar) to help to support citizens whose needs are greater than their own.'

On a second piece of blue Basildon Bond, he has written 'CMP JOB APPRAISAL'. He has written a list of my 'strengths', 'problems', 'personal characteristics', the 'type of work to go for', 'possibilities', 'jobs to avoid' and 'GENERAL CONCLUSIONS'. My 'problems' include 'organising time', 'organising work', 'keeping a sufficient distance to judge personal problems', 'problem-solving' and 'making decisions'. His key 'general conclusion' is that it's 'best for CMP to avoid jobs with erratic hours, commitment to spare-time study or lots of work outside office hours. Rather see spare time as a major opportunity for voluntary work.'

When I opened the letter, I sighed. Why did Dad have to be so pompous? Why was he always so stern? And who was he to say I was bad at organising my work and my time? Hadn't I got all As in my O and A levels? Hadn't I got a first? And he didn't need to quote the Bible to me! I was the one who was a proper Christian. He was just a wishy-washy member of the C of E. Now, the letter makes me smile. It's pithy. It's punchy. It's coolly analytical. It's Dad. If I were the one appraising him, I'd have to give top marks for his analysis of his second daughter, or at least of the person I was then. Most of all, it makes me feel the full force of something I often doubted. It's there in the last sentence, which is also the truest: 'To Christina with lots of love'.

Publishing was the first of the 'possibilities' on my father's list. I wrote to some publishers and applied for some jobs, but was told I needed experience. How, I wanted to yell, were you meant to get experience if they wouldn't give you a bloody foot in the bloody door? A couple of months after finishing my MA, I got a job in a bookshop in Guildford High Street. It was a relief to be lugging around boxes of books and putting them on shelves, instead of finding patterns in them or writing essays about their metafictionality, but I still wanted to work in publishing and it wasn't clear that working in a bookshop was going to get me in. Someone told me about a course at the London College of Printing. It was a Diploma in Printing and Publishing. It lasted four months and at the end of it almost everyone got a job. I told my father about it. 'Who's going to pay for it?' he said, in that tone of carefully controlled patience that suggested the other person in the conversation should tread very carefully indeed. I told him I'd get a grant. 'I wasn't,' he said, and the patience now sounded stretched to breaking point, 'talking about the fees.'

In the end, he agreed to fund the course, or at least the basic living costs for the length of the course, if I hadn't got a 'proper' job by Christmas. I hadn't, of course. I had been too busy going to the pub with my new friends from the bookshop: Patsy, who had never studied literature but seemed to have read more books than anyone else; Joe, a spiky-haired eighteen-year-old who wanted to be a playwright; and Adrian, who had just come back from six months in Berlin, and who wore sparkly scarves and had an earring and a ponytail. Patsy was the grown-up, with a house, a soon-to-be-ex-husband and a daughter. At weekends, we often met in her cottage in the Surrey Hills, which looked and felt like something in a fairy tale. The address was like a fairy tale, too: Yellow Cottage, Walking Bottom, Peaslake. For those months, I almost felt as if I was in a fairy tale, or perhaps the 'lost domain' of *Le Grand Meaulnes*, which I'd studied in French at school. In Alain-Fournier's only novel, the narrator wanders into a fancy-dress party in a mysterious chateau, a magical world he tastes and can't find again. For me, those months were a taste of a world without a treadmill, one where people weren't trying to climb a ladder to any kind of heaven.

My colleagues called me Ingrid. The manager, a man called Grant who had apparently been in prison for drug dealing, had heard that my mother was Swedish and decided I looked a bit like Ingrid Bergman. I didn't, but after running up and down four flights of stairs all day, I was slimmer than I'd ever been. My spots had cleared up. My mother told me that one of her colleagues' husbands had seen me in the shop and told his wife that I had 'lost that fierce look' I 'always used to have'. I wasn't sure whether to be pleased or affronted. I was certainly surprised when, on my birthday, the staff clubbed together to buy me a present. Grant chose it. It was black lace stockings and matching black lace suspenders.

It started with red lumps. First, on the day of Louise's wedding, where I was due to be bridesmaid, when I woke up and saw a scattering of tiny lumps on my chin. The dress, I thought, looked fine. It was sky-blue taffeta, a paler shade of the one I'd worn at the Castle Ball four years before. The dress hung well on my new, skinny frame. But my face did not look fine. I had been on antibiotics for my spots for years. We had all been on antibiotics for our spots. Caroline's started at Long Grove, with 'the pills'. Tom's started when he was thirteen and had left him with the kind of scarring they give James Bond villains. My mother thought it was a shame, but Tom brushed it off. No one who looked at the golden, sporting hero who loomed over everyone homed in on his skin.

I'd had spots since I was thirteen. They'd started with some little bumps on my forehead that made it feel like the skin of an avocado, and then with some tiny dots on my cheeks and chin. I had plastered my face with potions and creams. I had taken every type of antibiotic. I had braved discos and parties with tinted Clearasil, several shades darker than my skin. I had, at times, been miserable about my speckled face, but the sun usually calmed it down, and the past few months it had been relatively blemish-free.

Not now. Louise's wedding day was just the start of a battle that soon felt like a war. Every day brought new lumps, deep, throbbing wells of heat beneath my skin. I felt them as soon as I woke up and when I looked in the mirror I felt sick. The bumps were bad enough. They were a deep, dark red. Even with layers of foundation, they were impossible to hide. But the real problem was what happened next. Every lump was just waiting for the moment to explode, a volcano gathering the energy to erupt. The lump would throb for days until one morning I'd wake up and find it had turned into a head of pus which grew bigger and bigger until it had turned into a giant pustule. If I squeezed it, or even brushed against it by mistake, a see-through liquid would gush out and the next day I'd wake up to a fairy circle of tiny pustules next to the first one, which was now even bigger. I couldn't cover them up because whatever I caked over them, the yellow head poked through. I slathered on creams, but they made the skin around the pustules flake off.

It was disgusting. I was disgusting. By the time I moved into the attic in Tooting Bec, I felt sick from the moment I woke up to the moment I went to sleep. I had been looking forward to my new life in London, and a new course that would, I hoped, get me into a glamorous new world. The course was in a tower block by the Elephant and Castle. The lectures were mostly given by retired printers, men with tattoos who didn't feign an interest in the career prospects of middle-class youngsters who had pored over Milton and Keats. I couldn't look them in the eye. I couldn't look anyone in the eye. I knew that my raging, weeping skin made people want to look away.

I saw a dermatologist, who prescribed a drug called Roaccutane. He said my acne would get better, but first it might get worse. It certainly did get worse. Soon, I had red throbbing lumps halfway down my chest and halfway down my back. I had lumps on my eyebrows, lumps at the corners of my mouth, lumps on my jawline and lumps behind my ears. Every single pore on my face seemed to be turning into a bump that was turning into a pulsating cauldron of pus. I went back to the dermatologist. He peered at my face. He peered at his notes. 'Oh dear,' he said.

I didn't want to leave the house. I phoned in sick to my Saturday job at Foyles. I forced myself to go to church, because if you were a Christian you had to go to church. Priscilla had suggested we go to a church in South Kensington called Holy Trinity Brompton. It was full of the 'rahs' we now called Sloanes. Every member of the congregation seemed to have glossy hair, perfect teeth and skin like a peach. At the end of the service, I joined a queue for special prayer. A young merchant banker called Edward asked me what I wanted them to pray for. I tried to keep my voice steady as I told him about the battle that had broken out on my skin. I whispered that the dermatologist had said I might have polycystic ovary syndrome. I thought I saw Edward wince, but then he nodded and shut his eyes. 'Oh Lord,' he said, in a clear, ringing voice. 'We ask you to heal Christina's ovaries. Touch her with your spirit, Lord! Bathe her in your love!'

The group gathered round. Some laid their hands on me. Some held their hands above my head. 'Bless her, Lord' said a man in a suit. 'Oh yes, Lord!' said a woman in a Laura Ashley dress. 'Oh Lord, we trust in you!' said an Australian girl with long blond hair.

Underneath the canopy of prayer, I was gasping for breath. My cheeks were burning. My teeth started chattering and I started shaking. My teeth were still chattering when I got home.

In the end, I was referred to St John's Hospital for Skin Diseases, in a Gothic red-brick building behind Leicester Square. When the doctor saw my face, he invited students in to study it. I thought of *The Elephant Man*, which we had all watched as a family. At the time, I had felt so sorry for him I cried. Now I was the Elephant Man, or something like him. It had only taken a few months to turn from Ingrid with the black stockings (which I hadn't even had the nerve to try on) to a walking, talking medical textbook, but walking and talking, it has to be said, a lot less than I did before. Back in the attic in Tooting Bec, I spent a lot of time lying down, with my duvet pulled over my face.

The doctor prescribed a kind of ultraviolet light called PUVA, which I had to have in five-minute bursts, in a cabinet like a vertical coffin. I wore sunglasses on the Tube to get to and from the hospital. I knew they wouldn't actually make me invisible, but I hoped they would provide an extra layer of protection from the disgust I knew I now aroused. The treatment worked, or at least it worked for a while. It blasted off the bacteria and several layers of skin. It didn't blast off the scars.

My face was red and raw, but pustule-free when I went for an interview to be a publicity assistant at A & C Black, a publishing company in a Georgian house in the heart of Bloomsbury. When I left, I could smell real filter coffee in the corridor and hear operatic arias wafting in from the drama school next door. I took it as a sign. Oh Lord, I prayed, Oh Lord. Please, please, please, please, please.

I couldn't quite believe it when I got the letter. I had a job! In Bloomsbury! And I could walk down the street and not feel like the Elephant Woman! I moved, with Priscilla, to a basement flat in Pimlico. I started going to cafés and art galleries and having friends round for bottles of Chardonnay and bowls of pasta. Now I knew I had been wrong to doubt God. 'God is to be trusted,' I'd written in my Bible, 'the God who called you to have fellowship with his son Jesus Christ, our Lord.' 1 Corinthians 1, verse 9. Yes, I thought one night, as I was washing up after having friends for supper. God is to be trusted. 'He heals the broken-hearted and binds up their wounds,' it said in Psalm 147. And it was true! God had seen my broken heart and he had bound up my wounds.

I have a prayer journal from that time. It has a black faux-leather cover. It's one of the books on that printing course I actually made and bound. In it, I've written my hopes and prayers. I pray for my friends who aren't Christians. I pray for Caroline. I write long lists of the friends I've seen. 'Lord Jesus,' I've written, a few months into the new job, 'I thank you for the richness of my life. I thank you for my friends and I thank you for all the wonderful opportunities you have given me. I am just so excited and stimulated by all that I am learning and discovering. I LOVE LIFE.'

For years, I had known it was my duty to tell other people about the Lord. Now, I actually wanted to. I had seen that God kept his promises. I had often doubted it, but now I knew it was true. I joined 'the Earls Court Project' at church, an evangelistic programme aimed at drug users, prostitutes and homeless people. We met on Friday nights in a basement in Earls Court. The homeless people smelled of urine. They were often covered in scabs. I knew what it was like to be covered in scabs. When I gave them cups of tea and the sandwiches I'd made, I often put an arm around them. I thought perhaps they felt unlovable, and wanted them to know that they weren't.

At Bible Study, a girl called Karen told us that God had called them to start an outreach project for homosexuals. God loved them, she explained, but the Bible made it clear that homosexual acts were wrong. I knew this already because Bev was now engaged to a man called Jeffrey who had been healed of his homosexuality. That night, a group of people prayed for me. A man called Jason told me that he had had a picture of me walking towards a pub in Earls Court called the Coleherne. As I approached the pub, he said, there were angels at the doorway, welcoming me inside.

The first time I walked in, I wanted to run away. I'd never seen so many men in one room and I'd certainly never seen so many men in black leather. Quite a few of them were wearing peaked caps. Many of them were wearing chains and studded belts. Some didn't have tops on and some were wearing leather trousers that didn't seem to have a seat or crotch. Everyone stared at Karen and me as we walked in and I tried to look calm as I followed her to the bar.

Jason had told me that the Lord wanted me to be there, so I gripped my orange juice and marched over to a bald man in a cap.

'Hello, I'm Christina,' I said. 'Busy here tonight, isn't it?'

The man stared at me, and then nodded. 'Douglas,' he said. There was an awkward pause. 'I'm queer as a coot,' he added, 'but I find you very attractive.'

I didn't know what to say. Of the possible lines we had discussed in the prayer group, no one had suggested this. I asked him how long he had been coming here. About two years, he said. When I asked him why, he looked surprised and then said it felt like a kind of home.

I took a sip of my orange juice and told him I knew what he meant, because I felt something similar with my church.

Was I, he asked, religious?

No, I said. Religion, I explained, was about an institution. I wasn't religious, but I did have a personal relationship with God.

And was I, Douglas asked, happy? For a moment, I was shocked. Of course I was happy, I said, but being happy wasn't the point.

Wasn't it? said Douglas.

No, I said.

Chapter 13

Kangaroo

The first book I had to promote at Faber & Faber was *Safer Sex*. I was a bit disappointed. I'd been hoping to start with a book by a young poet, someone following in the footsteps of T. S. Eliot or Sylvia Plath. But my responsibility, it said in my new job description, was to promote the medical list, the children's list and some fiction and non-fiction. And actually, I thought, as I flicked through the catalogue, I'd publicise books about Apache helicopters if they asked me to. Any book, in fact, that had the Faber logo and name.

When I'd seen the ad in the *Bookseller* for a press officer at Faber & Faber, my heart had skipped. The ad was for a maternity-leave cover, and I had a permanent job, but I didn't care. Who wouldn't, I thought, give up security to work at Faber & Faber? This was the kind of job I had dreamt about, not sending out press releases about *Who's Who* and the Blue Guides. 'We are Wobegon!' wrote one of the editors at A & C Black on my leaving card, an allusion to the Garrison Keillor novel that was then one of Faber's biggest hits. I wasn't. I was touched by the kind comments on the card, and by the leaving present, a blue ceramic bowl I still have in my sitting room and a box set of *The Marriage of Figaro* on LP. But I couldn't pretend I wasn't thrilled.

The previous three or four months had been bumpy. Literally bumpy, because the lumps and bumps on my face had come back. They weren't as bad as they had been before, and they weren't all over my eyebrows and my neck, and there weren't as many yellow pustules, but when I caught sight of my face in shop windows, car wing mirrors, or even saucepan lids, my stomach churned.

At the Tuesday night prayer meeting for the Earls Court project, I had told Karen and Virginia that I couldn't believe God was putting me through this again. The Lord, said Karen, was asking me to give up my will. The Lord, said Virginia, wanted me to give up my pride. He would heal me, she said, when I learnt to give up my concern with my appearance. Karen had a picture of God preparing a crown for me. Virginia had a picture of God as a shepherd, and me as a lamb. The Lord, said Karen, was doing something very special. He was leading me through a wilderness experience. He wanted me to be broken for him.

I told Karen that I didn't want a fucking wilderness experience. I had nearly been broken too many times and I didn't want to be broken again. Karen looked as if someone had hit her. I saw a flash of panic in her eyes and felt as if I had taken something precious and smashed it to the floor. I said I was sorry, sorry, sorry and later, when we walked to the Tube, she prayed for me and sang in tongues, on the pavement in the Brompton Road.

When I heard I'd got the job at Faber, I thought perhaps this was the end of the 'wilderness experience'. Perhaps this job was my reward. But I wasn't sure what to make of *Safer Sex*. According to the subtitle, it was 'a new look at sexual pleasure', but what it really seemed to be about was not getting AIDS. When I saw the ads on TV with icebergs, talking about 'a deadly virus', I thought about Douglas and all those men in black leather I had met in the Coleherne. I felt a shiver running through me and hoped they were OK.

Safer Sex had a whole chapter on 'self-pleasuring'. It said that a good way to get an orgasm was to sit on a washing machine. I didn't know you could get an orgasm by sitting on a washing machine. I hoped I wouldn't have to explain to the authors that I'd never had an orgasm and that I'd only kissed my only boyfriend, and that had been six years before.

In the office I shared with one other press officer, I tried to give the impression that it was no big deal for me to be taking phone calls from the authors of books I'd studied, and to be organising launch parties, and going on tour, and staying in expensive hotels. I met Seamus Heaney, who had one of the sweetest smiles I'd ever seen. He had the voice of a very wise Irish farmer, and made you think that everything would always be alright. I met Harold Pinter, whose eyes were cold and who made you feel it wouldn't. I met Ted Hughes, and nearly gasped. It was like finding yourself in a current you knew would sweep you out to sea. It made me think of the poem Sylvia Plath wrote about her first meeting with her 'big, dark, hunky boy'. In that poem, 'Pursuit', she compares him to a panther. 'One day,' she says, 'I'll have my death of him.'

At parties, my boss, Joanna Mackle, charmed everyone, in little black dresses and Philip Treacy hats. The editorial director, Robert McCrum, introduced me to Mario Vargas Llosa, whose smile reminded me of a crocodile, and to Derek Walcott, whose smile was a mix of international jet-setter and cheeky schoolboy. Four years later, when he won the Nobel Prize, I remembered how he had taken my hand and bitten it. His glittering eyes suggested it wasn't just a friendly nip.

I hosted a party at the Garrick Club for a dentist-turned-wine merchant called Robin Yapp who had written a book called *Drilling for Wine*. He supplied a range of vintage wines for guests to try, and put explanatory labels next to the bottles, and silver spittoons. I ignored the spittoons and tried them all. When I got back to the Pimlico basement, I threw up over the kitchen floor. As I lay down next to the acrid pool, I felt the world spinning and remembered the bit in *Brideshead Revisited* when Sebastian Flyte vomited through Charles Ryder's window. 'It was,' said a passing Etonian, 'because the wines were too various.'

The wines were certainly 'various'. They were various at the parties, at the dinners, and at the launch dinner I hosted at L'Escargot for a book called *Misogynies* by Joan Smith. The guests were all women, apart from Joan's husband. The waiter gave the wine list to him.

At a dinner for Kazuo Ishiguro's *The Remains of the Day*, I sat next to the chairman of Faber & Faber, Matthew Evans. He said he had just met the strangest woman. She was an American, and a born-again Christian. 'She said,' he told me, 'that the Lord was in control of her life!' And it wasn't, he added, as if she was a redneck. She was a literary agent! 'Isn't that extraordinary?'

I felt something turn over in my stomach. I desperately wanted to say 'how weird!' and change the subject. I took a gulp of water and turned to him and said: 'I'm a Christian, and I believe that, too.'

Two and a half months after I started at Faber, I had a strange pain in my left ankle and one in my left wrist. I was packing clothes and books into boxes to move from the basement flat in Pimlico to an attic flat in Blackheath. I struggled to finish the packing, and then to get the boxes down the stairs. The next day, I went to the doctor, who told me he thought I had tendonitis and needed to rest.

I didn't see how I could. I had a long, long list of things to do. I booked a minicab for 7 a.m. the next day to take me to a bus stop at Greenwich. When the bus stopped at Southampton Row, I half-walked, half-hopped down the passage to the Faber offices in Queen Square. By the time I got to my desk, I wanted to scream with the pain. I realised I wasn't going to be able to ignore the doctor's advice, ticked as many things off my list as I could in a day and got a minicab all the way home.

For a week, I hardly moved. The pain spread from my left ankle to my left knee, and then hit my right ankle and right knee. When I stood up, I felt as if my kneecaps were being twisted by someone who was trying to get me to confess to a crime. I thought of the Little Mermaid, and that family trip to Copenhagen when I was wearing a T-shirt with my name on it. I remembered how, in the story my mother used to read us, the mermaid left the sea to walk on dry land, but felt as if she was walking on knives.

I phoned Karen from church and told her I was desperate. She was silent for a moment, and then she said that the first time she'd prayed for me she had felt there was a curse on my family. She thought this might be the root of the problem. She said she had sensed a 'spirit of death' and thought that this was confirmed by the fact that I so often wore black.

When she said this, I felt my whole body convulse. It was like the time the dentist's hand slipped when he was doing a filling and I thought the pain was going to knock me out. It was true that I had felt cursed. I had felt like Job, with my dashed hopes and my sore and weeping skin. Like Job, I had cried out to God. Like Job, I had battled to believe in God's goodness and that had sometimes felt like a battle with life itself. But it had never occurred to me, not even for a second, that my family might actually be cursed. How did that happen? How could God allow such a thing? How could anyone love a God who did?

I tried to go back to work. I got a minicab all the way, but when I got up from my desk to go to the loo, I ended up crying as I crawled on the floor. I got a cab to University College Hospital, and waited three hours at A & E. Eventually, a registrar did some blood tests. He said it could be rheumatoid arthritis, but there didn't seem to be any swelling in the joints. It could be an autoimmune disease called lupus, which attacked the organs and the joints. Or it could just be tendonitis. If it was tendonitis, it should clear up in a few weeks.

Every morning, I got a minicab to the bus stop. The hospital gave me some walking sticks and I used them to prop myself up as I waited for the bus, and then propel myself down the alleyway to Queen Square. I tried to stick to one cup of coffee, so I wouldn't have to worry too much about how I was going to get to the loo. At lunchtime, one of my colleagues brought a sandwich to my desk and in the evening kind Brian from sales, who lived in Lewisham, dropped me off on his way home. I tried to keep smiling. My mother had taught me that it was important to keep smiling. But every night, after I'd waved goodbye to him, I hauled myself up the stairs and howled as I collapsed on my bed.

On Christmas Day, my mother told me that she had

bought a second-hand Ford Fiesta for me to use until I got better. It was the same colour as the Triumph Herald we'd had in Rome and then in Guildford, the colour of a summer sky. For me, it was the colour of freedom, or a kind of freedom, but the first time I drove through central London, and manoeuvred the Fiesta into the tiny Faber car park, I hardly dared breathe.

Now I had a car, I could get back to church. I couldn't stand for the hymns – since I felt my knees were being twisted when I did – and sang to a forest of backs. After one service, Karen and Virginia prayed for the curse on my family to be broken. They took me through all the verses in Deuteronomy about curses. 'I have now,' it said in Deuteronomy 30, 'given you a choice between a blessing and a curse.' I told God that I chose blessing. I repented of every sin I thought I might have committed, and every sin I thought my family might have committed, too. The only big sin I could think of in my family was Tom having turned his back on the Lord. It made me sad that Tom was still so anti-Christian. I asked God to forgive him. I asked God to forgive me. By the end of our prayers, when we were all exhausted, Karen and Virginia told me that the Lord had broken the curse. The pain, they said, would now go.

It didn't. When my flatmate, Fiona, found me sobbing in my room, she asked two people from her house group to come round to pray. A man with a beard called Andy and a German girl with blond plaits called Ase marched around the attic flat and kept saying, in very loud voices, that Jesus was Lord. The kitchen and bathroom were fine, said Andy, but when he got to my bedroom, he stopped in front of an African batik I had bought at Brixton market. He peered at it closely and frowned. There was, he explained, a spirit behind it that didn't come from the Lord. I should, he said, destroy it and do Bible Studies on 'glory' to remind me of God's power.

Andy had a word from the Lord. He said that God knew that I felt all the lights had gone out in my life, but I should trust that the sun would rise again. Ase had a picture of a kangaroo doing a backflip. She also had a word of knowledge. 'I know the plans I have for you,' she said, quoting Jeremiah, 'plans to prosper you, and not to harm you, plans to give you hope and a future.'

I left Faber, after eleven months. The girl whose maternity leave I was covering wasn't coming back, but my boss said this gave her the opportunity to 'restructure' the department. On my last day, they gave me a pair of earrings and a lovely card.

I wasn't sure what to do. I didn't know how I was going to get another job when I couldn't walk more than a few yards without needing to sit down. I had heard about a kind of course called a Discipleship Training School, run by an organisation called Youth with A Mission. It lasted four months and cost about £1,000. The idea was that you went to one of their centres in New York, Paris or

Milan or, if it was in England, in Harpenden, Nuneaton or West Sussex, and learnt how to be a powerful witness for the Lord. Ever since I'd started going to the youth club at Millmead, I'd heard stories about how people had had their lives transformed by a YWAM DTS. I wanted *my* life to be transformed. I needed it to be transformed. If it wasn't, I didn't know how I'd carry on. I found out that there was a course in St Helens, in Merseyside, that started in three weeks. From the £1,600 that Mormor had left each of her grandchildren when she died, saved up from her pension, I had just enough left.

The day before I drove up, I phoned my doctor's surgery. My father had paid for me to see a rheumatologist, who had found out that the blood tests I'd had done at UCH had never been looked at, and had been lost. A year after they were taken, a secretary told me over the phone that they had been found, and that I had lupus.

Chapter 14
Basket

Wolf. That's what *lupus* means in Latin: a wolf. The disease was called lupus by the thirteenth-century physician Rogerius because the rash it often causes on the faces of the people who have it makes it look as if they have been bitten by a wolf.

I didn't want to look as if I had been bitten by a wolf. I didn't want to cry wolf either, and certainly not to my parents. I thought it was too much for them to have two daughters with an incurable disease. I thought perhaps, since the blood tests were a year old, there was a possibility they were wrong. I decided I'd better have new ones done in Merseyside and only tell my parents if the results were confirmed. But I wasn't sure how I was going to manage the drive. I couldn't seem to stop shaking and thought I might crash the car.

The Discipleship Training School was in a Victorian school on the edge of St Helens, on a run-down estate.

When I drove up to it, I almost laughed. I couldn't quite believe that the place I'd just emptied my bank account to stay in looked like a prison. The books we'd been told to read in advance sounded like the kind of books you might give someone in a prison. They had titles like *Glad Surrender, Celebration of Discipline* and *Sit, Walk, Stand*. It struck me that even obeying the title of that one would be a challenge for me, but at least I could sit without too much pain.

The girls' dormitory was up a steep flight of stairs. I was relieved when Noleen, the course leader, said I could sleep in a room with bunk beds on the ground floor. Noleen was one of the fattest human beings I'd ever seen. She was from the American Midwest. She wore huge jeans and baggy sweatshirts and had spiky dark hair. I had expected someone who looked fiercer, but she had quite a mellow air. She had sent us all an information pack, which included a typed list of 'The Marks of a Disciple'. Am I willing to serve? it said. Am I willing to learn? How well do I submit to those who are over me? Am I learning to examine my life? Do I give in easily? How do I handle discouragement?

Well, I thought, when I read that. You may well ask.

I have the information pack in front of me now. 'DTS St Helens, England, September 1989', it says on the cover, next to a silhouette of a church next to some tower blocks. 'A Discipleship Training School', it says, 'is designed to draw each student into an intimate relationship with God.' The emphasis of the school, it explains, is the formation of 'a consistent Christ-like character'. One of our great needs as Christians, it adds, is 'to understand the ways of God'.

I have the timetable, too. It starts each day at 7.30 a.m. with breakfast and continues with Quiet Times, Praise and Worship, lectures, 'small groups', reflection, evaluation and 'evang/work' through till bed at 10 p.m. On the first morning, according to my prayer journal, we studied Luke. We were told we should be more like Mary, who responded to the news that she would give birth to Jesus by saying, 'I am the Lord's servant.' I tried to repeat the words in my head. I am the Lord's servant. I am the Lord's servant. I tried to believe that he was in control of the blood tests that had been lost, which meant that I had missed a year's treatment for a disease where treatment mattered a lot. I kept repeating the words of Psalm 71, which said: 'Though you have made me see troubles, many and bitter, you will restore my life again.'

On the second day, during the prayer and worship session, Noleen asked if anyone needed prayer. I put my hand up and heard myself telling the entire school that I'd just found out I had a disease called lupus. A woman with frizzy hair said her mother had been healed of lupus. A girl called Becky said she had a sense that God was going to use it for good. I opened my eyes to look at her. I couldn't stop gazing at her clear blue eyes and her translucent skin.

That afternoon, I went to see the local GP. I told him about the blood tests that had been lost and found, and asked if he could arrange some new ones. The doctor, who had greasy hair and a bushy beard, told me that he was a Christian. He said that everything worked for the good of those who loved Christ Jesus.

I drove to the hospital to have the blood tests. The nurse said the results would be ready in two weeks.

Late at night, when the last session of praise and worship had finished, I read books about suffering. I read *Something More* by an American writer called Catherine Marshall, about her quest, through many tragedies, for a deeper relationship with God. I read *The Cost of Discipleship* by Dietrich Bonhoeffer, a Lutheran pastor who plotted to overthrow Hitler and died in a concentration camp a month before the end of the war. I knew that what I was going through was nothing compared to them, but it didn't seem to help.

I looked up lupus in a medical dictionary. It said it was 'an autoimmune disease in which the body's immune system, for unknown reasons, attacks the connective tissue as if it were foreign, causing inflammation'. It 'caused a variety of symptoms', including 'a red, blotchy, butterfly-shaped rash over the cheeks and bridge of the nose'. Most sufferers, it said, experienced 'fatigue, fever, loss of appetite, nausea, joint pain and weight loss'. There might also be 'anaemia, neurological or psychiatric problems, kidney failure, pleurisy, arthritis and inflammation of the membrane surrounding the heart'. The disease could be 'life-threatening if the kidneys are affected'. There was 'no cure'.

The night before I went to get the results of the blood tests, everyone prayed for me. A number of people had words of knowledge. I have them written down, on a piece of lined foolscap, in childish handwriting that isn't mine. A man called Dave said he could see a road, with me on one side and God on the other. The traffic had stopped and God was asking me to cross over. A woman called Brenda said she had a picture of a basket. The basket was moving slowly backwards and forwards, but the Lord was under it, and was going to carry me along the path. A man called Neil said that Jesus had been with me through every tear I shed.

The doctor told me I definitely had lupus and I had it for life. He said I should read up on the disease, because it was important to know what to expect, and to get symptoms treated before it was too late. He said he didn't think I should be working. I should be settled in one place, so I could get some proper medical care. It was important not to overdo things, because if I did, it might cause permanent damage.

When I got back to the school, I lay down on my bunk. I felt too numb to cry. I felt as if my future had shrunk to this building that looked like a prison. I didn't know how to tell my parents. I didn't want to tell them on the phone. I tried to stop my voice cracking as I arranged to meet them the next weekend at a pub in Pimlico for Sunday lunch.

I had rehearsed what I was going to say. I told them that they mustn't worry about me, and that I was sure God would use my illness for good. My mother started to cry, and then kept swallowing in the way you do when tears are leaking from the corners of your eyes, even though you're trying to stop them. When she managed to talk again, she said that on the way to the pub they had passed a road called Lupus Street. She said that when she'd seen the sign she'd said that she hoped to God it wasn't lupus.

I had never heard my mother use the word 'God' as a swear word. The nearest I had ever got to hearing either of my parents swear was when my father was trying to assemble an IKEA wardrobe and shouted 'oh hang!' Now, he had the same furrowed face he always had when my mother had a migraine.

A few days later, I got a letter. 'My heart is too full,' wrote my mother, 'and heavy to allow me to express what I feel. I just wish that this burden could have been given to me instead of you. There is no point in asking any questions like why you? Why me? Why us? I have been through this once before.'

My father also sent me a letter. I have both letters, his in blue fountain pen, and hers in blue biro, both on blue Basildon Bond. His letter is addressed to 'my dearest Christina, and deeply loved youngest child'. He says that Caroline 'has had to be brave over many years, and the pain for her parents has been deep indeed. And now,' he says, 'we have the same pain for your sake.'

'For nearly all of my married life,' he says, 'I have suffered great pain as I worried about our diplomatic life, and Caroline's unhappiness from the age of one. Your mother is a brave and wonderful woman, and my greatest pain has been to see her unhappy. She is radiantly brave now.

'Happiness,' he says, 'will return to all of us one of these days – sooner than we think, because it is always there in the sky and the rain and the flowers and the sunshine.'

When half the Discipleship Training School went to run a mission in Marseille, I stayed behind in St Helens. We did 'open-air outreach' in the town square. We went to youth clubs. We spoke at schools. We took services, in the local Methodist church, and Catholic church, and Anglican church. I spoke at a youth club, to a group of boys and girls in tracksuits. Afterwards, three of the girls wanted to find out more. I gave them each a Mark's gospel and invited them to the school for supper. At the end of the evening, I asked if they wanted to invite Jesus into their hearts. First Joanne, then Sharon, and then Tracy whispered that they did. We prayed together, in the corner of the assembly hall that was now a canteen. When they left, their eyes shone.

I spoke to a group of fourth-years about 'God's love for a broken world'. According to the notes in my prayer journal, I talked about famine, oppression and wars, and ended with a message of hope. I gave a talk at a coffee bar run by the local church. I gave my testimony in the town square. There were two giant speakers in the square and as I spoke I could hear the words I'd just said echoing back.

At the end of the course, before we went home, we prayed for each other in turn. A man called Desmond with bad acne scars thanked God for my evangelistic gifts. A teacher called Peter prayed that I would be a light for God in the media and the arts. Glamorous Carla's husband, Neil, had a picture of a whip being cracked in the middle of a group of people, dividing them into two halves. He said that I had the strength to give God's 'demarcation of justice and truth'. He said I would be that whip.

When I got back to Nelson Gardens for Christmas, I didn't feel much like a whip. Instead, I felt like a teenager who was stuck at home with her parents and had no idea what to do. I kept working my way through my pile of Christian books in the hope that I would stumble on the answer.

One day, when my parents and Caroline had gone to work, the phone rang. The person at the other end of it was crying. It took me a moment to realise it was Tom.

Tom was working for a firm of actuaries in Guildford. He liked his job and was good at it. He had lots of friends, both at work and out of it, friends from volleyball, friends from wine tasting, and friends from school, university and golf. He had bought a tiny flat in a pretty wooded area outside Dorking, and liked inviting people round for elaborate meals and good wine. When I got over to it, I found him in his pyjamas and his hair was standing up in tufts. For weeks he'd had a virus he hadn't been able to shake off. His eyes were dull. They made me think of my guinea pig, Conker, who had caught pneumonia and how my heart had flipped over as he gazed up at me from his straw.

I knew Tom had struggled with anxiety in his final year at Lancaster, but I'd never seen him like this. He told me that he couldn't cope. He didn't know how he could carry on working while he felt so ill. He thought he would lose his job and his flat. He knew that it would really upset Mum and Dad, but he didn't know what to do.

I drove him back to Nelson Gardens. We watched *Moonstruck* together as he lay on the sofa and gnawed his thumb. When my mother came home from work, she sat at the kitchen table and cried. She was, she said, a sunny, outgoing person who liked coffee and cake and shops. She didn't know what she'd done to produce three grown-up children who were all miserable, and ill.

After Caroline lost her job at Cornhill Insurance, my mother helped her apply for jobs. She applied to the Department of Transport, Guildway Ltd, St Luke's Hospital, Surrey Constabulary, the Post Office, Boots, Webster's bookshop, Bookwise and C & A. I know, because I have a red lever arch file in front of me, saying 'CAROLINE EMPLOYMENT', and it's jam-packed. She was, it's clear from the applications, willing to do anything.

When the job centre suggested that Caroline apply for a different job at Cornhill Insurance, my mother put a letter in with the application form. The letter is in the file. 'It may seem impertinent to you to apply for a job with a firm from which she was asked to resign,' she writes, 'but whatever happens, I should like to set the record straight.'

She gives details of Caroline's breakdown and her time at Cornhill. 'I know she was never very fast,' she says, 'but she was accurate and her spelling was good.' She explains how, under the stress of being moved to the new audio typing pool, Caroline had another breakdown, which she tried to hide. 'Since Caroline did not want to tell the office,' she says, 'she struggled on against all odds.' My mother explains that Caroline is now registered as disabled but is 'very well' and says that 'several psychiatrists have given her a good prognosis and been impressed by her courage and ability to hold down a job.' She says that she has been told about a 'job introduction scheme' for people who are registered disabled, 'in which the job centre pays most of the first six weeks' salary and the employer is under no obligation to keep the candidate on if not satisfied'. If the Cornhill were willing, she says, 'to try Caroline again, even on a temporary basis, we would be most grateful'.

Unfortunately, the Cornhill was not willing. It was eighteen months before an employer was. Caroline was thrilled to be offered a job in Milwards shoe shop. In the file, there's a handwritten letter from her new boss. 'Dear Miss Patterson, I am very pleased to welcome you to our shop and hope you will be very happy with us.' Caroline was certainly happy to have the job, but she wrote a letter to Tom, who was then helping out at a summer camp for disabled people in America. 'I am finding work at Milwards shoe shop very difficult,' she says, 'especially finding the shoes. The manageress has been very kind to me. She is very nice but she told me on Friday very nicely that I was too slow. I enjoy dealing with the public and am good at it, it is just that I don't think I'm very good at the job. I am on a six-week trial. If I don't pass it, I mustn't worry too much.'

She didn't pass it. It took six months for her to get another job, this time as a part-time assistant in the home furnishings department in Marks & Spencer. She loved the job. She loved the uniform. I have a photograph of her smiling in it, framed on my desk. I also have a Post-it note which I think she must have stuck on the till. 'Sale,' she has written. 'Read card / amount – key in / Press enter twice / customer to sign printed paper /check customer's signature'. I can hardly bear to look at it. Press enter twice.

The job was a work experience scheme for people with disabilities. When Caroline finished her stint, my mother wrote to the manager, praising the scheme and begging him to keep her on. He thanked her for her kind words, but said it was important for Caroline 'to seek permanent employment'.

In the file, there's a green form for the job centre. It's filled out in capital letters, but the handwriting is my mother's. In response to the question 'What limits does your health place on the work you can do?', she has written: 'I HAVE TO BE ON PERMANENT MEDICATION (LARGACTIL/LITHIUM) SINCE MY FIRST BREAKDOWN IN 1973 BUT I DO NOT WANT TO BE REGISTERED DISABLED.' On the final page, the applicant is asked to give details which 'may affect your availability for work'.

Underneath it, my mother has written: 'SINCE I WAS ASKED TO RESIGN FROM THE CORNHILL INSURANCE AND FROM MILWARDS SHOE SHOP I HAVE FOUND IT VERY DIFFICULT TO FIND PAID EMPLOYMENT. I HAVE SPENT SIX YEARS TRYING TO FIND ANOTHER JOB.'

Six and a half years after Caroline left Cornhill Insurance, she was offered a job as a part-time cleaner in the kitchens at the University of Surrey. The wage was £2.57 an hour.

When she passed her six-month probationary period, we all went out for a Thai meal. Now she was coming up to the end of her first year.

Four days after Tom told me he couldn't cope any more, and on the day my mother woke me to say he shouldn't be left on his own and I sat with him, as he told me, again and again and again, that he thought he would lose his job and didn't know what to do, Caroline rang my mother from the university. She said that she had been called in by the personnel officer. She had been told that her work wasn't up to scratch and asked to resign.

When my father got home from work, I overheard him telling my mother that he wished, for her sake, that she'd never met him.

The next day, when I woke up, my left arm had gone dead. Within a few days, I had pain in my fingers, pain in my wrists and pain in my arms. My fingers hurt so much that it was hard to write, but in my diary, in shaky handwriting, I wrote this:

God, if you're listening, and if you care for me at all, please, please answer my prayers. I have tried to follow you for eleven years. I have given up romance, relationships, sex, because I didn't want to displease you. I have tried to share my faith with others. I have sought the truth, even when it has not been easy. But we all have our breaking-point, and I'm not sure that I want to make that choice any more. The Bible says we will not be tested beyond our ability to endure, that our God will supply all our needs, that He heals the broken hearted and restores the weary. I have not found this to be true.

Tom was signed off work with depression. My parents doubled the dose of Caroline's pills. I knew I had to be well for them, but the pains just kept getting worse.

I stopped praying. I stopped going to church. A few weeks later, in my diary I wrote this:

I want to believe in a loving God. But I do not believe you are just, and I do not believe you are good. Let those who do, continue to enjoy your good gifts, but I have had enough.

Fuck off, God. Go and inflict your poisonous blows on somebody else.

Satan, you've won. Let me have my life back.

Part III

Chapter 15

Lifeline

'Do you,' said the doctor, 'feel like Job?' Her tone was crisp. Her hair, flecked with grey, was drawn back into a neat bun. Her eyes, appraising me through thick-framed glasses, were a deep, clear blue. It was my first appointment with my new GP. I glanced down at her notepad and wondered what she had been writing. Surely it wasn't normal for doctors to mention Job? I let the silence hang and then I nodded. 'Yes,' I said.

We had all been shocked when my father announced that he was buying a flat at the Barbican. He would, he explained, get a 'golden handshake' when he retired from the civil service, and had decided that he would take out another mortgage and invest it in a property, and that this would be somewhere he could stay when he was in London – and somewhere I could live. At first, I thought I must have misheard him. I knew my mother had almost wiped out her savings in buying the seventeen-year-old

Fiesta. A meal out was still a treat. But then my father reminded me of how we'd all gone to the Barbican Centre when it opened, and how I'd said I couldn't imagine anywhere more exciting to live. And that was when I realised that he had just made the biggest financial commitment of his life for me.

My mother drove me to IKEA. When we arrived, we had coffee and a bun, as we always did. Before we left, we had meatballs. My mother stopped to look at everything. She always stopped to look at everything. I usually wanted to look at everything, too, but now I just wanted to leave. In all our trips to IKEA, every summer of my childhood, I had dreamt of the moment I'd be buying things for my first home. I hadn't thought I'd be doing it while sitting in a wheelchair pushed by my mum.

We borrowed the wheelchair from IKEA, but I also had one at home. I hated it and tried not to use it. I had a disabled badge now, so I tried to park as near as I could get to wherever I was going, and then half-staggered, half-ran into the building and on to the nearest chair. Sometimes, I used walking sticks. Sometimes, I used crutches. They made me feel like a tragic orphan in Dickens or perhaps like Richard III declaring that it was now 'the winter of our discontent'. I agreed with him. Now is the fucking winter of my fucking discontent. I wanted to yell it from the rooftops. I also wanted to yell it from the floor. If you're not using walking sticks or crutches, people don't understand why you sometimes have to sit on the floor in the queue at Safeway, because if you don't, you're going to have to scream.

The flat my father bought was in a concrete block next to a subway. The bedrooms were both overlooked by the office block next door. When my mother unlocked the front door to it, I knew I should feel grateful. I knew I was incredibly lucky to have the opportunity to live in a flat in central London, and to have parents who cared about me enough to make a passing teenage dream come true. But all I could think about was the pain in my hands, and arms, and knees. I couldn't help much with the boxes. Tom, who was still off work, carried most of them. When he dropped my favourite ceramic bowl, I couldn't stop staring at the scattered shards.

Now, sitting opposite a woman with a neat bun and sensible glasses, I thought of that broken bowl. That's what I wanted to say. It's broken. Everything is broken. I had thought it would be beautiful, but it's smashed to pieces on the floor. I had thought I would be on that vinyl chair, in that tiny consulting room, for ten minutes. I was in there for nearly an hour. She asked me about my medical history, so I told her about the acne, and the headaches, and the insomnia, and the vitiligo, and the sickness, and the tiredness, and the migraines, and the colds. I told her about the Raynaud's, which made my hands and feet go blue. I told her about the pain, and how it started in one wrist and one ankle, and spread to the other wrist and other ankle, and then settled in my knees. I've been kneecapped, I wanted to say. I've been poleaxed. I've been felled.

She asked me about my family. I thought if I had to talk about my family's medical history then I'd probably never leave. But my mother had taught me that you should always be polite to doctors, so I told her about Caroline, and her breakdowns, and her schizophrenia, and how desperate she was now, and about Tom, and his post-viral anxiety, and his depression, and how desperate he was now, and about my father, who had told me one night that he was worried about having a heart attack, and about my mother, who was usually cheerful, but who had said, when Caroline lost her job, that she wanted to die. And I told her, because she seemed to want to know everything, that I had lost my faith.

That's when she asked me if I felt like Job. When I told her I did, she asked if I'd like some counselling. She said that a vacancy had just cropped up with the psychotherapist at her practice. I could, if I wanted to, go and see Mrs Jones.

Mrs Jones had short, mousy hair and piercing grey eyes. I felt they could see straight through my ribcage and into my heart. I didn't want to talk about my pain. I was sick, sick, sick of talking about my pain. I had told people at church, who had promised me healing, which hadn't happened, and seen doctors, who had prescribed drugs, which hadn't helped, and consulted homeopaths, who had given me little white pills which brought me out in boils, but had no effect on the burning, twisting sensation in my knees. I had seen herbalists, who had made me boil up bags of stinking herbs, and acupuncturists, who had pricked me with needles. I had repented of any sin I, or my family, might have committed. I had had demons cast out. And none of it had made the tiniest pinprick of difference. I didn't see how a woman in an A-line skirt and a cardigan was going to help when they had all failed. But she was here, and so was I, and there didn't seem to be many other options.

Mrs Jones didn't speak much. She seemed to want me to do the talking. So I told her about my pain, and my sister, and my brother, and about how I'd tried to serve God, and now hated him. She nodded, as if it was perfectly normal for someone to sit there, on a vinyl chair, and tell someone you've never met in your life that you hate God with your heart, soul and mind. She kept saying things like 'And how did that make you feel?' It made me feel like a character in a Woody Allen film. It made me want to run screaming into the street, though I couldn't run, that was the problem, I couldn't even fucking walk.

At the end of the session, she said a few things that made me think. She said that the impression she had of my family was of great pain, but also a desire to protect each other from pain. She thought I was making a big effort to keep the pain hidden from my parents, and that I had a deep sense of guilt. She sensed that there was a feeling in my family, because so many of the problems kept coming back, that crises were 'immobilising' and 'permanent'. She said she thought that no one really knew the pain I was in, and that I was ashamed of it. This could be a 'safe space' to talk about those feelings, and if we talked about the emotional pain, perhaps that would help the physical pain, too.

I didn't know what to say. I thought Mrs Jones was probably right that crises in my family seemed 'immobilising' and 'permanent', but that was because they were. I didn't know why emotional pain would have anything to do with physical pain. I was in emotional pain *because* I was in physical pain! She should try feeling as if she had been kneecapped and see how happy that made her! And it was ridiculous to talk about my 'guilt'. It wasn't *my* fault I had a sister with a mental illness, or a brother who seemed to have a tendency towards anxiety and depression. It wasn't *my* fault that I was ill and now crippled, and it was insulting to suggest it was. Who the hell was she to pronounce on me and my family? And it was mad, mad, mad to suggest that I felt shame. It made me feel sick. It made my cheeks burn.

First once a week and then twice a week and then, for a while, three times a week, I spent fifty minutes with Mrs Jones. Once a week, I'd see her at the doctor's surgery, in a room with a blue carpet and black vinyl chairs. Twice a week, I'd drive over to her Georgian house in Brentford and sit in a room with flowery curtains and peach walls.

In heavy traffic, it was an hour and a half each way. It felt, I sometimes thought, like a full-time job. Just a job that wasn't paid. Behind that door, there was always the same carefully blank face. For entire sessions, Mrs Jones hardly spoke. The silences made my heart thump. I was sick of the sound of my voice, sick of the contents of my head.

One day, she suggested I lie down on the couch. Oh my God, I thought. It was still a thrill for me to say that. Oh my God, oh my God, oh my God. This means I'm a basket case. I'm officially neurotic, a shrieking hysteric, a fruitcake. I said yes, because I always said yes to people in authority. But when I lay down and closed my eyes, I felt lighter. It was a relief not to have to see those cool, grey eyes staring back.

One Thursday afternoon, I told her about a conversation I'd had with my mother. She had been pushing me in my wheelchair around St James's Park. 'Did you say wheelchair?' said Mrs Jones. For the first time, she sounded shocked. Yes, I said. Surely I'd told her about the wheelchair? And how I hated it, but how, if I wanted to go for a 'walk', or to a museum or gallery, a wheelchair was the only way to do it?

'A wheelchair,' said Mrs Jones, 'gets a lot of attention, doesn't it?'

I felt as if I had reached out to shake someone's hand and that they had instead raised a fist and smashed it in my face. For a while, I couldn't speak. 'Do you think,' I said, and I tried to keep the anger out of my voice, 'that

I'm exaggerating the pain? Do you think,' I added, and now I knew my voice was icy, 'that I'm *making it up*?'

Mrs Jones said that she wasn't suggesting that I was making the pain up. She was wondering whether the pain was the work of 'the unconscious'. She said it could be the unconscious's way of making up for an earlier lack of attention, because of Caroline. It could be about anger I didn't know how to express, and so directed against fate, or 'God'.

I wanted to shout and scream and punch her in the face. What the fuck did she mean that I was 'directing' anger against God? Hadn't she heard a word I'd said? *Of course* I was angry with God. Who wouldn't be, after how he had treated me? And what on earth was this psychobabble about the 'unconscious'? Couldn't she see I could hardly move because I was in so much pain? How the hell could my 'unconscious' do that? Did she think I was an idiot? Did she? Did she? Then I started crying and couldn't stop. And then I was very surprised to hear myself saying that if Caroline suffered, so should I.

I met Patrick at a friend's private view. Vanessa was a talented artist with a bohemian wardrobe and a private income. She was one of the few friends I kept up with from church, largely because she was extremely relaxed about her faith. 'I've never let it stop me doing anything I want to do,' she said one night, over poached salmon at her Pimlico flat. Her love life had certainly been more lively than mine. It was seven years since I'd had a boyfriend, the same stretch of time as the famine that 'consumed the land' of Egypt in the Bible, and Jacob's wait for Rachel, when he ended up with her elder sister, Leah.

Patrick and Vanessa were old friends. He was ten years older than her, sixteen years older than me. He had curly dark hair, kind eyes and what my mother always used to call a Roman nose. While staring at a watercolour of a sunset on a sea, we discovered that we were both freelance, which really meant that we were both unemployed. I had gone on a course, paid for by the jobcentre, called 'Starting Your Own Business', where we were all told that we could be entrepreneurs. It certainly sounded better than saying I was on benefits. Patrick had worked for many years at the BBC and was now trying to get work as a freelance producer. No one could say that either of us was trying very hard.

We discovered we had the same computer, an Amstrad PCW 9512. His wasn't working, and he asked if he could use mine to update his CV. Two days later, he arrived with a jar of Nescafé and a packet of chocolate digestives. He spent much more of the day chatting than tweaking the CV. Soon he was coming round to use my computer several times a week.

'I really like you,' he told me one day.

'I really like you!' I told him back. It was partly a reflex. I'm fine, thanks, and you? I did like him. I thought he was funny and warm and good company. I didn't want to tell him that he didn't make my heart beat faster and that I thought you should only go out with someone if they did.

We started seeing films together, and cooking meals together, at my flat and at his. He invited me for a weekend at the family cottage, a couple of hours away from London. We sat by a fire in 'the snug' and when he started kissing me, I didn't want to pull away. It was like opening a delicious bottle of wine I'd forgotten and now couldn't put down. But I still thought you should only go out with someone if you thought you'd want to marry them. Otherwise, you might end up hurting them and the thought of hurting anyone filled me with a sense of sick panic.

I wrote him a letter, telling him that I was very sorry, but I didn't think I could go out with him, because I couldn't see it working as a serious, long-term relationship. I found a copy of the letter recently and was so appalled I threw it out. It was like something written by a Maharaja who had been asked for his daughter's hand, researched the suitor's prospects, and graciously declined. Patrick must have thought so, too, because he laughed and told me to lighten up. So we carried on going out, but not going out. He wasn't my boyfriend and I wasn't his girlfriend, but it was hard to tell because we were kissing and cuddling and even touching parts of each other's bodies I'd never touched, or had touched, before.

Patrick told me that he had slept with lots of women before he found God, but since he was now a Christian, he couldn't sleep with me. I was confused. Surely, in that case, he shouldn't be going near me, since I had told him I was no longer a Christian? He wanted to have sex, but wasn't allowed to. I wanted to have sex, but couldn't since he wouldn't. One day, at his cottage, we did. It was, I thought, a bit uncomfortable, but I could see how you could get to like it. Afterwards, Patrick said he was sorry and that he shouldn't have done it, and that we shouldn't do it again. I wasn't sorry at all. I was just relieved that, at twenty-six, I was no longer a virgin.

I was starting to panic about how I was going to earn a living. I did an evening class in copy-editing. I did some unpaid work in the publicity department at the Women's Press. I wrote off to publishers and asked to do some proofreading, and did it so badly that one of the publishers left a message on my answerphone telling me off. I wrote features, on spec, and sent them to magazines like *Ms London* and *Nine to Five*. The one I wrote for *Ms London* was about British girls who went to work as cleaners on Greek islands, based on a lone trip I'd made to Poros a couple of years before. The headline I gave it was 'Olive Oil and Orgasms'. I thought it sounded sophisticated, but I still had no idea what an orgasm was like.

I applied for a job as a proofreader at an advertising listings magazine called *Loot*. The same week, I applied for a two-day-a-week job at the South Bank Centre to do 'literary PR'. The interview at the South Bank was the day before the interview for *Loot*.

I still sometimes wonder what would have happened if it had been the day after. It takes me back to my teenage anxieties about shops with bananas and shops with baked beans. Would I have spent years proofreading ads for second-hand Zanussi freezers and Nissan Cherries? Would I have measured out my life in price points and typos, as the twisting pains in my knees got worse? It was a few years before the film *Sliding Doors* came out, offering two different futures to a heroine played by a perky Gwyneth Paltrow, depending on whether she caught or missed a train. Now I see that afternoon at the South Bank as my sliding door.

I was interviewed by the press officer, Ros Fry, and the literature officer, Maura Dooley. Maura was a poet. She had a mass of dark curls and huge brown eyes and looked, I thought, just as a poet should. She had started the literature programme at the South Bank and revived Poetry International, a festival first started by Ted Hughes. She had also helped to resurrect the Poetry Library, first opened by T. S. Eliot in Piccadilly in 1953, and moved to the South Bank two years before. It had the biggest collection of contemporary poetry in the country, and a 'lost quotations board' where you could put a quotation you vaguely remembered, and hope someone would help you track it down. This, of course, was life before Google.

When I heard Maura talk, at great speed, about poets she loved, and when I walked into the Poetry Library, and saw people gazing at patterns of words on open pages, as if in a trance, and when I saw the Voice Box, the clean, white canvas of a room next to the Poetry Library that was used for readings and events, I felt a strange throbbing in my chest, as if something that had been dormant was coming back to life.

For so long, I had felt like an intruder. At church, and house group, and Network, and the Christian Union, and YWAM, and on my evangelistic missions to Perugia and St Helens, and in gay pubs and coffee bars for the homeless, I had felt like someone trying to recite a script I always got wrong. When I read Marlowe's *Doctor Faustus* at Durham, I thought I had found someone who understood how I felt, but the confusing thing was that Faustus was shackled to the Devil and I was shackled to – well, I couldn't say, because that would be blasphemy. When Faustus yells, 'See, see where Christ's blood streams in the firmament!' I wanted to cry, but I wasn't sure why. I couldn't say, or even know, that Christ's blood was blocking my view.

For years, I had studied the Bible and tried to twist the world to its truths. I had gorged on 'Christian books', tales of triumph and salvation spun out of gossamer threads that hung together until the last page and then floated away. I had been with Dante in his hell, worried about Milton's sexy Satan and joined Tennyson in trying to 'trust that good shall fall / At last – far off – at last, to all,' and that every winter would 'change to spring'. I had felt, in fact, but not allowed myself to acknowledge, that the poets and the writers of fiction and plays, the ones who were inching through a fog and making guesses as they went, were the ones who were getting somewhere near the truth.

When Maura called to tell me I'd got the job – not even a job, but a part-time freelance gig – I felt like someone who had been clinging on to an iceberg, who'd been thrown a lifeline by a passing ship. I felt, in fact, as if I was on the way home.

Chapter 16

Deliverance

My mother kept every press release and every leaflet. In her files, there's the full archive of my South Bank years, and the full archive of my published writing. I haven't looked at these leaflets for years. They're colourful and seductive and so beautifully designed I think they could be in a museum. When I flick through them, it's a shock to see the photos of all those writers and poets as they looked thirty years ago. Many are now dead. Giants of literature – Seamus Heaney, Doris Lessing, Octavio Paz, Susan Sontag, Miroslav Holub – all gaze out at me and trigger vague memories of conversation and laughter. I wish I'd kept the kind of diary where you actually say what you do and not just what you feel.

It makes me think of Nora Ephron's essay 'I Remember Nothing'. In it, she lists some of the people she met. There was Eleanor Roosevelt. There was Groucho Marx. There was Jimmy Stewart, and Cary Grant, and Jacqueline

Kennedy Onassis, and Robert Morley, and Dorothy Parker. She would like, she says, to be able at least to summon a few anecdotes, but she can't remember anything about the meetings at all.

It wouldn't be true to say I remember nothing, but I can only summon feelings and flashes. With Seamus Heaney, for example, I remember that every time he did an event, the queue to get a book signed snaked around the building and almost everyone in it claimed to be his cousin or friend. I remember his face, the face of a man who had expected to be digging peat, and his eyes, which always seemed to crinkle in the corners as if he was suppressing a smile. And I remember his voice. He could have read the phone book and we would all have felt as if we were listening to Shakespeare.

There was a car park next to the building, so I could drive, in my sky-blue Fiesta, to the Festival Hall and get a lift up to the office and try to spend as much of the day as I could sitting down. I didn't want to tell my new colleagues about the pains in my legs. I didn't want them to know about the life I had left. One evening, when a group from the press office went to the Archduke wine bar across the road for a drink, everyone started swapping stories about when and how they had lost their virginity. I felt a prickling in my cheeks and knew they had gone pink. 'You're very quiet!' said one of the senior press officers. I smiled and took a gulp of my wine. I didn't want to tell them that it had only been a couple of months since I'd lost mine.

Maura and her colleagues organised about 120 events a year. I went to most of them and read books by as many of the writers as I could. The poems, short stories and novels piling up on my bedside table felt like a new flavour of chocolate I had just discovered and couldn't resist. Maura told me I didn't have to be so conscientious. I was, she reminded me, only being paid for two days a week. I didn't know how to explain that I felt that I had been let into a magical kingdom, a lost domain, a golden city on a hill. Try keeping me out! I'm in, I'm in, I'm in.

Maura had already published several poetry pamphlets and was about to publish her first collection. Her deputy, Lavinia Greenlaw, was also a poet and about to publish hers. Alan Bisset, a wry Scot who smoked roll-ups and shared outrageous snippets of gossip when he got back from his fag breaks, was writing comic novels. I was working with writers! I was writing press releases about writers, which wasn't quite the same, but it made me feel part of a literary community. When Maura, Alan or Lavinia invited me to join them for a San Miguel in one of the Festival Hall's many bars, I felt a rush of pride and something like relief. I made it! I got away. I found my tribe, or at least I am allowed to sit with this tribe. I am not worthy, or at least I am not a writer, but I am happy to sit at their feet.

When Lavinia left the South Bank for a part-time job that would enable her to write more, I applied for her job and got it. Now I was automatically part of the trio that drifted off, at the end of the day, for a 'swift half'. Now I had to introduce writers on stage and make small talk with them afterwards, over dinner or drinks. My knees still hurt when I walked, but I was so absorbed by what I was doing I often didn't notice the pain. I was still seeing Mrs Jones twice a week. On Tuesday and Thursday lunchtimes, I'd make a mad dash in the Fiesta across the river to the doctor's surgery, pray (but now only metaphorically speaking) for a parking space and practically hurl myself on to the couch. I was still slightly scared of Mrs Jones. She was the only person in the world I still called 'Mrs'. I hadn't read Freud and didn't know much about the theory of therapy, but I sensed that the formal title was part of the cure, like the silences and the blank face.

Now, when I saw her, I talked about my colleagues and the writers I met. I didn't want to talk about my family. When Mrs Jones tried to steer me towards them, I would try to wrench the conversation back. I wanted to talk about my new life and new friends. I still felt that I was teetering on a tightrope between the world I had left and the one I had half-joined. Most of my Christian friends thought I was a traitor. Most of my new friends didn't know about my Christian past. When they talked about the bands they had followed, and even sometimes been in, I didn't want to tell them that I had swapped the Sex Pistols and Joy Division for 'Our God Reigns' and 'Come, Jesus, Come'. It was only a couple of years since the fall of the Berlin

Wall. I felt like someone who had been stuck behind the Iron Curtain, eating tinned food in nylon flares, and had just been ushered into a hypermarket jammed with so many different types of clothes and foods I had no idea how you were meant to choose.

In the months and years that followed, I met almost every living writer I'd heard of, and plenty I hadn't. When the last book had been signed, we'd go for drinks or dinner. Salman Rushdie and Umberto Eco swapped their verdicts on Italo Calvino, which made me grateful that I'd written an essay on his work as part of my MA. Eco made him sound a lot more fun than I did in my essay 'Angles of Refraction: A study of parody in the works of Italo Calvino', which quoted literary theorists, in French.

I couldn't believe how much the poets drank. Joseph Brodsky drank the minibar in his hotel room dry and then handed us the receipt, as if it was a certificate for an exam he'd passed. 'The strongest stay the longest!' said one Slovenian poet with a big, bushy beard as he held out his glass for a top-up. It was towards the end of Poetry International, which went on for ten days and ended every night with a buffet supper that sometimes didn't finish till the early hours. We were all struggling to keep our eyes open. 'Well,' I said, after an awkward pause, 'it depends what time the strong have to get up.'

Yevgeny Yevtushenko, who used to fill football stadiums with his poetry readings in Russia, invited me back to his hotel for a drink. So did James Dickey, the American poet laureate who wrote *Deliverance*. When he got back to South Carolina, he sent me a book about the American South and a letter saying that he would 'always remember' me. I never did go back to anyone's hotel, and I didn't know whether to be flattered or insulted that these old men – they were always old men – asked. The men I found attractive never asked me out. It never occurred to me that they could sense my terror and that terror turned to something like ice. I was shocked to hear, one day, that the men who worked backstage called me 'the ice maiden'.

No one had ever taught me how to talk to someone you were attracted to, but my mother had certainly taught me how to talk to anyone else. She charmed everyone with her polite questions and her laughter. She made everyone feel as if she was their best friend. I was good at making friends but had spent years on my guard: primed for theological argument among Christians and primed for the need to witness to those who weren't. Now, for the first time since I was fifteen, I could forget about both. I couldn't quite believe that I was allowed to talk about what I liked, with people who were trying new things, learning new things, doing new things. The literature department shared an office with people who worked in music, craft, the visual arts and dance. On Friday nights, a big group of us would wander down to the main bar. We'd all go to the private views. We'd get free tickets to concerts and dance.

During the Meltdown music festival programmed by the artist and musician Laurie Anderson, I was sitting in the bar when her husband walked in. He sat next to me and we talked for the next two hours. I didn't feel I could tell Lou Reed that I didn't know his work, but his name definitely rang a bell. At a lunch one day I sat next to a writer's beautiful girlfriend. When I asked her what she did, she gave a vague reply. It was only later I realised I'd been chatting to the star of *Dr Zhivago* and *Don't Look Now*. I wanted to tell Julie Christie that we had all been haunted by Lara and that Caroline hated the Bolsheviks as much as she did.

Sometimes, I'd meet Alan, and his girlfriend, Claire, and David from marketing and his girlfriend, Claire, and Claire from the crafts section and her boyfriend, Duncan, and friends of theirs who weren't called Claire. We'd go for a drink, or to a pub for Sunday lunch. Sometimes, as the laughter echoed round the table, I wanted to yell with joy because I had finally found a group of friends who didn't make me feel like a freak.

My mother often bought tickets for readings, turning up sometimes with my father, sometimes on her own. She wasn't all that interested in the poets, but she liked seeing me introduce them. I told her she wasn't allowed to ask questions in the Q & A, or sit in the front row. Once, I saw her queue up to get a book signed by Stephen Spender. I knew she would never read a book by Stephen Spender. When she got to the front of the queue, I heard her say something in a voice that was almost a whisper. 'That,' she said, handing him the book to sign and glancing over at me to check I hadn't heard, 'is my daughter.'

In an old shoebox, I find a photo of her outside the Voice Box, clutching a book she has just got signed. Her smile is electric. Her head is slightly tilted, her eyes alert. She looks as if she is about to clap her hands. Sometimes, when I met her for lunch, or afternoon tea, she actually did clap her hands. There were times when joy fizzed out of her. It would bubble up and burst out. Almost every time we met, we'd have coffee and cake. She would sigh with pleasure after every sip of her coffee and every tiny bite of her cake. My mother made coffee and cake feel like a party.

In that shoebox, I find a photo of her stripping wallpaper. There's a photo of my father, too, chipping off tiles. My mother's wearing a white blouse and a cornflower skirt. My father's wearing a white shirt and black trousers. Neither of them ever owned a pair of jeans. They're in the bathroom of my new flat. I had thought I wouldn't be able to leave the Barbican flat. I knew what it had cost my parents to get it and couldn't bear them to think I was ungrateful. But Mrs Jones had said it would be hard to 'separate' from my family if I was still living in my parents' flat. She seemed to think it was important, for my life and health, that I did. So, over Sunday lunch one day, and with my heart racing, I told them about my plans. My father looked wounded. My mother patted his shoulder. I felt as if I had just announced a plan to murder the entire family.

Two weeks later, my father sent me a letter, on blue Basildon Bond. He would, he said, rent out the Barbican flat and increase his mortgage to help me with a deposit, to the same tune he had helped Tom. Over the next two pages, he set out information on building societies, their current lending rates and his recommendations. Like all civil servants, he ended with a summary. I should, he said, regard this 'unpaid consultancy' as a birthday gift. With his help, and on a salary of £17,000, I managed to buy an ex-local-authority flat in what used to be the attic of a Victorian house in Camberwell. It was £58,000. I should have filled the street with bunting for being able to buy my own flat on less than the average wage. I didn't, but I did throw a party. I also threw out the swirly carpets, stripped off the woodchip paper, got someone to blast off the Artex and painted everything white. I filled the flat with colourful kilims and furniture I picked up at markets.

The flat had its own section of garden, so far away it felt like an allotment. The previous owners, Ed and Kath, left their gnomes as a moving-in present and for months I didn't dare move them, since I knew they often went to visit Gill next door. My father put up a trellis and planted a clematis and roses. There's a photo of him, in a sports jacket, standing next to a yellow rose bush. His smile is strangely shy.

Once, when I was waiting for the bus to the Elephant and Castle, a woman shrieked when she heard my accent. 'Do you live round 'ere?' she said. 'Wiv a voice like that?'

If my neighbours were surprised by my accent, they managed to hide it. The Nigerian across the road kept inviting me to join him for prayer sessions, which I kept politely turning down. Fred and Daisy in the basement had lived there since the thirties and liked inviting me in for cups of tea. Fred had been a handyman for the council. My downstairs neighbour, whose snores and sneezes I heard through my floor, was a boxer. Gill, who lived in the attic flat next door, hoped to follow Ed and Kath to Essex, but she often invited me to join her and some of 'the girls' for a pizza in the Walworth Road.

Yes, I said to the woman at the bus stop. I do live round here. I wanted to tell her that I was happy to be there, happy to have my own place, happy to have a job I loved and happy, happy, happy because, four years after they started, the pains in my knees seemed to have gone.

Chapter 17

Carousel

I fell in love with a man at work. It was the first time since Jonathan, the first time for ten years that I had felt that soul-deep yearning for another human, that throbbing, humming, fizzing, buzzing, energising, paralysing, brain-jellifying compulsion to hurl myself into someone's arms and sink into their flesh. I thought of him every minute of the day and through the night, as I hugged my pillow and begged for sleep.

There was a problem. There was always a problem. He was married. And I had absolutely no idea what he thought about me.

One day, he brought me an exhibition catalogue and I thought it must be a sign. I still have it. Would you believe I still have it? I took it from him as if he were handing me the keys to a padlock on his heart. I once sat next to him during a concert and felt as if, like Krook in *Bleak House*, I might actually burst into flames. I was on fire.

Everything was on fire. Someone had struck tinder, struck a match, struck gold. I thought I couldn't live without him. I honestly thought I couldn't live without him. And we had only had a handful of conversations.

I was nearly thirty. I was panicking about being nearly thirty. As my birthday loomed, I sent out invitations to a party. 'Growing Panic at Grosvenor Park,' I put on them, 'as Christina approaches thirty!' I added a skull and crossbones, to underline the message. I was joking and not joking. One by one, my friends were starting to pair off. I smiled when they told me, smiled at their weddings and later smiled when they handed me wriggling infants smelling of clean cotton and milk. I didn't know how they could do this thing that felt to me like scaling an entire mountain range without an ice pick or a rope. How was it possible for someone you liked to like you? How did you let each other know? How did you get from a stumbling conversation to a kiss, a weekend, a life?

My friendship with occasional benefits with Patrick had fizzled out when he realised that I wasn't lying when I said I didn't want a romance. Or at least that I didn't want a romance with him. He was angry. I was confused. I had told him, hadn't I? I wanted to want him, but I didn't want him. I wanted Martin, the poet who'd done a reading at the South Bank and who had actually broken through the barbed wire and flirted with me. I once drove past his house late at night just to see if the lights were on. I drove home, feeling like I had in one of my first assemblies at primary school when I realised I was sitting cross-legged in a puddle. I calmed myself down by reading Wendy Cope's poem about cuddling a phone book because the name of your beloved is in it. The poem is called 'Going Too Far'.

I wanted someone urbane, intellectual, sensitive; someone eloquent, thoughtful, honourable, wise. Oh, and tall. Certainly, taller than me. When I talked about it with Mrs Jones, she said I seemed to want someone like my father. I hated it when she said things like that. Yes, my father was brilliant and handsome and successful and articulate, but he was also autocratic, intimidating and sometimes a bit awkward. Mrs Jones knew we often clashed. Why on earth would I want someone like that? Was she working her way through some A–Z of Freud?

Martin was a crush, a bug, an obsession. I told all my friends about him: about the conversations we'd had on the night he did the reading, about how I'd mustered the courage, for once in my life, to invite a man I was attracted to for supper with some mutual friends, about the postcard he'd sent to thank me, suggesting we go to see a movie when he was back from his holiday, and how I'd waited and waited and waited and checked my answerphone as if it were the pulse of a patient in intensive care. I told all my friends, and several of my colleagues, every tiny detail. I know because I've found six pages on A4 paper, outlining the rising and falling arc of my hope.

Martin was a crush and a crushing disappointment,

but my colleague, who I still feel too coy to name, was something else. I've been in love four times in my life, and this was one of them. By 'in love', I mean the pathological definition: the racing heart, the wrecked appetite, the trembling, the sleeplessness, the anxiety, the panic, the despair, the madness. That's it: the madness. You don't think you can function any more because you're exhausted from all that howling at the moon.

I was exhausted by the effort of trying to control my emotions and by the lack of sleep. I was also exhausted by the repetition. In one of my sporadic diary entries, which are mostly just emotional outpourings, I mention the many friends and colleagues who have counselled and advised me through a love affair which only seems to have happened in my head. I seem to have told everyone everything. I'm an open book. I'm a bleeding heart on a sleeve. Reading those pages now, I feel both mortified and protective. 'I love him,' I've written. 'In every way, I love him. I adore his intelligence, his calm, his voice, his humour, his quiet consideration, his kindness, his serenity. I delight in the thought of him. I delight in his company. Just being near him makes me almost faint with desire.'

O daughters of Jerusalem, I adjure you, if you find my beloved, tell him I am sick with love. That's what this reminds me of. The Song of Songs. The Song of Solomon. I've read Keats, I've read Eliot, I've read Heaney, I've read Plath, but what runs through my veins is the book I have read most. I want to put an arm around that girl, who makes me think of Dorothea in *Middlemarch* and Anne of Green Gables and a whole range of characters in Thomas Hardy. It was Elizabeth-Jane in *The Mayor of Casterbridge* who concluded that happiness was 'but a mere episode in the general drama of pain'. Certainly, what I've written, in such neat handwriting that I hardly recognise it, has a touch of Tess of the D'Urbervilles in a winter turnip field. I know, I write, that the man I love won't leave, or be unfaithful to, his wife. 'I don't know how to live with the horrible loss of this potential,' I've written. 'I feel as though this is my only chance for love, and for a happiness based on love, and I won't get it.'

Love in its pathological form certainly tends to foster that feeling. But what makes me sad now is the sense, in all my flirtations, which weren't really flirtations, that what was possible for almost everyone was not possible for me.

I had a row with my boss. Maura had left, to go and run a big literary festival, and Alan and I mourned her loss. I didn't have the confidence to apply for her job. The woman who did was pregnant when she got it, so I ended up covering her maternity leave before she arrived. By the time she did, I felt I could do the job, and loved it. It was boring going back to being the deputy. It's always boring going back to being a deputy when you've done the big job. This wasn't my new boss's fault, but I probably acted as if it was.

One day, when she asked me how I was getting on with a task she had set, I told her that I was 'bored out of my fucking mind'. As soon as I said the words and saw the look of shock on her face, I wanted to take them back. I'd never spoken to a boss like that before, and I haven't since. I think I was more shocked than she was. Sorry, sorry, sorry, sorry. I wanted to prostrate myself on the ground. I phoned her later at home and said I was sorry again. She was gracious, but it was too late. Within three hours, I had pain in my left hand, my left ankle and my left knee. Within four hours, I had pain in my right knee and back.

That weekend, I went to my friend Caroline's wedding. I couldn't miss it since we'd been close friends since we were five. I told her I'd sprained my ankle. That, I explained, was why I had to spend the whole day sitting down. In my diary that night, I wrote: 'Please can the pain go. Please, please, please, please, please, please, please, please, please, please, please.'

I couldn't beg God any more. At first, when I had told him to fuck off and out of my life, I thought he was still there. My hate couldn't blast him out of existence, even if I wished it would. Now I didn't know. Perhaps he was, perhaps he wasn't? If he didn't answer people's prayers, if he didn't care about people's lives, what difference did it make? I had begun to think, on balance, that he probably didn't exist. I had been hoodwinked. I had been blackmailed. I had been tricked. But who, then, do I yell out to now?

My doctor and Mrs Jones both agreed it was clear that the pain had been triggered by the row. It was clear, they said, that this was deep emotional pain. My mother said that was ridiculous. What I needed was to see more doctors. I should get more blood tests. It might be a virus. It might be a virus that nobody had yet found. The most important thing, she said, was to stop indulging in all this psychotherapy, which was clearly making things worse.

My doctor signed me off work with 'polyarthralgia', which really just means an awful lot of pain. She hoped, and I hoped, that resting, and having extra sessions with Mrs Jones, and perhaps trying to work out why my body had done this, would make the pain go. It didn't. After two weeks, still in as much pain as before, I went back to work. I could still drive and park. I could limp from my car to the lift and from the lift to my desk. Colleagues brought me sandwiches and cups of coffee. It was like being back at Faber. Five years on, I didn't seem to have any more idea than I had then of how to get rid of the pain once it had set in.

My mother suggested I join them in Sweden. My parents still went to the cottage with Caroline every summer. My mother was sure that a rest would help. A week among the pine trees, fresh Swedish air and Swedish sunshine would surely work magic where everything else had failed.

It was fifteen years since I had been to Sweden with my family. I thought back to all the rituals that had marked our annual pilgrimage: the cleaning, the packing up, the jangling chains as my father parked the car, the search for the cabin, the coffee and cheese rolls on deck, the Agatha Christies, the horizon bobbing up and down, the first glimpse of land. I thought of the drive through Gothenburg and then out on to the open road: the cows on the mossy sea's edge, the stop for *vetebröd* and pear-flavoured *läsk*, the 'Sydney Bridge', the lane through the forest and then the sight of our cousins, waiting at the mailboxes, rushing up to the car. I thought of the excitement and the tastes and the smells and the hope. That's what I couldn't bear to think about: the hope.

I had never flown to Sweden. I had never flown anywhere in this much pain. By the time I got to the baggage carousel, I wanted to lie down next to it and scream. Once I'd grabbed my suitcase, I staggered out of the building and collapsed on a bench. I watched blond families wheeling their luggage past: parents in T-shirts and jeans, toddlers with tiny rucksacks, clutching toys. I wondered what it would be like to go on holiday with a man you loved, and with children you had made.

When my parents found me crying on the bench, they looked embarrassed. My father patted me on the shoulder and stared down at my suitcase. My mother handed me a carton of apple juice. When I said I didn't want it, she started humming. Only Caroline looked how I felt. Her big, soft face crumpled up with sadness, and for a moment I felt I could see into her heart and that she could see into mine.

All week, they waited on me. In the garden, among the birch trees where I'd played with Anna and Carl Johan, they brought me coffee and cakes. My mother had stocked up on *pepparkakor*, and *vetebröd, sockerkaka* and *kringlor*. She drove me right down to the beach at Frosakull where we all used to swim, and I managed to make it over the sand dunes and down to the sea. The water was so cold that, for a while, it shocked me out of my pain. I splashed around and thought of Caroline on the beach, the summer after she came out of 'the unit', and how everyone else had been running around in swimsuits, but she had been walking like a robot, in navy trousers and a navy shirt and in my mother's sunglasses and hat.

Back in the garden, staring out at the forest and listening to the grasshoppers, I wondered how someone who had so many friends, and such a loving family, could feel so alone. I thought that there was so much I loved about my life, but that there seemed to be something inside me that was determined to make sure that good things couldn't last.

My mother paid for me to see a doctor at the health centre in Halmstad. The doctor said, in fluent English, that he didn't think the pain was 'systemic', but that I didn't look like a 'psychosomatic patient' either. Normally, he said, psychosomatic patients had 'shoulders up to their ears'. They smile manically, he said, and hardly mention the pain. I, on the other hand, was very concerned about it, and very analytical. But he would look at the blood tests and we would see.

Two hours later, the results were ready. They were very good, he said. I was very healthy. There was no sign of lupus or any connective tissue disease.

I asked him if he had any idea at all what was wrong with me. The doctor shook his head. 'I have to be honest,' he said, in the sing-song tones that all my English-speaking Swedish relatives used. 'No.'

I asked him if he had seen any similar cases. He shook his head again. 'I'm afraid not.' He shook my hand and wished me luck and my mother paid the bill.

When we got back to the cottage, I lay down on my bed. I felt tears trickling down my cheeks but tried not to make any noise. My mother knocked on the door and asked if I wanted anything to drink. She was sure, she told me when she saw I was crying, that the pain would go. She was sure a doctor would find out what was wrong. She would pay for me to see a physiotherapist, or perhaps a neurologist. Someone would have an answer.

In my diary that night, I wrote that I was giving up on my dream of having a family of my own. 'Anyway,' I wrote, 'the world needs no more mad, sad Pattersons.'

No more mad, sad Pattersons. Be careful – be very, very, careful – what you wish for.

On my last day in Sweden, we went to Växjö to see Auntie Lisbeth and Uncle Hans. We drove to cousin Peter's flat, my parents with Caroline in one car and me in the car with my uncle and aunt. I asked Auntie Lisbeth about Anna, who was now working at the Swedish Ministry of Defence.

'She has such energy and drive!' I said. I hoped I'd managed to keep the envy out of my voice.

'She does,' said Lisbeth, 'but so do you!' I was quiet for a moment. Sure, I thought. I can hardly walk across a room. My energy and drive, I told her, had been somewhat tempered by events.

There was a long silence. 'I always worried about you,' said Lisbeth. Uncle Hans put a hand on her arm. 'Lisbeth,' he said in a warning voice, but she carried on. 'I always told Anne that you shouldn't have to suffer because of Caroline. Caroline and Tom were always so close, but I told her that someone needed to stand up for you.'

I was so shocked I couldn't speak and then we arrived at Peter's. He was waiting by the front door. As we all leapt out to greet him, I tried to sound as normal as I could, but I felt as if I had just been handed a ticking bomb. That night, when we got back to the cottage, I wept until my pillow was wet.

The next day, my mother drove me to the airport. We stopped off at IKEA on the way. She told me, over meatballs, that I should stop the psychotherapy. It was self-indulgent, she said, to talk endlessly about what had happened to me, cooking up imaginary grievances and 'raking up the hot coals of the past'.

I stopped chewing and put down my fork. I told her

that I was sick, sick, sick of therapy, that it was difficult and painful and embarrassing, and that I had nothing left to say about anything that had happened to me. I told her that I didn't do it as a hobby, but because the medical stuff didn't seem to make any difference and this seemed to be the only thing that offered me any hope at all of getting better.

We drove in silence to the airport. We sat in silence as we waited for my flight details to come up. In the end, my mother broke it. She told me that I had been brainwashed by my doctor and therapist. Between them, they had cooked up a theory that was stark, raving mad.

Perhaps it was the word 'mad' that did it. I didn't want to hurt her, but I would not have five years of searching, digging, combing, weeping, begging for something easier and quicker, but ploughing on because there wasn't something quicker, tainted with that word.

'Ask Lisbeth,' I said.

'Ask Lisbeth what?'

'Ask Lisbeth what she thinks.'

My mother begged me to tell her, and so I did. And then my mother said that she had failed in every way. She had failed with all of her children, and she would go back to her dysfunctional family, and hope to be killed in the car on the way. And I got on a plane and thought I had broken my mother's heart.

Chapter 18

Excellent Tour

On her thirty-seventh birthday, Caroline went to the summer palace of the Tsars. She stood where the Grand Duchesses had stood, gazing at the autumn sunshine shimmering on the lake and the trees around it turning to russet and gold. She posed for photos in the courtyard, framed by a sprawling, baroque wedding cake of a building, an elaborate patchwork of white and powder blue, studded with gilt curlicues and tiny onion domes. She wandered through the rooms where her beloved Romanovs had dined and slept and played, and perhaps wept. In the photos, she looks joyful, but dazed.

None of us could believe it when my parents announced that they were going to make Caroline's dream come true. There are no captions in the red album labelled 'RUSSIA MOSCOW OCTOBER 1995', so I'm not sure what all the photos are. But it's very clear when we reach Caroline's birthday. There's a photo of a bed in a hotel room. On it, there's a book about the Romanovs, open at a photo of the Grand Duchesses. On the bedside table, there are six birthday cards. One has white roses on the front. I've found it in the file labelled 'CAROLINE LETTERS AND CARDS'. 'To dearest Caroline with lots of love,' it says, 'and wishing you a fabulous birthday in this most fabulous of cities (and the location of so many of your happiest thoughts), your loving father.' Underneath, he has written the place and the date: St Petersburg, 12 October 1995.

His diary fills in more of the detail. It's as laconic as usual, but what hits me is the tone. He even allows himself some capital letters and exclamation marks. 'RUSSIA!' he has written at the top of the page. 'Thrilling first day in Moscow. Excellent tour included. Overwhelming first impressions of Red Square. Terrific METRO TOUR. Bolshoi with Caroline. Poor seats but enjoy SNOW WHITE.' The next day the register, if anything, ramps up. 'KREMLIN TOURS quite fantastic with the world's best guide (Vera). Imperial Armoury breathtaking. Then fish sandwich and wonderful concert in an old palace.' The next day is his birthday. '"Happy Birthday" from our nice group for my 64th. Then wonderful train through countryside to Sergiyev Posad, the heart of Old Russia. The definitive highlight. NIGHT TRAIN.'

He is thrilled to arrive the next morning at 'Anna Karenina's station'. Tom, Caroline and I had been shocked by the dramatic end of the TV series, which we'd watched on Saturday nights, with peanuts and R. White's lemonade.

My father hadn't. He loved all Tolstoy's work – and Dostoevsky, Lermontov, Turgenev, and Gogol – but *Anna Karenina* was his favourite book and he had read it several times. Perhaps that's why he seems to have been as excited as Caroline to arrive in St Petersburg. 'Stay at the three-star Moskva,' he writes. 'Wonderful location with a view of the Neva. Excellent tour all round the sublime city, and another excellent guide (Galina).'

The next day is the big one. 'Perfect golden day for Caroline's birthday,' he writes. 'Wonderful trip to Pushkin and Pavlovsk to see the summer palaces of the Tsars. Anne and I leave Caroline "at home" to enjoy *Eugene Onegin*.' At this point, he runs out of space in his tiny Letts diary and adds an asterisk. At the top of the page, next to another asterisk, he writes 'tremendous sets, but a podgy Tatiana'.

As always, my mother packs in a lot more detail. 'Sunrise over Neva and a glorious day,' she has written in her own diary. 'We celebrated Caroline with lots of cards, her Tsar book and a nightie. She was thrilled.' She then launches into a full account of the day: the 'magical tour' that started with an 'interesting ride past Stalin-built flats' and through 'the countryside full of lovely birches and autumn colours', the sudden glimpse, when they got to Tsarskoye Selo, of 'this gorgeous blue and gold palace where the Tsars had lived'. My mother had bought a permit, so she and Caroline could take all the photographs they wanted. After the tour, they walked through 'a beautiful park with a lake' and then got a bus to the Pavlovsk Palace, built by

Catherine the Great for her son, Paul I. 'What a birthday for Caroline!' she writes. And then, after taking Caroline back to the hotel, she's off to the Mariinsky Palace with my father to see *Eugene Onegin*. 'We thoroughly enjoyed it,' she says, 'the singing was good, the theatre magnificent and the set superb, but Tatiana was much too stout and old to be creditable.' I assume she means 'credible', though it's also possible that Tatiana was just not good enough.

In the photos, Caroline is also pretty stout. Her weight and girth have crept up and up. She's wearing huge, baggy dresses, coats like tents, jackets that make her look twice as wide as my mother. It must have been an effort to drag that bulk around. It's a credit to her that she's smiling. It's creditable, in fact, that she's smiling. I've always been grumpy when I put on half a stone.

Her extra weight, like so much else, was not her fault. By this time, she had been on Largactil for twenty-three years. Weight gain is just one of its many side effects. I never heard her complain about it. Not once. When Tom prodded her stomach and teased her about the size of it, she just laughed, because she loved Tom and he could do what he liked.

Caroline had a boyfriend. Tom had had a series of short, intense romances that hadn't translated into anything you could call a relationship. I had had a series of short, intense romances, but these had mostly happened in my head. Our elder sister put us to shame. She met Richard at church. She had started going to Millmead some years before. Unlike almost everyone else there, she wasn't militant about her faith. In fact, I never heard her mention it. If anyone ever promised her that the Lord would heal her, I think she probably kept quiet until they changed the subject. In matters of faith as well as romance, my sister seems to have been more sensible than me.

I've found a CV that says 'I belong to Millmead church young people's 20+ group' and a biographical note that says her leisure activities include 'a deep commitment to the Christian faith' as well as 'spending time with my boyfriend Richard and my other friends, English classic literature, holidays to Russia and to visit my family in Sweden.' The 'holidays to Russia' make me smile. She only went once and I never heard her lie. She must have been planning more.

Richard was twenty years older than her, and several inches shorter. He worked as a gardener for Surrey County Council. He had what we would now call 'learning difficulties', but he didn't have any difficulties communicating his love for Caroline. Every night, he called her and they chatted on the phone. When he came round to Nelson Gardens, they would sit on the little sofa in the room that used to be my bedroom, watch videos and hold hands. I don't think they ever did much more than that. I don't think their Christianity would have allowed it. But what do I know? Honestly, what do I know? I can only make some guesses.

Caroline was deeply fond of Richard, but it was clear where her passions lay. It was the Romanovs she truly loved. Nicholas, yes, Alexandra, yes, Alexis, yes, but most of all the Grand Duchesses: Olga, Tatiana, Marie and Anastasia. It's clear from the huge pile of books I've found in Tom's garage, but it's also clear from the blue lever arch file, neatly labelled by my mother: 'CAROLINE'S RUSSIAN PAPERS'. In it, there are photocopies of photos of the Russian royal family, photos I haven't seen before. There are clippings from newspapers about them, including one from *The Times* about 'how Romanov family photographs are captivating the Russian public'. When you see some of them, you can see why. Here's Nicholas, carrying Alexis in a sailor suit. Here he is, bathing in the Gulf of Finland. Here are three of the Grand Duchesses, and Alexis, all casually dressed, at Tsarskoye Selo. Tsarskoye Selo! After reading those diaries, I almost feel I have a stake in it.

There are postcards from George Gibbes, thanking Caroline and my parents for hospitality at Nelson Gardens, and inviting the family to various services at St Nicholas House. There's a Christmas card, announcing that St Nicholas House is now closed, but saying that the 'historical collection' of Father Nicholas (Charles Sydney Gibbes, 'sometime tutor to the Imperial Family') has now been transferred to Luton Hoo. That one is addressed 'To Anne, John, Caroline, Tom and ?' I like the honesty in that '?' I can't help thinking it expresses quite a lot.

There are press clippings about the assassination of

the Romanovs and 'the search for the grave'. There's a subscription to the Imperial Russian Historical Society. 'Breathing new life back into Old Russia' is the slogan. That's my sister. Born in Bangkok and brought up in Guildford after four years in Rome, she sure as hell did her bit to breathe new life back into Old Russia.

She had given up on her dream of getting a job. After she lost her washing-up job, we all agreed that it was probably better for her to take a break from the search. Caroline wanted a job more than anything, but the evidence seemed to show she couldn't manage one. Or at least that she couldn't keep one. And hope deferred, as the Bible says, makes the heart grow sick.

In the 'CAROLINE EMPLOYMENT' file I've found an 'Action Plan'. It's from something called the Employment Training Agency. It lists Caroline's employment history and her qualifications. Under the 'action steps', it says Caroline should be at the 'NSF Bookshop three days per week until placement can be found'. The NSF Bookshop was a centre with a second-hand bookshop, run by the National Schizophrenia Fellowship in Godalming. It was a place where people with a mental illness could help out, drink coffee, and be with other people who understood their struggles. According to the leaflet I've found, it helped 'the client directly or indirectly to cope with life in the community' by offering 'life skills training' and 'occupational sessions'. For Caroline, it became a second home.

It was run by an extraordinary woman called Pam

Sedgwick, who dedicated her professional life to supporting people whose lives had been buffeted and reshaped by their experience of mental illness. She built a loving, supportive community of people who felt they had found kindred spirits, felt they had found kith and kin.

The biographical note I found that mentioned Caroline's 'deep Christian faith' was from a thick wodge of A4 paper, spiral-bound and with a laminated cover. On that cover, there's a picture of the Romanovs and the kind of decorative border I found on the Cup of Sorrows. Underneath the photo, there's a title and an author. 'THE FAMILY LIFE OF THE LAST ROMANOVS BY CAROLINE PATTERSON'.

'Having read the diaries, letters and poetry of the Russian Royal Family,' she says in the introduction, 'and seen the watercolours and the exercise books, I have been absolutely fascinated by the beauty of their photographs, especially of the daughters. This has led me to try to learn how other families are united in a deep Christian love.' Her investigation, she says, has been 'fascinating', but 'frustrating' because 'there was not very much material about the Romanovs'. She can't bear to think about the 'waste' of the fact that there are 'hundreds of albums gathering dust in the secret archives'. Her greatest dream, she says, is to 'glimpse into the Kremlin archives' in Moscow. 'These photographs,' she adds, 'mean more than anything in the world to me.'

I don't think she was joking. And she's right that the

photos – photocopies here, of course – are enchanting, glimpses of the Romanovs' family life that their fellow citizens, or rather subjects, would never have seen. There's one of Alexandra cradling a baby and gazing at it with the intensity of a Da Vinci Madonna. There's one of Olga and Tatiana, wild-haired in their nighties, staring out from the two arms of a single armchair. There's one of a tiny Anastasia, plump in a sailor dress with a straw hat and a cheeky smile. 'Anastasia,' writes Caroline, 'was a great chatterbox and seized on one of Gibbes's most exasperated moments. He told her to shut up and she asked him how to spell it and adopted it as her nickname.' Anastasia put her new nickname on one of her exercise books: 'Shut up! Tobolsk 1917–1918'. The book, says Caroline, 'is now in Luton Hoo museum, having previously been owned by George Gibbes, Sidney's son who was kind enough to let me examine it.'

Kind enough to let me examine it! Now I'm the one who's in awe.

Caroline's account of the romance of Nicholas and Alexandra, and the family life that followed, is beautifully written and studded with detail and personal touches. Following quotes from Nicholas's diary after Alexandra has accepted his marriage proposal, she comments: 'I very much admire the closeness and sincerity of Nicholas and Alexandra and find the comment of George V of England very moving: "I must say, I never saw two people more in love."' Nicholas and Alexandra had their honeymoon at

Tsarskoye Selo. 'Words cannot describe,' wrote Nicholas in the diary Caroline quotes, 'what bliss it is for us to both live in such a lovely place.' She also quotes from Alexandra's diary. 'Never can I thank God enough for the treasure he has given me for my very own and to be called yours sweetly. What happiness can be greater?' Their love, Caroline writes, 'derived from the spiritual values of Christianity'. But they were, she adds, 'to bear great troubles later on in their lives'.

In her chapter 'introducing the Imperial children', Caroline writes about the gardens at Tsarskoye Selo, 'fragrant with lilac, and lakes, statues and terraces'. She quotes Charles Gibbes's description of Olga, whose 'manners could be a little brusque' and who 'liked simplicity and paid little attention to dress'. I'm not surprised to read Caroline's comment: 'I very much like the sound of Olga.' Like my father, she hated shopping and had zero interest in clothes.

In a chapter on Alexis, Caroline quotes Anna Vyrubova, a lady-in-waiting and confidante of Alexandra, who was imprisoned after the Romanovs were killed. 'I saw the Tsarevich in the Empress's arms,' she says. 'How beautiful he was, how healthy, how normal with his golden hair, his blue eyes and his expression of intelligence so rare for so young a child.' This, says Caroline, is 'ironic' since he soon started bleeding from his navel. She talks about the Tsar's pride in his 'chubby, rosy, wonderful boy'. She mentions Alexis's sense of mischief and the dinner where he 'plunged under the table and took off one of the maids of honour's slippers, presenting it with pride to his father as a trophy'.

She paints such a charming picture of this family, blighted by the illness of one of their children, that I want to read more. Instead, she moves to the 'background history': the strikes, the demonstrations, the riots 'against the absolute rule of the Tsar', the massacre of peaceful protesters he apparently didn't authorise. 'He was,' says Caroline loyally, 'basically a kind country squire who only wanted a peaceful family life.' She then leaps straight to 'correspondence of the four daughters and family recently released by the Russian archives'. There are affectionate, and heavily misspelled, letters in English from Tatiana and Olga to 'my sweety darling Mama'. There's a letter from Anastasia to 'my golden, good, darling Papa', saying that she has sat with a soldier and 'helped him to read', but also that 'Olga is hitting Maria, and Maria is shouting like an idiot'. She sends him '1,000,000 kisses' and signs the letter 'Your dearest and truly loving daughter, thirteen-year-old servant of God'.

The next letter she quotes is also from Anastasia, to her tutor, Peter Petrov: 'This afternoon we all went for a ride, went to church and to the hospital and that's it.' From 1914, the Grand Duchesses, along with their mother, treated wounded soldiers at a military hospital in the grounds of the Catherine Palace at Tsarskoye Selo. I want to read more about this. I want to read about those months when the family was imprisoned in their own palace and then in a house in the foothills of the Urals, where they were marched to a basement and shot. Olga was twenty-two. Tatiana was twenty-one. Maria was nineteen. Anastasia was seventeen. Alexei was thirteen.

I want to read about all of this, but these chapters are missing. The version I have ends with a letter from Alexandra to Olga. 'You are the eldest and must show the others how to behave,' she writes. 'Learn to make others happy, think of yourself last of all. Be gentle and kind.' It's the next sentence that makes me want to cry. 'When you see somebody sad, try to cheer them up and show them a bright sunny smile.'

The trip to Russia was two months after the holiday in Sweden. If my mother still wanted to 'get killed in the car', she hid it very well.

Now, more than ever, and perhaps really for the first time, I understand why Caroline fell in love with this family, this smiling mother, this handsome father, the boy who bore his illness so bravely, the girl who couldn't be bothered with clothes. I see why she was transfixed by those photos of parents and children in bright northern light, standing by lakes and silver birches, enjoying the sunshine before the storm.

The biographical note at the beginning of *The Family Life of the Last Romanovs* lists Caroline's 'accomplishments'. They include 'voluntary work, Godalming NSF

Bookshop, playgroup facilitator, St Saviours church, support volunteer, Oxfam, Guildford'. It follows that with 'publications'. Next to that, she has written 'The Family Life of the Last Romanovs, a 100-page book researched, typeset and self-published. The theme explores and reflects a warm family life.' The biographical note also mentions two things I didn't know. Caroline's book won her an Outstanding Learner Award from the National Organisation for Adult Learning. It was also 'the centrepiece display' in an exhibition at the Godalming Museum.

Chapter 19

Getting Out of Your Own Way

In the end, it was magic that got rid of my pain. Sunshine and magic, or something like it. The leaflet I have in front of me, with my name written neatly at the top, uses slightly different words. It mentions 'Rei', defined as 'universal like the rays of the sun, life-giving and non-limiting', and 'Ki', 'the indivisible substance of which the universe is made'. Opposite this definition there's a bald, naked man with diagrams showing 'the seven major chakras'. In the diagram, the chakras are like trumpets. Sound the trumpet! Healing is on the way.

After the trip to Sweden, I booked a seven-day 'holistic holiday' on a Greek island called Skyros. If my pain was emotional, psychic, hysterical, or whatever word you'd use to describe something that seemed to baffle every single doctor, then surely, I thought, a 'holistic' break in the sunshine was my best hope of a cure? I would, I decided, do anything. I'd pay anything, I'd go anywhere. I'd bash cushions, wear tie-dye pantaloons, eat rice cakes, do primal screams – I'd do whatever the fuck it took to get rid of the pain.

On the ferry from Athens to the island, a bald man called Michael told me about reiki. His eyes glittered when he talked about the miraculous effects of this healing energy on people's bodies, minds and lives. Reiki, he said, had changed his life. The reiki teacher, Jenni, a huge American with three chins and flicked-back hair, said it had changed hers. She had, she told us, spent years in hospital and had a series of operations on her spine. Then she discovered reiki and now she was a 'reiki master', devoting her life to the practice of this sacred art.

I tried not to laugh the first morning when we were all told to walk around the room and pretend to be trees. I tried even harder when we were split into groups to do 'image work' and then had to tell each other about the pictures we'd had of ourselves as lions or gazelles. Jenni gave a brief introduction to reiki and explained that it had been discovered on a mountain in 1922 by a Japanese monk. It sounded ridiculous. It *was* ridiculous. It didn't stop me joining the others in drawing and saying the reiki symbols, which we were not allowed to share. We had to practise repeating the words in our heads as we took it in turns to lie down and hold our hands above each other's 'chakras'. As I lay there, aware of hands hovering above me, I felt as if someone had heated up the blood in my veins. When it was my turn to do the 'healing', I felt tingling in my hands.

Why? I honestly have no idea why. Reiki, according to the Wikipedia definition, is 'used as an illustrative example of pseudoscience in scholarly texts and academic journals'. It is, in other words, famous for being nonsense. Was it a kind of mass hypnosis? Mass brainwashing? Mass hysteria? If it was, it seemed to be a lot more effective than the versions I had tried before. And also a lot more fun.

When we weren't lying on the floor, or hunching over people who were lying on the floor, we sat and chatted in the sun. In the evenings, we went to tavernas, ate grilled squid and drank retsina. I shared a tiny apartment with a woman who worked as a speechwriter at the EU. On the way back to my room one night, I found her on a bench with a Shakespearian actor from her creative writing group. They were kissing under the stars.

I don't know if it was the reiki, or the sunshine, or the laughter, or if it was just because, as Hamlet says, 'There are more things on heaven and earth, Horatio, than are dreamt of in your philosophy', but by the end of the week I could do the fifteen-minute walk down to the beach. I went home feeling cheerful and happy, and believing that the pain could go, which it did.

I still dreamt of being a journalist and was now reviewing more than sixty books a year. It was Maura who had suggested, when she read my press releases, that I do a sample review and send it off to the *Literary Review* and the *TLS*. When my first review was published, I felt like cutting it out and framing it. My mother didn't frame it, but she did start a 'CHRISTINA WRITING' red lever arch file. By the time we cleared her house, those files of my writing took up three shelves.

After doing some book reviews for the *Observer*, I was asked to do a monthly round-up of first novels. I was still helping to run more than 100 events a year at the South Bank on top of a full working week. 'I don't know how you manage to read all those books!' wrote my mother in a postcard. 'Your fame has spread and a friend of mine rang this morning to ask if it was actually you who had written those excellent reviews in the *Observer* and my heart swelled with pride! Dad and I are so proud of your achievements.'

Dad and I are so proud of your achievements. I should have tattooed this on my heart.

My mother wasn't sure what to think when I started going out with a man I met in the bar at the South Bank. Stephen was so striking that people turned to look at him. He had shoulder-length dreadlocks, high cheekbones on a sculpted face and haunting brown eyes. He looked, I thought, like a pharaoh, but one who turned into a cheeky schoolboy when he smiled. He dreamt of making documentaries, but was actually unemployed. He was also barely literate because he had hardly been to school. He had been brought up, or not really brought up, in care and had ended up living on the streets as a teenager, joining a gang that burgled offices in Soho and paying for it with a couple of years 'inside'. He only let this slip when I asked him, over a delicious dinner he'd prepared, where he'd learnt to cook and there was a long, long pause.

Stephen was only the second man I slept with. For the time I was with him, I felt safe and loved. My heart still stirs with a kind of love when I think of him now.

It was just a few weeks. For me, it was always just a few weeks. Or even just a few days. My next relationship, though that isn't quite the word, spanned several weeks, but involved only two actual meetings. I had been shocked when a famous, and famously handsome, writer had called to ask me out for dinner. I'd met him at the South Bank several times, but hadn't noticed a flicker of interest, and probably wouldn't have believed it if I had. We met in a chic restaurant in Notting Hill. I was shocked when I saw the prices on the menu and even more shocked when he ordered champagne. At the end of the evening, he kissed me. He told me I was irresistible and I didn't even try to resist him. Like every other scalp of every other Casanova, I thought I'd be the woman to win him over. It didn't take long to find out I was wrong.

I was walking on to the stage of the Queen Elizabeth Hall to introduce the Mexican poet Octavio Paz when I realised I was limping. I thought I must have done something to my ankle. At the end of the evening, I only just managed to hobble to the car.

The next day, there was a publishing dinner I was desperate not to miss. When I made it up the stairs and to the private dining room in Soho, I was excited to find my name tag next to Doris Lessing's. I wanted to tell her that I had read *The Golden Notebook* as a teenager in the sand dunes in Sweden, and that it had felt like a life-saving drug. I wanted to quiz her about her life and her books, but I couldn't concentrate on anything because of the pulsating pain in my left foot. When she saw me wincing, she offered to drive me to A & E. I thought I couldn't possibly let Doris Lessing drive me anywhere, and propelled myself down the stairs by hanging on to the handrail. When I got to the pavement, I propped myself against a lamp post and hailed a cab.

It was seven years since I'd gone to University College Hospital, with the pains in my knees that had had me crawling on the floor. That was when they lost the blood tests and didn't find them for a year. This time, the doctor who examined my foot thought I must have sprained my ankle. He sent me away with painkillers and crutches and told me that if I kept moving, it would get better. I did, and it didn't. By the end of the week I had pain in both ankles and both knees and in my fingers and arms.

It was a year since the pain had last gone. I'd thought I had finally beaten it. Now I felt as if a silent, vicious, nameless enemy had managed to hunt me down.

I didn't want to talk to Mrs Jones. I felt I had nothing, nothing, nothing more to say about my pain, or where it might come from, or how it might go.

In search of another miracle, I booked another 'holistic

holiday', this time in southern Spain. I drove to Stansted, left my car at the airport and was picked up at Malaga. I didn't leave the building or its grounds all week. Once again, there was sunshine, there was beauty, there was delicious food and there were kind people, but this time there was no magic. This time, there was an American psychotherapist called Bernie, running a course called 'Getting out of your own way!' I was desperate to 'get out of my own way'. I wanted to find and destroy whatever it was that was tripping me up, knocking me down, wiring my nerves to an electrical circuit in some weird version of the Milgram experiment that seemed to have been specially designed for me. I wanted bows and arrows. I wanted secret symbols. I wanted wands. Bernie, unfortunately, wasn't offering them. He told me he thought the pain in my joints had something to do with anger. He said he thought I felt angry and ashamed and that the pain was my way of punishing myself for my anger. He said I had to accept that the pain wasn't some alien force trying to ruin things for me, but a part of me, and I couldn't put a deadline on it going away.

As I allowed his words to sink in, I felt even more ashamed. I felt as if my shame and rage were written on my body, written on my cells, written on my bones. I felt as if I had a poison inside me, and this was the poison that sometimes crippled me and sometimes exploded on my face.

When I picked up my car from Stansted and set off

down the M11, I kept thinking I was going to crash. For the first time in my life, I felt that something inside me was actually trying to kill me. I gripped the steering wheel and tried to keep the car straight, but I felt as if I was fighting a force that was stronger than me.

The next day, when my mother called, I could hardly speak. She called back a few minutes later and said that she and my father were setting off to London to collect me. They drove me back to Guildford and we all sat on the sofa together and my mother held my hand.

My doctor phoned through a prescription for an antidepressant called Prothiaden. It's one of the old types of antidepressant, the tricyclics, often used in a low dose for pain relief, and one she had given me when my arm had gone dead six years before. It made me tired and dizzy and sick, but it also knocked me out. In the days and weeks that followed, the pain left my fingers, and then my arms, and then my back and then, six weeks after it had come back, it left my knees.

When I look back at those days, even when I write about those days, I feel some of the shame flooding back. For so many years, I was mortified by the pain that kept flaring up and tripping me up. I was mortified in every sense. I was deeply embarrassed to have such a strange, recurring illness, or imaginary illness, one that burst out at inconvenient moments like a jack-in-the-box that was also some kind of Joker. I was also, to paraphrase the dictionary, subdued, suppressed, subjugated, controlled and punished by it. The word 'mortify' comes from the Latin *mortificare*, meaning 'to kill or subdue', which in late Middle English became 'put to death', 'deaden' and 'subdue by self-denial'. *Mortis*, of course, means 'death'. Even now I feel reluctant to write about this part of it. I feel ashamed, in fact. But I have to be honest. There were times when I wanted to die.

The first time was when my skin burst out, when I was twenty-three, and felt like a leper. You're meant to feel attractive when you're twenty-three. When your whole face has turned into a weeping, throbbing, suppurating mess, one that intrigues dermatologists and attracts pity from medical students, that's quite a challenge. The acne, like the physical pain, came and went and came and went and was only finally controlled (suppressed, subjugated but not punished) by a drug that I was told was given to women who wanted to be male. In the meantime, I tried different cocktails of drugs. I tried a range of antibiotics, which didn't work. I tried Roaccutane twice, but had to give it up because I thought my head was going to explode, which the leaflet listing side effects called 'cranial hypertension'. I tried several versions of the pill, which felt like a waste since I hardly ever had sex, and seemed to have no effect at all on my skin. I filled a bathroom cabinet with lotions and creams prescribed by dermatologists, including one they really do give lepers.

I tried homeopathy and special diets, acupuncture and

facials, Chinese herbs and hypnotherapy, 'body work' and 'detoxing'. In the end, I went to a dermatologist in Leeds, who put me on a hormone-blocking drug that's used for transgender transitions. It gave me a severe headache for about four days a month, but I thought forty-eight days of pain a year was a small price to pay for clear, or quite clear, skin.

What strikes me now is the sheer, exhausting effort of trying to look normal, and behave in a normal way, as I tried to stop the pain in my body bursting out and the poison, or whatever it was, erupting on my face. For months, I would be fine. I had an enviable job. I was working ridiculous hours, but doing work that was interesting and getting noticed. I had lots of friends. I've always had lots of friends. My mother taught us all the art of friendship and my friends have often kept me going when almost everything else seems to have failed. But there were times when none of this seemed enough. Sometimes, when the pain hit again, or when my skin exploded again, or when I felt I would never find love, I thought: that's it. Enough already. Living is just too damn hard. Sometimes, I thought about what I would do to end things. It was the thought of my parents that stopped me.

Or at least that's what I thought at the time. Now I don't think that's quite true. When I look back, I see a jerky path, a two-steps-forward-one-step-back kind of path, with big leaps and sudden slides and another long, slow ascent and another sudden slide. It reminds me of the graph my mother did of Caroline's medication. It also reminds me of Beckett: 'You must go on. I can't go on. I'll go on.'

During my interview at the Poetry Society, I couldn't stop wriggling in my chair. I had never had cystitis before and had no idea it could be so distracting. I could hardly concentrate on the questions, which were being asked in an attempt to work out whether I was suitable for the role of 'Poetry Places Co-ordinator', running a national scheme of poetry residencies, funded by the lottery. When I was offered it, I asked if I could do it four days a week. On the fifth day, I wanted to try to be a journalist. I still loved working with writers, but I knew that what I really wanted to do was write.

I had cystitis because I'd spent a good chunk of the week having the best sex of my life. I'd met Winston at a fast-food stall at the Elephant and Castle, on the way back from a bad date. I'd had to compose my face when I spotted the man I'd arranged to meet, in a bar in Soho. He was several inches shorter than he had said in his ad, which I'd found in the 'lonely hearts' section in the *Guardian*. He had a sulky face and cold eyes. He also had no manners. After a tense hour of sullen answers to my polite questions, I left feeling depressed and hungry. When my bus reached the roundabout at the Elephant, I decided to stop off for some rice and peas. I had just been served when a man in a leather jacket sauntered up to me.

'Do you want to go for a drink?' he said. Winston has a

smile that's very, very hard to resist. He has a gap between his front teeth. He also has a swagger and sweetness I've rarely seen in a human being, a set to his shoulders that says: my heart is open, but cross me at your peril. He's six foot four and, as he once said of his cousin, Doug, built like a brick shithouse. Doug lived in one of the projects on the Bronx. Winston's mother, a Jamaican matriarch adored and feared by all her offspring, had sent him there after a spell in a young offenders' institute. 'That will saart you out,' she told him and, after several months surrounded by crack dealers and gun-runners much bigger and meaner than Winston, it did.

We went to a pub under the arches that turned into a lock-in. We went to the Old Gin Palace in the Old Kent Road. Winston leaned across the table to kiss me and I felt as if I melted into his impressively solid chest. We held hands as we walked back through the bleak estates to the Walworth Road and then back to my flat. I was surprised when he lay on the floor and asked me to walk on his back. He had, I later discovered, broken his back twice, once when he fell off a roof, smashed through a glass ceiling and landed on a purple coffin, and once in a motorbike accident at the Elephant and Castle, where I'd just bought my rice and peas. Winston's accidents, I soon discovered, were as colourful as his life. He had worked as an electrician, a bar tender, a barista and a musician. He had played drums with Stevie Wonder. He had grown up round the corner from the Elephant and gone to school in Peckham, but was now living in the South of France. He was back to visit his mum.

Winston lit up my life from the moment I met him. Some people just do.

I started the new job, in a ramshackle building in Covent Garden, with colleagues who were friendly and fun. I saw Winston as he bounced between Antibes and Walworth. One night, in a pub, one of his friends said, 'Who's the posh bird?' Another said, 'How's Fluffy?' in a faux-aristocratic voice. I had no idea his friends called me Fluffy. Years later, I discovered that I was still listed as Fluffy in Winston's phone.

Nine months after I started the new job, I sold my flat and moved. My father was with me when I saw the old school converted into apartments in Stoke Newington. The one we were standing in had a tiny kitchen and bedroom, but the main room had a mezzanine and the ceiling was two storeys high. Through the big classroom window, you could see a garden full of silver birches. They made me think of Sweden, and of the five birches my father had planted in the front garden when we arrived in Guildford from Rome. One, he said, for each member of the family. 'I don't think you could do better than this,' he said, and I thought he was probably right.

Six months later, the director of the Poetry Society told us he was leaving. This time, I decided that I wasn't going to refuse to apply for a job just because it would be embarrassing if I didn't get it. My colleagues cheered when I did. One of them told me I was going to be the first woman to run the Poetry Society since Muriel Spark in 1948.

Two days after I heard I'd got the job, I went to Guildford. My mother had bought some sparkling wine. She poured four glasses, and a glass of Appletiser for Caroline. My father raised his glass. 'To Christina,' he said, 'and the new job.' We all clinked glasses, but Caroline knocked hers over and smashed it. 'Why,' she yelled, before storming out, 'do you always make such a fuss of Christina?'

Chapter 20

Beloved

I laughed when I saw the sign. 'Queen Bee'. It was the finance manager, Eamonn, who made it and stuck it on my pigeonhole. It made me smile because I couldn't pretend I wasn't loving being the boss.

Since I had been at the Poetry Society for eighteen months, I already knew some of the things I wanted to change. I changed them quickly. Some were organisational. Some were about working practices. Some were symbolic. The offices had a clear-out, and a fresh coat of paint. Some of my colleagues weren't very happy when I said that we'd ditch the loud rock music during office hours and make sure there was always a human to answer the phone. They cheered up when I told them I didn't want people at their desks after 6 p.m. We could get things done during working hours and no one was paid enough to do more.

The Poetry Society was (and is) in a tall, thin Victorian

building in a side street in Covent Garden. It was originally a home for market traders but in the sixties was used as the office of the radical magazine the *International Times*. The Poetry Society moved into the building in 1992, from much larger, grander offices in Earls Court. It was in financial difficulties and the only way to deal with them was to sell up.

Money was still tight, and I spent a lot of my time staring at budgets and trying to find ways to keep things afloat. Staff salaries were shockingly low and I wanted to pay my colleagues more. People worked at the Poetry Society because they loved poetry and because they wanted to share that love, through the society's education work, publications, events, or work in schools. We were all jammed into offices on the top two floors. The next floor was a 'poetry studio' with a daffodil-yellow floor. The ground floor was the Poetry Café, a cosy room with battered wooden tables, a mini poetry bookshop and poetry-related art. It was also a bar. If you want to build relationships at work, then it really, really helps to have a bar.

On Fridays, we'd all stop for 'the 5.45', and wander down to the Poetry Café for wine and beer. We'd huddle in the corner, swap anecdotes and release some of the tension of the week. Some of my colleagues had already become my friends. I had worried that my new role would affect our friendship, but it didn't. My colleague Lisa and I still often went to the wine bar round the corner and howled with laughter over each other's dating disasters. Lisa still makes me laugh more than almost anyone. As perks go, it's hard to think of one that's better than spending every working day with people whose company you seek out when the work is done.

I started a staff poetry reading group, and we took it in turns to bring along a poem we liked. In winter, we dissected Philip Larkin or Simon Armitage in the basement, over Chilean Chardonnay or San Miguels. In the summer, we mulled Carol Ann Duffy or Ted Hughes over margaritas on the roof. I've always loved parties and I organised as many social events as I could. I set up a series of members' dinners in the Poetry Café, hosted by poets and with themed food. I set up wine tastings, run by our IT manager, who used to work in the wine trade. I put on a series of 'intimate' poetry readings in the poetry studio. They had to be 'intimate' because the venue was so small. Winston turned up for one halfway through, in full leather bike gear and with clanking chains. He sat down, fell asleep and started snoring. I signalled to Lisa to prod him. He jerked awake with a juddering snort and looked around the room with the air of someone who expected to be at a bikers' convention but found himself at a Bible Study. At the end of the reading, when I asked the audience if they had any questions, he stuck up his hand. 'Can I read a poem of mine?' he said. With Winston, the surprises never stop.

With Andrew Motion, who was then the poet laureate, I helped organise a Golden Jubilee poetry competition for the Queen. The meetings were at Buckingham Palace. It felt quite surreal to be discussing how to target 32,000 schools while gazing at portraits of past monarchs. Once, when a military band in the courtyard started playing James Bond medleys, I got the giggles. Every time I saw my colleague Martin's mouth twitch, I felt a delicious wave rising up, clamped my mouth shut and stared down at my notes. When I met the Queen, at the award ceremony, it was clear that I wasn't the only one who had giggled at Buckingham Palace. The poet John Agard, who flirts with everyone, flirted with her and I could see from the glint in her eye that she was charmed.

There were plenty of boring parts of the job, of course. I once sneaked out of a meeting at the Qualifications and Curriculum Authority when a man wouldn't stop talking, and went to Caffè Nero for coffee and cake. I always felt less cheerful on a day when I had to fill out a funding application, tick boxes for the Arts Council or write a report for a sponsor. I often think of my mother's request to put 'she cleared the loft' on her grave. No one would ever put 'she liked admin' on mine. But every time a sponsor said yes, or an application for a grant was successful, I would nip out for bottles of cava and Kettle chips. We'd all stop work and raise a glass. We'd stop work so often, in fact, and I ate so many crisps, in the office, and in the Poetry Café, and in the wine bar round the corner, that I put on a stone.

What I loved was the social part of the job. I loved

chairing events with poets at festivals and going on the radio to talk about poetry, and sometimes on TV. I loved seeing poets work in schools, and particularly in inner-city schools where some of the children didn't think they were good at anything else. I sat in poetry workshops in law firms, hospitals and prisons and learnt something from each of them. When the Mayor of London's office asked us to organise a poetry competition, I suggested a poetry slam instead. I'd heard about these spoken-word poetry competitions, in front of live audiences, from someone who had been to one in New York. When I saw the children perform their poems, in theatres, church halls and at a big festival in Victoria Park, I thought I couldn't be prouder if they were mine.

If I were to pick one image of that time, I think it would be of all of us, sitting on the roof, talking about poetry and sipping home-made margaritas in the sun. It was golden. That's what I've always longed for: for things to be golden, and they were.

I had never really known what to talk about with my father, but now I talked about work. When I had problems with staff, or poets, or the board, I sometimes asked him for advice and was surprised to find his suggestions nearly always worked. When I had to write a business plan for the Arts Council, to say why I thought we needed extra funding, he read it. I had never seen a business plan before, and wrote it after going on a two-day course. The

Arts Council gave us a 42 per cent increase in our grant, which meant I could give the staff a pay rise. I was almost as pleased when my father told me my business plan was 'really good'.

I thought it was a shame that it had taken so long for us to be able to talk to each other, without feeling the conversation was an argument one of us had to win. I thought back to all the times in my childhood when my father had come back from work and asked me about my day. I'd say 'fine, thank you' and that sometimes seemed to be all there was to say. I remembered how he sometimes asked me questions I was sure he knew the answer to, because I'd already heard my mother tell him. And how he always used to ask whether we were enjoying a TV programme, or an ice cream, and how I thought it was obvious if you were enjoying something, and didn't need to say.

I remembered the rows at mealtimes, and the 'elbows off the table', and the 'don't eat with your mouth full', or 'with your left hand'. I thought of how when he was telling us something it sometimes sounded like the Chancellor's Budget speech. I remembered how he would furrow his brow when my mother had a migraine, and how he would tell us that if we didn't have anything nice to say we shouldn't say anything at all.

I thought of all these things and felt sad that we had so often sparked each other off. Now I could see that something between us had been misfiring, and that this was partly because we were wary of each other, but also because we were both, strangely, shy. Now I saw what other people saw and talked about: a brilliant man who thought deeply and cared deeply, a man who set the highest standards because he believed that you should always do your best. Now that I was talking to him properly for the first time, I realised that I didn't just love him because I was his daughter. I liked him. I really liked him.

So when he phoned to tell me he had cancer of the colon, I felt a cold fist squeezing my heart.

In the days that followed, I carried on walking around and doing my job, but felt as if I had been injected with a drug that had frozen my veins. My father had tried to sound positive when he told me the news. We wouldn't know how things stood, he said, until he had his operation. My mother had hardly been able to speak because she had lost her voice. It wasn't the first time she had lost her voice when she couldn't find any words.

I've found them in her diary. 'Slept badly,' she writes the day after the trip to the hospital, 'and cold sweat twice. Woke up to the horrible knowledge that John has colorectal cancer. It hits you as you wake up.'

My father's diary entry is matter-of-fact. 'NOT GOOD NEWS from Prof Marks. Suspected rectal cancer with radiotherapy and two (?) operations in prospect. I must get used to it. Write to resign from Perkins and Capita RAS.' He was a school governor and was on interview panels for public appointments. He must have been feeling pretty bad to resign from both straight away. It's the entry a few days later that moves me more. 'Quite a blissful day! (Though with less good moments.) I cut the back lawn and feel up to a wonderful trip to Vann where the gardens really are paradise. Woodland spring bulbs etc. Wonderful white fritillaries.'

For nearly three years, Caroline had had something like an independent life, living in a tiny housing association flat ten minutes' walk from my parents. They still saw her every day. They helped her with her shopping and her bills. She still went three times a week to the NSF Bookshop in Godalming. She sometimes helped out at Oxfam in Guildford High Street. When she wasn't doing any of those things, she saw Richard and her friends. It was ten years since she had done any paid work, but she seemed to have been better off without the stress. She had been well, or relatively well. Life had been good, or at least better.

The visits she looked forward to most were from Tom. She would lay out the coffee and cake before he turned up and they would sit together on the sofa, watching her favourite videos. He called her 'the Crow'. Tom had a nickname for almost everyone. He called our mother 'Ma' or 'the mater' and our father 'the old boy' or 'the big Chief'. He still often went round to Nelson Gardens, to have Sunday lunch with my parents or hunch in front of the TV with my father to watch the football or the rugby. They could sit for hours in silence, with just the odd grunt or cheer.

When Tom heard the news about his cancer, he wrote him a letter. I've found it in the 'TOM LETTERS' file. 'Dear Dad,' it begins, 'I was obviously very upset to hear the news about your cancer on the phone tonight. It came as a horrible shock, as you never really think these things are going to happen to your nearest and dearest.' He says how nice it was to see him on Sunday, and that he was pleased that they had watched the football. 'I just wanted to say that you have been the most fantastic father to me all my life and I love you dearly.'

When my mother told Caroline the news about my father, she had to give her Valium. She had started feeling breathless a few weeks before. She had also, she told my mother, started getting pains in her legs and was finding it difficult to walk. 'Told her a bit but tried to reassure her,' my mother has written on the day of his diagnosis. The reassurance didn't work. Caroline started having panic attacks. She stopped sleeping. My mother arranged an emergency appointment with the doctor, who increased the dose of her medication and gave her more Valium. She still didn't sleep.

On the day of my father's colonoscopy, my mother sat with Caroline in her flat and 'tried to reassure her' before dashing back to the hospital to pick my father up. From then on, her diary is a mix of hospital appointments for my father, Caroline's panic attacks and my mother's attempts to look after them both.

My father had always been a big, strong man, but now

he looked pale and frail. I was more shocked when I saw Caroline. I was always shocked by her size, but now her once-skinny legs were red and swollen and on her face I saw raw fear. I took her for a drive to Compton, a pretty village outside Guildford where we used to go for Sunday walks, and to the Watts Gallery for tea and cake. I stopped the car just a few yards from a table outside the café, but by the time she sank down on the bench she was out of breath. When I brought the tea and cake to the table, she tried to smile. 'That looks delicious,' she said. I could see from her eyes that she was in pain.

When she walked, she said, she felt she couldn't breathe. She had pains in her thighs and calves. She found it difficult to stand, and difficult to get up the stairs. She also couldn't get into the bath. My mother had had rails put up, but she still couldn't manage it. My mother had to sponge her down.

The day after my father had his colon removed, Caroline was taken into hospital. They did blood tests, X-rays and cardiograms. They told her she had a hole in the heart. They said this had made her heart bigger than it should be, and had led to something called cardiomyopathy. They put her on Coversyl, frusemide, Aldactone, aspirin and digoxin. She was already on Largactil, Disipal, Diazepam and Seroxat.

On my father's first night out of hospital, when he was trying to cope with his colostomy, my mother got a phone call from Caroline, and had to leave. She sat by her bed all night while Caroline cried. My mother could hardly understand what she was saying, but she kept saying the words 'schizophrenia' and 'God'.

I was surprised when my father called me at work. He thought you should never make, or take, personal calls at work. When he had needed to call my mother about something when he was working at the Cabinet Office or the Treasury, he would wait till lunchtime and call from a pay phone in the street.

He told me that Caroline had collapsed while she was washing up at 'the bookshop'. The ambulance had taken forty minutes to get there. The paramedics had done their best.

I lay down on the floor of my office. My head was wedged against the filing cabinet, but I didn't think I could move it. I heard a wail, and realised it was coming out of me. Eamonn knocked on the door. He had a pile of tissues in his hand. I told him, but the words sounded ridiculous, that my sister was dead.

I had never been to a funeral. When Mormor died, my mother flew out to the funeral on her own. When Mama May died, I was too crippled with pain to get on a train. I was sad when Mormor died, and even more sad when Mama May died. I was sad when Morbror Arthur died and then when Moster Agnes died, but I wasn't all that surprised because they were old. When Caroline died, I felt as if the world had flipped over and we were in a new landscape covered with dust and rocks.

We went to the registry office to register her death. It was an Edwardian building round the corner from Millmead Church, the place where I'd found God and where Caroline still went. I mean had gone. Had gone. Had gone. Had gone. Caroline had gone and I had to change my grammar.

It was just up from the River Wey, where my father used to take us punting. He had loved punting at Cambridge and was keen to show off his skills. Once, he got his punt tangled up in someone's fishing line and spent half an hour coiling up the line before handing it back to its owner. 'I'm so sorry,' he said. I was huffing and sighing, but when I heard him say that, I stopped. I didn't think I'd ever heard my father say sorry. Afterwards, he took us to the Jolly Farmer next to the boathouse for half a shandy and a baked potato. I always looked forward to that baked potato. Even after every house had a microwave, and pubs and restaurants started serving warm potatoes with no skin to speak of, it remained for me the one, true potato, a melting buttery mush of comfort, with a crispy skin to crunch. Comfort after fresh air on the river with my father, slicing wood through the water, proud of his punting, proud of his brood.

There wasn't much sign of comfort at the registry office, where we sat on plastic chairs as my father filled out the forms. When he got to the box marked 'occupation', he paused. It was eighteen years since Caroline had worked in an office, but he nodded, as if he had made up his mind about something that had been troubling him, and wrote the word 'typist'.

We didn't go to the Jolly Farmer. Instead, we went to the funeral parlour and looked at leaflets about coffins. In the end, we chose one made out of beech. After we chose it, I suddenly thought that maybe the coffin would be too small, maybe coffins always came in a standard size and Caroline wouldn't fit in it. When we left, I wanted to run back and tell them. Later, I told my father. He said I didn't need to worry about that, and that the undertakers knew what they were doing.

On the morning of the funeral, I went to M&S to pick up the sandwiches for the wake. The woman at the counter looked at my receipt and then at a big black book. 'Sorry,' she said. 'There seems to have been an error. I'm afraid there's nothing listed here.' I kept showing her the receipt and she kept shaking her head. Please, I said. I can't tell my mother that there are no sandwiches for her daughter's funeral. Please, please, please, please, please.

In the end, she found some. Tom waited in the car outside while I picked them up.

When Uncle George turned up at Nelson Gardens with Auntie Rosemary, and then Uncle Maurice with Auntie Bell, it was a shock to see them all in black. For a moment, I couldn't think what they were doing there. I thought: so, it's true. The world has flipped and it's not flipping back.

When we got into the big black limousine, I looked out

at the other cars, which we were holding up, and thought of all the funeral cortèges I had seen, and how I'd wondered about the people inside them and what it was like to wear your grief on your car and clothes and sleeve, and to know that you could only do that for one day.

It took a while to get to the crematorium, but when we did, there were so many people waiting outside the chapel that I wasn't sure they'd all get in.

When I saw the coffin, I felt something surge through me that was like an electric shock. I saw my mother's face and wanted to wrap her in my arms and tell her that it wasn't true, it had all been a terrible mistake. We watched as the coffin was lifted out of the hearse and my parents followed the vicar as he walked behind it and Tom and I followed them. When the first hymn struck up, I tried to keep my voice normal, but I wanted to fill the chapel with my wails. The Lord's my Shepherd, I'll not want, He makes me down to lie. Yea, though I walk in death's dark vale. So this was what death's dark vale was like.

My father did the reading, from Revelation, chapter 21. His voice shook when he said, 'He will wipe every tear from their eyes' and 'there will be no more death or mourning or crying or pain.' When the coffin went through the curtains, and to where I knew there would be flames, I wanted to run after it and stop it.

Afterwards, we had a service of celebration at Millmead. It was more than fifteen years since I had walked through those glass doors. I thought of the leather jackets and the volleyball, and how Jackie, and Sam, and Barry, and Chris had been so friendly. I remembered the first time I heard the pastor, David Pawson, and how half an hour had felt like a minute.

I had only ever heard choruses in that church, but a pianist was playing 'Jesu, Joy of Man's Desiring' as we filed to our seats. Bach. My father's beloved Bach. I looked around and gasped. On a Tuesday afternoon, there were more than two hundred people. All there for Caroline.

We sang 'Praise, My Soul, the King of Heaven'. After the opening prayer, there was a reading from John, chapter 14, verses 1–6. 'Do not let your hearts be troubled . . . In my Father's house there are many rooms.' We sang 'Will your anchor hold in the storms of life?' It's listed in the service sheet as 'a hymn which Caroline loved'.

One by one, we went up to the microphone. Tom went first. His voice kept cracking, but he managed to read out the message he had written for Caroline. He remembered, he said, the 'wonderful last day' they had together at Stonehenge. 'I don't think you would believe it,' he said, 'if you saw how many people have come to say goodbye to you. They have all come because they thought so much of you.' His voice broke and I thought he wouldn't be able to continue. He swallowed and paused and then started again. 'I know,' he said, 'you thought jobs and tasks were difficult, but you had a real gift for making friends.' He thanked her for being 'an absolutely fantastic sister'.

My father read out the letter he wrote, two days after

Caroline died. I've cut it a bit, but here it is. At the top, in capital letters, he has written MY FAREWELL MESSAGE TO CAROLINE.

Dearest Caroline,

I loved you with all my heart. I was there when you were born at the Bangkok Nursing Home on the 12th October 1958. I took you to Godalming, where I was born, on Wednesday 12th of July 2000, and saw you alive and happy for the last time. The next day you were taken away from us.

I have your passport in front of me. The only stamp in it is the Russian one. For Mum and me as well as for you, that tour in October 1995 was one of the highlights of our lives.

Then in August 1997 you moved to new independence at 36 Elgin Gardens, where your beloved Richard gave you such faithful support.

Mum has been quite heroic in keeping you going in your flat during these last hard weeks when you had your heart problems and I had my operation followed by chemotherapy. But they were hard times for us all.

When I think that I shall never again hear your eager 'Hello, Dad' so full of love and gladness to see me, I have a feeling of unbearable loss. But the wonderful memories will be with me for the rest of my days, however long or short. I was so proud that I was able to resume giving you lifts to Queen Street in the last few days. On our final drive you said that there would be no more golf course walks in Sweden for us. You were right. We both knew then that those walks are treasured memories. So are the fish and chips you shared with Mum and me on our last Saturday together.

You do not get your place in my 'illness message' album. You were then too ill to write. But in your final Father's Day card you wrote that I was the best father in the world. I do not deserve that. But I could not have loved you more.

My mother didn't speak. My mother couldn't speak. I didn't know how I was going to, but I did. I said that, when I was a child, I didn't realise all the battles Caroline had fought, and that some of them were battles she couldn't win. I said that I didn't understand why she was suddenly sent away, or why, when she came back, at first just to spend the nights at home, she looked so frightened. I said that what she wanted, more than anything, was to lead a normal life. She didn't even want to say that her mother was Swedish, or that she was born in Bangkok and then lived in Rome. I said that all she ever wanted was to be ordinary.

I said I remembered how hard Caroline had worked at school, when she was on so many pills that she sometimes slurred her words, while she had to watch Tom and me get As in everything. I remembered how she had tried so hard to learn to type, and then managed it, and how much she had loved her job at Cornhill Insurance. I read a paragraph from a letter she'd sent Tom in America, when she was working at Milwards shoe shop, but having trouble finding the shoes.

I said that after she gave up trying to find, and keep, a job, she was much, much happier. I said that she loved people, and was very good at listening and talking, and was interested in so many things. I said she was the only person I'd ever met who honestly thought it didn't matter how you looked. I said that she never worried about the spots the pills gave her, or about how fat they made her, because she thought that what mattered was your heart.

I read a poem. It was Raymond Carver's 'Late Fragment'. It's only five lines long.

And did you get what you wanted from this life, even so?
I did.
And what did you want.
To call myself beloved, to feel myself
beloved on the earth.

I said what I'd only just realised, and now knew to be true: that my sister was the bravest person I knew.

Chapter 21

The Rainbow in the Sky

My mother took photos of everything, and so it's all there in the album: the trip to the registry office, the evening wake at Nelson Gardens, a forlorn Richard sitting on the sofa with Tom, both in black suits and black ties. After that, there are photos of Caroline's flat and of Tom and my father helping to clear it. Hanging over her bed there are four framed photos of the Grand Duchesses.

There's a photo of my mother sitting in the empty flat, just before they leave it for the last time. In photos, my mother is always smiling. Even here, she's trying to smile, but in her face there's such sorrow I can hardly bear to look at it. It makes me think of the Cup of Sorrows. Take this cup away from me.

A few pages later, we're all having lunch at Tom's. 'Tom cooked us a delicious roast lamb Sunday lunch in Dorking' says the caption. A couple of weeks later there's a photo of Tom eating meatballs. 'Tom and I went to IKEA, where we had a very nice day. He bought an Anton desk.' As always, she's putting her best foot forward. She's trying to sound upbeat. There are coffees with friends. There are trips out. Here's my father, surrounded by white roses, against a backdrop of green fields studded with oaks. 'John and I went away for a few days between chemotherapy treatments. First we visited Chartwell.' And then we're by the grave, on the plot my parents had bought for themselves in the Swedish section of Brookwood Cemetery. We're standing next to a patch of green turf with a hole that has just been dug for the urn. My parents are in black suits and so is Tom. I'm in a purple skirt and a black leather jacket. My mother's caption is: 'We all sang "Now thank we all our God".'

A few pages on, there's a photo of my mother at a warehouse, standing by slabs of granite. The caption is hardly necessary: 'Choosing a memorial stone for Caroline's grave'. Every few pages, the album returns to the grave. There are photos of it in the snow. There are photos of my father next to it, planting spring bulbs. 'John in the flooded Swedish cemetery before his next operation,' my mother has written. The operation was the reversal of my father's colostomy. Here he is, lying in a hospital bed in a blue dressing gown, surrounded by tubes. In the next photo, he's in the sitting room at Nelson Gardens with a white slatted box. 'Tom gave John a weather centre,' says my mother, 'and fixed it up in the back garden.' It was a box full of thermometers and gadgets, to monitor temperature, humidity and atmospheric pressure. I've just discovered that it's called a Stevenson screen, since it was designed by Robert Louis Stevenson's father. My father read us the whole of *Kidnapped* and *Treasure Island*. Clever Tom, to have given him his own weather centre, designed by the father of the man who wrote *Treasure Island*. None of us ever forgot the hush in the house as we waited for the man on TV to tell us the forecast and how we could tell what it was just by looking at our father's face.

My mother wasn't all that interested in the weather, but she did take a photo of a rainbow against a grey sky, behind the house across the road. It was after my father's operation. 'Prof Marks rang later to say that the op had gone well,' she has written, next to a photo of my father outside the hospital, 'but the cancer had gone to the lungs.' You can see why she wrote, next to the photo of the house, 'The rainbow in the sky did not promise luck.'

My parents made the most of things. They always made the most of things. Between my father's trips to the hospital for chemotherapy, they went on as many trips as they could manage. They clearly went to a lot of gardens. My father's photo album from this time is nearly all photos of gardens and plants. There's page after page of daffodils, snowdrops, crocuses, roses and my mother. And there's page after page of photos of the grave, sometimes in sunshine, sometimes in frost, sometimes in rain. The flowers and bulbs my father planted on it were often eaten by foxes or deer. Sometimes they were washed away. My father kept planting new ones. He wanted beautiful flowers on my sister's grave.

My parents couldn't face a Christmas at home without Caroline and went to Tuscany. There's a photo of my mother standing in a hotel foyer next to an Italian nativity set, just like the one we always had on the Chinese cabinet in Nelson Gardens. There's a photo of my father in a piazza overlooking Florence. It's a grey, grey day and it looks as if it's about to rain.

We all spent a weekend at a hotel near Gatwick. Nothing, and I mean nothing, dimmed my mother's love of a bargain, so I think it must have been on special offer. There's a photo of Tom and my father lying on twin beds watching TV, but my father's pale face confirms my mother's caption: 'The men watched rugby in Tom's double room, but John was not at all well.' The colostomy reversal had not been entirely successful. My father often had to rush to the loo and sometimes didn't make it in time. Some nights, he had to go every half hour. Sometimes, he wanted to cry with the shame of it. He said he tried to think of Caroline's courage, and that this spurred him on.

My mother often cleared up after him. For better, for worse, in sickness and in health, but no one had said anything about scraping shit off trousers, off beds, off carpets and off the bathroom floor.

My parents went on their first ever cruise. They flew to Athens and boarded the *Ocean Majesty*, for a week on the

Black Sea. I'm pleased to see photos of my father sitting on the deck, 'enjoying the sun' and at a dinner table with a bottle of wine. Perhaps he even allowed himself a second glass? Now he's lying on a bed in their 'comfortable cabin'. He's reading Zadie Smith's *White Teeth* and he's smiling. I'm irrationally happy that he's smiling. Now he's at the Livadia Palace in Yalta and now here's my mother in the palace garden, in trousers. I've hardly ever seen a photo of my mother in trousers. Here they are again, in Istanbul and in Kusadasi and then back on the ship.

Three months later, I went to Helsinki with my parents for a long weekend. When the stewardess on the flight told my father he couldn't use the loo because the seat-belt lights hadn't yet been switched off, I thought I might actually knock her to the floor. I got him in the loo and stood outside it. Fight me, I thought. If you touch him, if you get in his way, you are dead. But that, of course, was the problem, the shadow hanging over us, the valley of the shadow we didn't want to name.

In Helsinki, we went to an exhibition on the 'Golden Age of Russian Art'. We went to the Lutheran cathedral and the Rock Church and on a day trip to Tallinn. At a food fair in the harbour, we had smoked salmon and blueberries and I thought of the salmon we used to eat on the veranda at the cottage, and the blueberries we picked and ate with the *filmjölk* that looked sweet but tasted sour. I knew that we would never do any of those things together again.

For my father's seventieth birthday, my mother booked a big room at the Angel Hotel in Guildford High Street and invited twenty of their closest friends. There were ten couples, and they had all been married for nearly half a century. My mother handed each person a collage of photos from the seven decades of my father's life. She had written a speech to go with it. She had told Tom and me that she wanted the evening to be 'upbeat'.

In the speech, which I have in my 'DAD' box file, squeezed between work files in my study, she quotes a letter he wrote his parents from prep school when he was seven: 'I got nine runs by five wickets and I got a gold star in class and am trying to do my best.' She quotes his first letter from boarding school when he was eleven: 'Dearest Mummy and Daddy, I am having a lovely time here. The work is lovely except for the Latin and the Greek is fair. The food is very good and the sausages are excellent.' She quotes a paper delivered to the Classical Society in Cambridge just before he met my mother, when he talked about a conversation he'd had with a Dutch medical student at Delphi. 'I had,' he'd said, 'denounced the Swedes rather vigorously.'

She quoted a piece in the *Scotsman*, which described my father as 'a tall, modest man, who speaks in a cautious civil service manner'. She talked about the things my father did after he retired: becoming a school governor, joining the Community Health Council, volunteering at the Citizens Advice Bureau, working for the civil service recruitment and selection board, doing a German course with the Open University, going to University of the Third Age classes, travelling, gardening, reading and watching sport with Tom. He and Tom, said my mother, 'both love observing the weather and talk enthusiastically about the level of rainfall'. Then she asked us all to raise a glass.

Two weeks later, we all went up to Northumberland, for a seventieth birthday meal with my father's sister and brothers. We stayed with Auntie Bell and Uncle Maurice, in the house that Uncle Maurice had designed with its own football field, where we used to spend every Whitsun half-term. My mother had booked a big table at the local pub and gave a version of the speech she had given at the Angel Hotel. Everyone clapped and then my father spoke. One by one, he addressed each person around that table. When he got to Tom, he said he was one of only two people in the world he could be with in totally comfortable silence. I could see Tom blinking away tears as my father thanked him for introducing him to Sky Sports.

Then my father looked straight at me. He said that hearing the news, in a hotel room in Glasgow, that I had been made director of the Poetry Society, and feeling I had got the recognition he felt I'd always deserved, had 'transformed' his life.

I had to focus on my knife and fork. I wanted to smile, but I was finding it hard to swallow.

The next day, my father said he wanted to take me for a walk. We set off, down the path we always went on from Auntie Bell's, across fields full of sheep, dotted with trees with leaves that were now fading from gold to pale yellow. I could see that he had planned what he was going to say. I was still shocked by what he had said the day before. I gazed at the sheep and then asked him if he meant what he had said about my job. My father paused. We both looked out to the horizon, and then he said he did.

'Who,' he said, 'do you think were the natural leaders around the table yesterday?'

I thought I knew the answer, but I didn't want to say it. 'I'm not sure,' I said.

'You and me,' he said. 'There were lots of very bright people round that table, but only you and I are the natural leaders. Mum always shines, but she doesn't want to be unpopular. That's why she turned down every opportunity to take a more senior role in her school. Tom's got a brilliant eye for detail and is very good at his job, but he doesn't want to be the boss. There aren't all that many natural leaders, but you're one.'

I felt something ripple through me that I realised was joy, but then I felt so heavy I almost had to stop. I told my father that I couldn't really claim the credit for my leadership qualities, and that I had clearly inherited them from him.

My father turned to me and gave me a smile I hadn't seen before. He said it always used to irritate him when people said how clever he was, and that no one could take any credit for their brains. He said that he never met a finer man than his own father, who had both intelligence and charm. He said he knew he didn't have that charm, but I did. I was lucky, he said, that I had inherited it from my mother.

When we arrived back at the pathway that leads up to Auntie Bell and Uncle Maurice's house, he said that I had good judgement and must trust it. To sum up our conversation, he said, because he is, or was, a civil servant and civil servants like summing things up, I should trust my judgement and be myself.

That evening, over supper, he glittered. I knew he could be very witty, because other people said so, but we didn't often see this at home. I wondered how much people outside the family had seen of this brilliant, funny man we were seeing now. I thought that soon nobody would, and the thought felt like a stone in my chest.

In bed that night, I thought about what my father had said. I had always thought he found me disappointing, but it sounded as though he didn't. Now I knew this, I wasn't sure how I was going to carry on in a world that didn't have him in it.

I carried on running poetry events, and writing reports, and doing reviews. I carried on seeing friends, and going to parties. And at weekends, I went to Guildford to see my father.

Once, when he was having his chemotherapy in hospital, I gave him a new edition of *The Penguin Book of English Verse*. He was so pleased he phoned my mother, and read her a poem.

When I heard that the cancer had spread, I had a migraine for a week. I didn't know how I was going to get through the days at work, but I knew my father would want me to, so I did.

By Christmas, which we all knew was our last Christmas together, my father's cancer had started to spread to the brain. He was still driving, but one day, when he came back from a trip to Guildford, to buy us each a Christmas CD, he drove over the flowerbeds and we all knew he couldn't drive again.

On Christmas morning, Tom drove him to Brookwood to light a candle on Caroline's grave. While they were out, I tried to scrub the brown, smelly patches he'd left on the carpet. When he got back, I tried to get him to change his trousers, but he wouldn't, so I scraped the patches off with a knife.

My mother had lit the *änglaspel*, or angel chimes, the candles that send bronze angels flying round in a circle, striking bells. She had made a pot of coffee and laid out the *pepparkakor* and the mince pies. We all sat in the sitting room and tried to smile as we passed around each other's presents. When my father tried to give us our Christmas CDs, he got, he said, 'into a muddle'. In the end, he sorted them out. He gave me Bach's *The Art of Fugue* and an envelope with £100 in cash. He knew I was about to go on holiday with some friends and on the envelope, in big, shaky letters, he had written: 'For Christina and Goa'.

Three months later, he was taken into hospital and then into a hospice. I drove down to see him every Sunday. Sometimes, he wanted me to cut his nails. Sometimes, he just ate sweets. He was bald from the chemotherapy, and had a swollen stomach that was caused, the doctor said, by a build-up of fluids his body couldn't process, and also, perhaps, by the sweets. He looked, I thought, like a giant baby. I remembered the car journeys of my childhood, and how we had only ever been allowed one sweet at a time. I remembered how, whenever we asked when we could have another one, he would only ever say 'soon'.

I told my father that I loved him.

He looked at me. He sounded impatient. 'It doesn't,' he whispered, 'need to be said.'

The next time I saw him, all he could say was 'Sting stang stong.'

He died on a Sunday morning, just after my mother had read him a poem. It was one they used to read together. It's called 'John Anderson My Jo', but my mother always changed it to 'John Patterson My Jo'. It's by Burns, who was from a village not far from where my father's grandfather was born.

John Patterson my jo, John,
When we were first acquent,
Your locks were like the raven,
Your bonie brow was brent;

But now your brow is beld, John,
Your locks are like the snaw,
but blessings on your frosty pow,
John Patterson, my jo!

John Patterson my jo, John,
We clamb the hill thegither,
And monie a cantie day, John,
We've had wi' ane anither;
Now we maun totter down, John,
And hand in hand we'll go,
And sleep thegither at the foot,
John Patterson, my jo!

My mother's diary entry is more pithy than the poem. 'The day my darling died.'

Before I drove down, I cleaned the car. I remembered that when I'd bought my Mazda MX5, after only ever having battered old cars, my father had surprised me by saying he thought it was a 'good idea'. He, who had had a Morris Marina, and then a Nissan Cherry, and then a Nissan Micra, said he thought it was important to 'cut a bit of a dash'. Not long after I bought the car, I washed it with a scourer. Yes, I really did wash it with a scourer. When the sun came out and I saw the swirls all over the silver paintwork, I felt sick. My father paid for it to be resprayed.

When I got to Guildford, there was a note from my

mother saying that they were at the hospice. At the hospice reception, I was told that my mother and brother were with my father in the chapel of rest. I had thought I didn't want to see him, but I took a deep, deep breath, opened the door and walked in.

He was wrapped in plastic under his clothes. His eyes were half open and I kept thinking they were going to open all the way. Tom asked to be left alone with him, and through the door, we heard his howls.

The week of my father's funeral, the newspapers were full of a book called *Baby Hunger*. The book talked about women of my age who had put their careers first, and left it too late. I was thirty-eight. The clock was ticking. I had tried so hard to meet someone. When Winston met a fellow biker at a party, and our on–off relationship switched firmly to off, I joined a dating agency called Drawing Down the Moon. I didn't draw down the moon, or a husband, or a father to my children, or even a boyfriend. I did have a few brief liaisons, mostly with men whose names began with R. There was a Robert and a Richard and a Ronald, but the truth was, they made my heart sink. It didn't seem like the best foundation for a successful family life.

I heard my mother tell a friend on the phone that the tragedy of her life was that she didn't have any grandchildren. Auntie Lisbeth had just had her first grandson. On the morning of the funeral, I asked her not to talk about the new baby too much when my mother was around.

In his 'funeral wishes', my father said that there should be a 'short address' by the rector of his church, 'or any other available clergyman' who knew 'a little bit' about him. There were to be 'no other personal comments or tributes'. He wanted 'the main point of the address to be that the greatest rewards come not from being in charge of thousands of people, but in trying to help individual vulnerable people'. The occasions, he said, 'when I was able to help sad people in the Godalming Citizens Advice Bureau were the most fulfilling of my life, and my many years of trying to help my daughter Caroline to cope with mental illness were my most challenging task, supporting my heroic wife.'

I spent most of the service just trying to stay upright, with my mouth shut. Afterwards, I stood outside the crematorium and people kissed me or shook my hand. I thought it was like a wedding line, but in our family we didn't have weddings; only funerals.

Chapter 22

Hot Cross Bun

Eight months after my father died, I got a note from the literary editor of the *Independent*. I had been reviewing and doing interviews for his pages for some time and had once told him that I dreamt of being a journalist. 'Since then,' he said in his note, 'everything has changed.' But his deputy was leaving, he explained, and he wondered if I'd like to apply for the job?

I must have told my father about the dream, too, because I've found a letter. 'Mum mentioned that you were thinking of journalism,' he wrote. 'I had been thinking in the same direction. I think that you write with an unusually sharp edge and clarity, and also in a very concise and down-to-earth way.' He ends his letter by saying: 'No doubt all observations from a father of this kind are suspect, but they are meant to be truthful and impartial.'

It was written in 1998, two years before I got the job my father said had 'transformed' his life, and which had certainly transformed mine. I wasn't sure I could love a job more. I loved my colleagues. I loved thinking about how to do things, and getting them done. I didn't want to leave any of this, or go back to being a deputy, but I had always known that what I really wanted to do was write. I knew how hard it was to get a job on a national paper and thought this was probably my only chance. So I applied for the job and, when I got it, felt a surge of excitement and a prickle of loss.

I felt nervous when I set off for my leaving party from the plate-glass office in Docklands that was my new work home. When I got to the Poetry Café, I gasped. There were fairy lights and candles. There was a whole bank of tables covered with plates of salmon blinis, goat's cheese bruschetta, mini quiches, roast beef rolls. There were bottles glinting in the candlelight. I had expected the odd bottle of cava, because everyone knew about my love of cava, but what I saw now was crate after crate of champagne. And there were so many people, I could hardly force my way through the heaving mass.

I was just taking my first sip of champagne when the ripple of an accordion burst through the hum. I glanced up and there, sitting in the open disabled lift, which was juddering its way up from the basement, were Eamonn, Peter, Chris and Martin. There, in fact, were the Bettertones, a band made up of mostly former employees of the Poetry Society, named after Betterton Street, the street we were in. They were playing 'Dancing Queen', because that was always the song that signalled 'the 5.45' and the end of the week. Ooh, you can dance, you can jive! We all bobbed and jiggled as we tried to shout to each other over the music and then swayed to their Klezmer and jazz.

After about half an hour, someone tapped a glass and summoned us all downstairs for speeches. The deputy director gave a speech, and then the chair of the board and then the director of literature at the Arts Council. Lisa spoke, too. She told me later that she had never given a speech before, but forced herself to do it because she wanted to say a public thank-you. I was so shocked I can't remember a single word any of them said, but I know what Roger McGough said, because afterwards he gave me the poem he'd written. 'This is the poem / you always wanted,' it starts, 'The one you desired / but could never afford / Unique, like yourself, / it stands out in a crowd / Stylish, witty / and self-assured.' The second paragraph is even kinder. I framed it, of course.

They gave me a red handbag and a life membership of the Poetry Society. They also gave me a leaving card, which was a version of our new membership leaflet, filled with messages from colleagues and poets. There was a photo of me, mid-flow, in a red velvet dress, surrounded by colleagues and poets, including a black and white T. S. Eliot, W. H. Auden, Philip Larkin and Ted Hughes. 'When Christina was Queen, the great and the good gathered to hear her legendary speeches' said the caption. The 'queen' was an allusion to the label Eamonn had put on my pigeonhole: 'Queen Bee'. I haven't looked at my leaving card for years, but now it feels like a postcard from a long-lost world. 'I've never had a boss who's come back from a day off sick,' said one colleague, 'and confessed she'd had a hangover the day before.' Another mentions the day our website disappeared and was replaced with one selling Viagra. Another said: 'I will never forget the first item on our SWOT analysis chart under Weaknesses: Kettle Chips.' My favourite comment was from a straight-talking Australian. 'Working with Christina,' she said, 'is like being part of one big, happy, cava-drinking family.'

Ooh, see that girl. Watch that scene. Having the time of her life. I had never, ever heard so many people say so many nice things about me. It was, I couldn't help thinking, like going to my own funeral, but without actually having to die.

Five weeks later, I was lying in the bath listening to the midnight news when my fingers brushed against something soft and springy. I couldn't think how I hadn't noticed it before. I went to my GP, who said she was sure it was nothing, but that I'd better get it checked out.

Two weeks later, I went to the breast clinic at Barts. The registrar washed his hands and then pummelled my left breast. I would, he said, need a mammogram, an ultrasound and a needle biopsy. He would try to see if I could have them all done in one day.

First, I had my breasts squashed against a glass plate. After that, I was called into a room by a woman with a clipped voice who told me to take off my top and bra and 'pop on to the couch'. She slathered a cold gel on my breast and then rolled a kind of wand over the cold area. She stared at a screen for a while and then asked me if I had anyone with me.

As I walked back out to the waiting room, I felt as if my whole body had been coated in that gel. After about half an hour, a man with a manic smile handed me an envelope and told me to wait. Then I was told to go into a little cubicle. After another wait, two doctors and a nurse walked in.

'There's a fifty–fifty chance you have cancer,' said one of the doctors. I heard the words and felt numb. Fifty–fifty. Toss a coin. Heads you lose. The man was trying to explain something to me, and I tried to concentrate on what he was saying. They could, he said, do a biopsy now, and the results would be ready in two days, but they wouldn't be 'definitive'. Or I could have a biopsy with an ultrasound, but the results wouldn't be ready for ten days.

My heart was thumping so hard I could hardly hear him. Two thousand years or ten thousand years. Pick a card. Any card. In the end, I asked for the needle biopsy now. The registrar jammed the needle in six times, so that he was as sure as he could be that we'd get a clear result. It hurt, of course it hurt, but I wasn't worrying about whether it hurt. I was worrying about whether it was what he thought it was, and three days later a breast surgeon told me it was.

On the first morning after my operation, a nurse told me that I had to get my own breakfast. She showed me how to clip the drips and drains to a metal trolley thing, and how I could use it to get myself to the room with the tea and the toast. The tea was in a giant pot and I didn't see how you were meant to lift it up if you'd just lost a big chunk of your breast and all the lymph nodes from under your arm.

When my mother walked on to the ward, I wanted to rip out all the tubes and tell her that I was fine, everything was fine, and everything would be fine from now on. She was wearing a cornflower-blue suit and a frilly white blouse. She looked as if she was on her way to a garden party and smiled in the way she always smiled when she was trying to cheer someone up. That day she didn't take any photos, but she did the next day, when she came back with Tom. There's a photo of Tom and me in the hospital courtyard. He's smiling. I'm smiling. I'm pale and thin, but I'm still smiling. Nothing to see here, apart from the plastic bottle on a tube hanging out of my fleece. It's about a third full of a red liquid that must, I suppose, be a mixture of post-surgical fluid and blood. Next to that photo in the album, there's a photo of the entrance to the hospital. 'Welcome to HOMERTON HOSPITAL' says the sign. It doesn't say 'hope you have a lovely time', which is just as well because I didn't. The nurses weren't kind. The nearest I got to a kind word was when one of them asked me, one afternoon just after my mother had left, why I was crying. She seemed surprised. She seemed irritated. Because I'm thirty-nine, I wanted to say, and I don't want to die. And because my mother has lost one of her daughters and her husband and that's enough. But I knew she didn't want to hear any of this, so I just said I was tired.

I still had the drain hanging off me when I went to interview Barbara Trapido. When I was working in the bookshop, all those years before, a colleague had taken me by the hand, literally by the hand, and to the bookcase where *Brother of the More Famous Jack* was sitting, full jacket out. She knew I would love it and I did. 'What is life,' asks the narrator at one point, 'but a progression from pimples to wrinkles, but for the getting of wisdom?' I had certainly had the pimples and was beginning to see some wrinkles, but I wasn't at all sure about the wisdom. I was still on my probationary period at work and terrified that I might lose my job. I was still feeling sick from the anaesthetic when I got on a bus to Tottenham Court Road to meet Barbara Trapido in a hotel bar. As soon as I got home, I transcribed the interview and wrote it up. After I emailed it through to my boss, I got on with my review of the latest novel by Rachel Cusk. My mother had taught me to be a workhorse and I am, I am.

The first time I went back to the hospital for the results

of the operation, they weren't ready. The second time, the surgeon told me that unfortunately they hadn't caught all the cancer and unfortunately it wasn't the grade they thought it was and I would need a mastectomy, chemotherapy, radiotherapy and five years on a drug called Tamoxifen.

In bed that night, I thought it would be better to die. I knew that was ironic, and that the whole point was to stay alive, but the price, I thought, was too high. I had read that Tamoxifen had horrible side effects. It gave you a kind of early menopause, thinned your hair and made you put on weight. I still hadn't had a relationship that lasted more than a few weeks. Who would want me when I was bald and fat and sick from the chemotherapy and when my body was maimed and scarred? And what would I do about work? Even if they let me keep my job, everyone would know I had cancer. I'd be the bald one, the tragic one, the sad spinster who was struggling on bravely, but who had left it, left everything, too late.

For the first time ever, I couldn't talk to my friends. What the hell did they know, with their lovely boyfriends and husbands and babies and hair and breasts? Instead, I went to the Bristol Cancer Centre, which someone had told me had helped a friend of a friend. I went, because I had to do something, but I didn't know what anyone could say that would make me feel that it would be OK to go through this, and go through it on my own.

I went to a talk about nutrition, where the speaker said

we shouldn't eat sugar, dairy products, processed food or red meat, or drink alcohol, coffee or tea. Instead, we should eat things like lentils and raw vegetables. We should, in fact, eat the kind of things you found in a book I'd seen in the bookshop, which I thought had the saddest title in the world. It was called *Vegan Cooking for One.*

I went to a talk on something called psychoimmunology, which seemed to be about the immune system and the mind. The doctor giving the talk said that stress, anger and misery were 'key contributory factors' in getting cancer. So, he said, was grief. A double bereavement, he said, was a 'classic precursor'.

The next day, I had a session with a doctor who told me that he thought it was a good idea not to have chemotherapy, since it affected your 'morbidity', or radiotherapy, since it caused cardiovascular problems, and then one with a nutritionist, who told me I shouldn't eat any of the things I like. Then I saw a healer who said that I had very 'forward-looking' energy, and that illness had been in my life to stop me going forward too fast. After that, I saw a therapist who said that cancer was an opportunity to think about what life was about. I wanted to tell her that I couldn't remember a day when I didn't.

I stopped eating chocolate, dairy products, sugar and wheat. I even tried cutting down on drink. Although I loved all these things, I thought this was something I could do that might help and wouldn't make me lose my hair. I didn't want people to know I was ill. At work, I only told the people who needed to know.

On the anniversary of my father's death, I went to the oncology department at Barts. I waited three hours and then the consultant came out and said they'd run out of time. Instead, I saw the registrar. He didn't think, like the doctor at Bristol, who was a GP and not an oncologist, that it was fine not to have chemotherapy or radiotherapy. He said that if the cancer came back, they might not be able to cure me.

The next week, I saw the consultant in his office. He looked as if he had just come back from a skiing holiday and talked in a tone that suggested he was being very, very generous in granting me a snatch of his time. He tapped my age and grade of cancer into a computer and showed me the different survival rates according to the treatments I had. He said that if I still wanted to have children, I should have two years on Tamoxifen and monthly injections of another drug that would put me into menopause. If the cancer didn't come back, this could be reversed. He wouldn't recommend that I didn't have chemotherapy, but I'd seen the figures, and it was up to me. He snapped his notebook shut to show our time was up. When I thanked him for his time I could see from the set of his mouth that I hadn't been grateful enough.

During the day, I edited reviews and opened sacks of books. In the evening, I googled pictures of mastectomies. At night, I dreamt about knives and scars.

I saw a plastic surgeon. 'So,' he said, in a slightly bored voice, 'you've had a mastectomy.' I glanced down at my breasts, which were still there. I wondered if he ever looked at the notes before he saw someone, or if he was just too busy.

I told him that I hadn't yet had a mastectomy but was hoping to discuss the different kinds of reconstruction I could have when I did. The examples I had seen online had ranged from Texas Chainsaw Massacre to child's first needlework class and attempts to pump up a stubbornly flat tyre. None of them had looked very appealing, so I asked if I could see some pictures of the kind he did. The surgeon looked at me as if I had just asked him to send me a CV. 'I am *not*,' he said in the voice our headmaster used to use in school assembly, 'going to rush around getting you examples of my work. I think,' he added, 'that your approach is rather heavy.'

Hefty. Ponderous. Lacking in levity. Pick your definition. Forgive me, Mr Very Grand Surgeon with the Dickensian name I can't disclose, for not taking this lightly. Forgive me, sir, for not prostrating myself on the ground. I suddenly realised I was sick, sick, sick of men with fruity voices telling me how they would hack, drug, inject and radiate me as if I was just another boring item on a production line, just another piece of meat about to go off.

'I'm not sure,' I said, 'how light-hearted you'd be if someone was about to cut off your balls.'

The next breast surgeon I saw was recommended by one of my mother's friends. He didn't speak to me as if he would rather be skiing. He said he might be able to take another section from my breast without me having to have a mastectomy. It would depend on the pathology reports. He had asked for them four weeks earlier, but they still hadn't arrived.

When he got the reports, he phoned me on my mobile. I couldn't believe that a surgeon had actually called me on my mobile. He told me that he thought we could try for a further 'excision' and that I could be in and out of hospital in a day.

I went to Guildford to have the 'excision', in the hospital Caroline had been in three weeks before she died. An hour before the operation, the surgeon discovered that my hospital hadn't sent the mammograms he had requested. It had, instead, sent an X-ray of an ankle. We never did find out whether the ankle was mine. I had the operation anyway and spent the night at Nelson Gardens, in my childhood bed. I didn't want to look under the bandages. When I did, a few days later, I saw something that looked like a hot cross bun. A poor thing, I thought, with its big, red, criss-crossing scar, but also a precious, beautiful thing, because it was my own.

Three weeks after the operation, I went for the results.

'The margins,' said the surgeon, 'are clear.'

As the words sank in, I felt as if I had been dipped in cool, clear water. I felt, in fact, as if I had been washed clean. Thank you, thank you, thank you, I said. I wanted to hug the surgeon. I wanted to kiss his shoes. I walked out and into the waiting room. I wrapped my arms around my mother's trembling frame. We could feel each other's bodies vibrate as we both cried with relief.

For five weeks, I had radiotherapy every day before work. When I finished the course, I started the Tamoxifen. It made me feel sick and tired and dizzy at first, but after a few weeks it was fine.

I kept my job. I kept my hair. In the ten months I was treated for cancer, I was off work for two weeks and three days.

Chapter 23

Queen Christina

'Well, isn't this lovely!' said my mother. We were drinking coffee and eating cinnamon buns in the main square in Stockholm's old town. The sun was shining and the gabled buildings around us – the colour of apricots, ripe olives and the cranberries in the garden at the cottage – were even brighter against the early summer sky. It was a year after the successful operation and I had just had my first 'all clear'.

The last time I had been to Stockholm was for a poetry festival with Maura, five years before. She was there to read her poems. I was there for the festival and the ride. It was November. I had never been to Sweden in the winter. The city gleamed in the silver light. It started snowing as we wandered around the old town and we grinned at each other as if we had stumbled into an enchanted world.

We stopped for coffee and a sandwich at a café in the main square. It was so packed we had to share a table.

When we ordered our coffee and food, the man at our table added his order to ours. It confused the waitress and it certainly broke the ice. The man told us that he was half Scottish and half Swedish and that he worked in London, but spent weekends at his flat in Stockholm's old town. He was, he said, a psychiatrist. His name was Matthew.

Matthew was the first person I'd met outside our family who was half Scottish and half Swedish. He was very tall, very handsome, very charming and very bright. When he asked if he could show us a bit of Stockholm, I turned to Maura with a look of such desperate yearning, she smiled and said yes. We went to Skansen, the island of old Swedish cottages and farmhouses brought together from around the country, and drank mulled wine in the snow. We had cloudberry liqueur in his tiny flat. When we got back to London, I met up with him again. The first time we met alone, he told me that he was a psychopath, but that I shouldn't worry too much because I'd find 'pockets of warmth'. When a psychiatrist tells you they're a psychopath, you should probably listen, but I didn't. I'm sure I don't need to say that it didn't end well.

I must have told my mother at least some of this, because in her diary account of our weekend, she writes: 'We walked to the Old Town, past the castle and back to the Stortorget [main square] where we had coffee, sitting outside "the Coffee cup" (where Christina had met Matthew the psychiatrist ages ago).' My mother had been excited when I told her about Matthew. She lived in hope, but my record didn't build it.

A few weeks after the operation that turned my left breast into a hot cross bun, a colleague took me out for lunch. I was still drinking very little and eating the kind of thing recommended in *Vegan Cooking for One*. My colleague ordered giant steaks and a bottle of Argentinian wine. It would, he said, put the colour back in my cheeks. What happened next certainly did. 'I'm afraid I've fallen in love with you,' he said, as he poured the rest of the Malbec into my glass. After a lingering kiss in a multi-storey car park, I decided I was in love with him. For the next few months, I would wait for the ping of his email, and then a few minutes more, to meet him outside the office. He was charismatic, erudite and funny. His company, I thought, was like champagne. It was also carefully rationed, because he was still living with the mother of his children. They lived separate lives, he said. He was going to leave her, he said. He didn't, of course.

I told my mother about my colleague, too. She didn't approve, but she still cut out and sent me pieces he wrote. She told me when she heard him on the radio. She kept telling me she'd heard him on the radio even after I'd walked away with what was left of my self-respect.

My mother couldn't understand why I picked such unsuitable men. I couldn't understand it either. But I still told her about my romantic adventures because they mattered to me and I mattered to her and because she was, and always had been, the most important person in my life. In Stockholm that weekend, we talked about everything as we drank coffee in the sunshine, had waffles at Skansen, drank G & T in our hotel room and ate prawn sandwiches bought on the harbour's edge. That night, we went to see *Cristina, Regina di Svezia*, an opera by Jacopo Foroni about Queen Christina. Every time a character sang 'Christina', my mother clutched my arm.

On our last evening in Stockholm, I told my mother I wanted to find out about Caroline's illness. I still felt I had a child's knowledge of what she had gone through and wanted to learn, and understand, more.

My mother said she would do what she could to help. The next time I went to Guildford, she gave me some papers and a diary she had found in Caroline's flat.

The diary was written in 1979, when Caroline was twenty and I was fifteen. I wasn't sure if I should read it, even though my mother had given it to me, and only read a few pages.

It's written in tiny handwriting that's very hard to read. It's full of detailed descriptions of TV programmes Caroline has watched, books she has read, and people she has met. It's full, in fact, of curiosity and joy. Some names crop up a lot: the Romanovs, the Brontës, Claudius from *I Claudius*, Derek Jacobi, who played him in the TV series, Siân Phillips, who played Livia, Janet Suzman, and lots of Caroline's friends, including some she hadn't seen since she was three.

As I flicked through it, I saw that two pages were Sellotaped together. I cut through the tape and saw something that made the hairs on my neck stand on end:

'Dear God, my only wish on earth is to be rid of Christina. The name Christina Patterson makes me want to choke with hatred.'

On the next page, my sister has written something she has crossed out: 'Let Christina die this year of cancer.'

Part IV

Chapter 24

Medium Rare

It was seven years between my first and second lump, which is a nice biblical span. As Joseph explains in *Joseph and the Technicolor Dreamcoat*, things can change quite suddenly. After 'seven years of bumper crops', he sings, the future 'doesn't look so bright' and Egypt's luck 'will change completely overnight'. He's interpreting Pharoah's dream about the seven fat cows that came out of the Nile and seven other cows that were 'skinny and vile' and how the seven thin cows ate the fat cows, but it 'didn't make them fatter like such a monster supper should'.

I was the baker in our primary school production of the Andrew Lloyd Webber musical, which I think we can all agree is rather a minor part. But I can still hum every tune. 'Close Every Door'; 'Go, Go, Go Joseph'; 'Poor Poor Joseph'; 'Grovel Grovel'; 'Any Dream Will Do'. I still find it odd that I can remember almost every note, and quite a few of the lyrics, of a musical I took part in when I was eight, but not all that much about last weekend. I also think that list of songs is quite a good synopsis of a life.

The years after that first lump were more 'Go, Go, Go Joseph' than 'Close Every Door'. Work was fascinating and I was doing well at it. I met masses of interesting people and was invited to masses of interesting parties and events. I started doing pieces for the travel desk. Free holidays! Not quite free, because I had to write about them and had to use my leave to go on them, but still the kind of perk most employees can only dream of. I took my mother to Croatia, Berlin and Vienna, where we drank bucketfuls of coffee and ate stacks of cakes. I took friends to St Lucia and Mallorca, to stay in villas I would never have been able to afford.

My romantic life continued to offer bursts of excitement and even entertainment, but mostly for my friends. Dating had switched online and turned into a giant marketplace where the rules had changed. It was like an Amazon warehouse, one where everyone was wandering around, pausing to unwrap a few parcels, chuck out the cardboard and then get back to their quest. People rarely looked like their photos. They blew hot – very, very hot – and then vanished. People repeated patterns, because people generally repeat patterns. I met an Egyptian who, for some reason, called himself Sean. He brought roses and chocolates on our second date and proved to be an Olympic kisser. His flat had a white leather sofa and a giant TV. Not my taste, I thought, but let's be open-minded. And, let's be honest, the sex was great. After a few dates, he disappeared. About a year later, he got back in touch and persuaded me to meet him again. Open-minded? Undoubtedly. Grovel Grovel. Any Dream Will Do.

I met a chef who arrived on our first date on crutches. He had had an accident while skiing, but it didn't stop him arranging an action-packed second date. It started with a ride in a speedboat on the Thames, continued with a visit to the galleries at Somerset House, and was followed by a comedy gig and then cocktails and dinner at the Delaunay. He must really like me, I thought, but at Piccadilly Circus he told me off for the way I kissed. On our third date, he told me that he was 'determined to hold out for something good'. This was just after we'd had really quite adventurous sex.

Poor, poor Joseph. But perhaps Joseph should have seen the signs, or at least read the runes.

And then, one sunny, July day, a group of fanatics planted some bombs. My train to Liverpool Street stopped at Hackney Downs, and a man told us that we wouldn't be able to get any further because of 'power surges'. It took a while to learn that two Tube trains that had just left Liverpool Street had been blown up. So had a Tube train travelling between Kings Cross and Russell Square. So had a bus in Russell Square, which a witness described as 'half a flying bus'. Like eight million other Londoners, I went home in a daze. The next day, I had a pain in my hand. It started in my fingers, and then spread up to my arm. It was deadline day at work and I was editing the books pages on my own. I still had a column to write, and five pages to put together. By 5 o'clock, my fingers wouldn't let me type. Within a couple of days, the pain was in both arms, both legs and my back.

The newspapers were full of stories about the actual victims of that terrible day and here I was, wandering around like Quasimodo – or not wandering around, that was the problem – even though I'd been nowhere near a bomb. There was a part of me that wondered if I was the fanatic, a fanatic without a cause. Or perhaps I, or my body, was the bomb? The trouble was, there was no way of knowing what would set it off.

Now an employer would make it possible to use technology to work from home. Not then. I was off work for three months. I thought it was ridiculous that I'd been off work with cancer for two and a half weeks, but with weird pain that no one could name for four times as long. It was crazy, it was baffling and it was boring. No one ever tells you that recurring illnesses, or conditions, or syndromes, or whatever you want to call something debilitating that doesn't have a name, are boring. The same pain. The same worries. Nothing new to feel or learn. And the horrible feeling that progress is an illusion. You're chugging along and things are OK, and then suddenly you're back where you started. Oh, that landscape. This is where I got stuck in that bog and it took me absolutely ages to pull myself out of it and scrape off the mud.

This time, it was an acupuncturist who helped me out of the bog. I didn't want to see her, because I'd seen plenty who hadn't helped before. Yana is, and was, different. The first time I saw her she asked me about my symptoms, so I told her about the pains in my arms and the pains in my legs, and then she asked me more, so I told her about the headaches and the insomnia, and the acne and the white patches under my arms, and about my hands and feet, which people always say are like blocks of ice. She took my pulse and looked at my tongue and told me about something called 'increased intestinal permeability' or 'leaky gut'. She said that a 'leaky gut' was a gut that wasn't absorbing food properly and was letting tiny particles of waste into the 'system', and that these tiny particles were being treated by the rest of the body as a kind of enemy. She said that the way the other cells reacted to the enemy was to attack it. This was what caused inflammation, and what doctors called an 'autoimmune response'. It was where the body started attacking its own tissue. It's where, in other words, you start attacking yourself.

I looked it up and saw that it was linked with a range of autoimmune conditions, ranging from lupus to rheumatoid arthritis and vitiligo. I also saw that it's listed on Wikipedia as a 'pseudomedical diagnosis'. I have no idea whether it's absolute nonsense or rock-solid science, but I have since read quite a few books and articles that seem to suggest that the gut plays a much bigger part in our health than doctors previously thought. All I know is that Yana started treating me and I got better. Every time I have a flare-up of pain or any of the other symptoms I sometimes get when I'm tired or upset or stressed, I go to see her. Every time, she has made me better. If I followed the principles in *Vegan Cooking for One* (which I haven't actually read and nor has Yana) I would probably have been able to see her less. I could treat my body as a temple and give up wine, crisps, coffee and cake, which are some of the things that cause inflammation, particularly when they mix with the cortisol that comes from stress. But I won't give up those things because they are, for me, part of what makes life worth living.

I had just been dumped when I went to my appointment at the hospital. It was the usual story: a charming man with a silver tongue who promised me the sun, the moon and the stars, but whose promises, as he later explained in the kind of tone you'd use to a tiresome toddler, were not meant to be taken literally.

He was right. When he told me, in his emails, and on our few, heady dates, that he loved me and wanted to be my rock, I believed him. When he told me that that wouldn't be possible after all, I cried, as he said, 'like a seven-year-old child'. That number seven again. Give me a child before he is seven. But I was nearly forty-six. As my now former lover had just reminded me, I was 'a middle-aged woman'. No one could give me a child now.

Anyone can fall in love with anyone. That was something Iris Murdoch said in her novel *The Black Prince*, and which I quoted in that dissertation on her work called

'Cheering Oneself Up'. I don't know if it's true, but I've certainly fallen in love with some wildly unsuitable people and this man was one of them. When he told me it was over, I did not think: well, that was a lucky miss. I felt as if I had just been barred from a place I had been queueing to get into all my life.

The next day, I had pains in my legs and pains in my arms. Here we go again, I thought. Punish yourself, why don't you? Take a blow and double it. If someone whacks you, make sure you also whack yourself.

I nearly missed the appointment at the hospital. I was preparing for an interview and nearly forgot. The last time I'd been to the clinic, they had tried to discharge me. It was five years after my radiotherapy ended, and after five years they think you're fine. When the young registrar told me I didn't have to come back, I felt a burst of relief and then a flicker of something else. He said that now I'd just need to have a mammogram every three years. Great, I thought, that sounds much better. But then I remembered that nothing had shown up on any of my mammograms. It had only shown up on ultrasound and MRIs.

'Please,' I asked the registrar, 'can I keep having the MRIs?'

The registrar looked confused and then said he would ask the consultant and phone to let me know.

He did phone and he said I could. I had the scan after a night in my lover's arms. I was used to it now: the cold liquid they shoot into your veins, the feeling of being trapped in a metal coffin, the drumming that feels like the drumming in your heart. I was used to needles, used to tubes, used to being prodded, used to 'popping on a couch' and lying where I was told to lie.

This time, it was a different registrar. He asked me how I was. I thought he was just being polite, but I told him about the pains in my arms and the pains in my legs, but not the pain in my heart. And then he told me about the shadows.

When I walked out of his room, I felt as if there was something in the air that made it difficult to breathe. A nurse tried to comfort me. She arranged for me to come to the 'one stop' clinic on Thursday, which sounded nice and cheerful, but there are times when it makes sense to be cheerful and times when it doesn't.

So much of cancer is a waiting game. You wait for results of biopsies and scans. You wait for appointments. You wait for operations. You wait for diagnoses and prognoses and treatments. If you like games, I suppose you'd say it's a mix of poker and chess and Russian roulette. I've never really liked games, and I had played this one before.

This time, it was clear that the breast had to go. The oncologist told me that my tumour was number two on a scale, which sounded as though, if it was a steak, it would be medium rare. I asked him if he thought I'd need chemotherapy. He made a face, and then said that if I was his wife or daughter, he'd say yes.

The breast surgeon told me that I would need to go on

a drug that would bring me into menopause. She said that there was a risk of getting cancer in the other breast and I might want to think about a double mastectomy.

After I saw her, I went to the dentist. I had been going there for twenty years, but I couldn't find it. I walked up and down the street where it used to be and, in the end, I got the number from directory enquiries and called it. The dental surgery was, it turned out, right in front of where I was standing.

A week later, I went to see the breast care nurse. She unclipped a plastic container and handed me a lump of something that looked like a giant tear. She told me to touch it, and I did. It felt hard. She showed me a bra, made out of lacy nylon, which had one normal cup and one that was designed to be filled out with something that was not flesh, which she called a prosthesis. There was something about that lace designed to cover plastic that made me feel as if I had something stuck in my throat.

I went to see the breast surgeon again, this time with a plastic surgeon. The plastic surgeon told me I could have something called a DIEP flap, where he would take flesh from the stomach and stick it in the space left by the breast. He would also take blood vessels from the stomach and connect them up to the blood vessels in the chest. Sometimes, he explained, this went wrong. If it went wrong, then the flesh where the breast used to be would go black and die. And the stomach, which would have a scar running all the way from one side to the other, could never be used to supply flesh again. But this was just a risk you had to take.

We talked for a long time about whether I should have one mastectomy or two. The plastic surgeon looked at my stomach and said there wasn't enough fat to replace two lost breasts. He said that sometimes you could take flesh from the bottom to make a breast, but that he didn't think I had enough flesh on mine. I couldn't have a new breast from the stomach and a new breast from the bottom, because I wouldn't be able to lie on my front or my back and I wouldn't be able to do much else.

And so, in the end, we agreed that I would just have one mastectomy, and I would have the breast rebuilt at the same time with flesh from my stomach. He would operate in about a month, he said. In the meantime, I should eat as much as I could.

While I was waiting for my operation, I did eat as much as I could. I was surprised to find that you could get sick of crisps and bread and pastry and chips and cheese and cakes. I had coffee and a big plate of pastries with Lisa, who always cheers me up, but when I went to the flat she shares with her partner and her five-year-old daughter, which is, and has the vibe of, a place where a whole family can cuddle up on a sofa, I had to leave. I had a Thai meal with my friend Rachel, who was on maternity leave. On my birthday, she had come round with her four-year-old and her baby, and a little cake she had baked for me, and I had gazed at her baby, at her blue, blue eyes and her skin that was like a peach. I told Rachel that I had to have a mastectomy and would then be brought into menopause, and she said it was too much to have to cope with a broken heart and this.

Winston came round with his son Daniel, who was now four, and his daughter Michele, who was born the day after my father's funeral. ('Thou met'st with things dying,' says the old shepherd in *The Winter's Tale* to his son, 'I with things new-born.' In this, I am much more like the son.) It was clear that they were under strict instructions from their father. They marched over, put their arms around me, and gave me a kiss. They had made me cards. Michele's had a picture of a blonde woman lying on a bed. Next to it was an arrow and the word 'Christina'. Inside, it said, in big, multi-coloured letters, 'To Christina, I hope you get well.' Daniel's had a picture of a woman with long hair and a big smile. Inside, there was another picture, which looked like a space-hopper with horns, long legs like claws and, in the middle, where the body should have been, two giant circles. When I looked at the circles, and then at him, he nodded. 'Boobies!' he said. I pulled him towards me and I stroked – I couldn't stop stroking – his beautiful, velvety cheek.

I told Yana, the acupuncturist, that I didn't know how I was going to get through this, and that I wasn't sure that the cure wasn't worse than the disease. Yana, who's one of the most hopeful people I've ever met, said I should see Richard, the therapist she had seen for three years.

Richard used to be a psychiatrist in the NHS. He lives

in a big house near Hampstead Heath and always wears a suit and tie. When I walked into his consulting room, full of books and pictures and tasteful *objets d'art,* I felt like a child. It was my birthday. As he ushered me in and showed me to my seat, I had a mad urge to quote the words of another Christina. 'Because the birthday of my life,' says Christina Rossetti in her poem 'A Birthday', 'Is come, my love is come to me.' But my love, I told Richard, has in fact left me, and now I'm facing this thing I have to face alone.

My cheeks were burning as I talked to him. I could not imagine a more embarrassing conversation to have with a man who looked like a headmaster, and one I'd only just met. I was mortified. That word again. From *mortificare,* to 'put to death'. But death was the problem, and so, what the hell? I told him that I hadn't managed to have a long-term relationship, which was what I had always wanted. I hadn't managed to have a family. I'd had two operations for cancer, and then I'd had a cyst on my ovary, which I'd had to go back into hospital to have cut out. It felt, I told him, as though all the bits of me that made me a woman were being gradually removed. I told him I felt like a failure as a woman. If I died now, I said, I would look back on my life and feel that I had failed.

Richard looked at me. I felt as if his eyes were boring into my skull. 'That,' he said, 'seems to me like a very harsh assessment.'

The burning in my cheeks got worse. 'I don't think it's harsh,' I said. 'I think it's true.'

Chapter 25

Jonah and the Whale

The night before my big operation, I started reading Martin Amis's *The Pregnant Widow*. I had been due to chair a big event with him a couple of weeks later. At my meeting with the breast surgeon and the plastic surgeon, I had asked if they thought I'd still be able to do it. They had thrown each other a glance I didn't quite understand. 'I think,' said the breast surgeon gently, 'probably not.'

After the operation, I understood. When my phone buzzed with a text, I couldn't reach out to pick it up. There were bandages all over my breast, or what used to be my breast, and all over my stomach, or what used to be my stomach. It looked and felt as if my body had been cut in half. When a nurse tried to get me to sit up, I felt as if she had just asked me to fly to Mars.

I stared at the pile of books on the bedside cabinet as if they were relics from another world. It was days before I could pick one up, weeks before I could read more than the odd page. I still had the words of Martin Amis buzzing round my head, the last words I had read before walking down to the operating theatre. I'd been surprised when a nurse told me to follow her. I had expected to be put on a gurney and wheeled down. As I set off in my hospital gown, which was made of the same diamond-patterned material as my old school-uniform blouse, I thought of Mary, Queen of Scots, and of Jean Plaidy's *Royal Road to Fotheringay*, which I'd read at school while wearing that blouse. I wondered what it would be like to know that you were walking to a place where you were going to have your head cut off, and not just a breast. I knew it must feel much, much worse than this, but I couldn't quite imagine how.

From the few pages I had read, and as far as I could tell, *The Pregnant Widow* was all about breasts. 'The secondary sexual characteristics in their Platonic form,' one of Amis's characters calls them, 'a sort of mystery. An end unto themselves.' I tried not to think about the words he had written, about the desire that a man has for the softness of a woman, and to wonder whether a man would ever have that desire for me again.

Five days later, Winston strolled through the revolving door of the hospital foyer to take me to my mother's. The place felt full of elbows and sharp corners and I was sitting hunched, with my arms wrapped around me, bony armour against a new, hostile world. As he strapped me into the front seat of his van, he wrapped me in the fake-fur blanket he used to keep his children warm. I felt as if I would need to be wrapped in that blanket for ever.

That night, I tried to make my childhood bed as much like the hospital bed as I could, by making a slope out of a pile of pillows. I couldn't imagine that I would ever be able to lie flat again. My stomach felt like a drum that had been pumped with air and stretched so tight that it was about to rip. I took a sleeping pill, but still couldn't sleep. When I finally did, I dreamt that I was lying on a bed in a room full of people who were also lying on beds, waiting to have a baby cut out of my stomach. The baby was very big and I was very uncomfortable. When I woke up, I was still uncomfortable but there was, of course, no baby there.

The next day, my mother bought a copy of the *Independent*, which had a piece I'd written about a trip to Cambodia a few months before. The headline on the front of the travel magazine was 'Christina Patterson is captivated by Cambodia', but now I could hardly remember being there at all. When I read the piece, I remembered the sign I'd seen outside Tuol Sleng prison, which said 'while getting lashes or electrification, you must not cry at all'.

A week later, Tom drove me back to the hospital. I was so nervous I couldn't think of anything to say and I could tell from the way Tom was gripping the steering wheel that he was as nervous as I was. The breast surgeon tried to look cheerful when she told me that it looked, from something called a FISH test, as though my cancer was

HER2 positive. This would mean, she said, that, on top of the hormone treatments, I would need chemotherapy and a year on a drug called Herceptin. The next two years, she said, would be 'critical'.

As the surgeon explained all this, I tried to concentrate on keeping my jaws clamped together, as if I was a dangerous dog that had been told that if I didn't control myself, I'd be put in a muzzle. When the breast surgeon left the room, I couldn't keep my jaws clenched together any more, and when I heard the noise that came out of them, which was like a wild animal that had lost its offspring or its mate, I thought it was terrible that something was making a noise like that, but couldn't stop.

When I got back to Guildford, my mother tried to smile, but with that look in her eyes that I knew meant she was trying not to cry. I went up to my old bedroom and switched on my laptop, and tapped 'HER2 + breast cancer' into Google, because I'd never heard of it. It said that it 'tends to be more aggressive than other types of breast cancer' and is 'traditionally associated with poor prognosis'. Although I agree with Susan Sontag that it's not a good idea to see illness in terms of a battle, I thought it would be hard not to think that there was a very big battle ahead. It seemed very unlikely that a man would fall in love with me now that I was covered in scars and soon wouldn't have any hair. Even if he did, he probably wouldn't want to get involved with someone who thought they might be fighting a battle for the rest of their life. I also thought it was disappointing that the thoughts that came to me were so unoriginal, and that I was thinking things like: why me? And what have I done to deserve this?

That night, when I was stretched out on the sofa, wrapped in a blanket, I told my mother that I would do my best to get through it. She pushed herself up from her blue leather armchair, found her handbag, fished around in it, and opened her wallet. Inside it, there was a yellow Post-it note. 'Philosopher's saying,' it said, in my mother's primary school teacher handwriting. 'What does not destroy me makes me stronger.' My mother told me that she had been carrying that note in her wallet for twenty years.

When I finally finished reading *The Pregnant Widow*, I realised that it made me feel like a piece of meat. But one thing Martin Amis said struck me. The most attractive people, he says, are the ones who love themselves. Looks, he says, improve with happiness. I thought it was the kind of thing a self-help guru would say. I also thought it was probably true.

In the past few months, I've looked at scores of family albums. In so many of the photos, I look ill at ease. Sometimes, I have a bad haircut. Sometimes, my skin is bad. Sometimes, there's just a sadness in my eyes. I can see that I am, broadly speaking, an attractive woman. I'm tall. I'm slim. I have a perfectly pleasant face. I can look at those photos now and think: why the hell didn't I appreciate what I had? As Norah Ephron says in her book of essays *I Feel Bad About My Neck*, 'Anything you think is wrong with your body at the age of thirty-five, you will be nostalgic for by the age of forty-five.' And now I'm nostalgic for how I looked at forty-five. But I still think there was something not quite right, and now I can see what it was. I just didn't feel comfortable in my skin.

I certainly didn't feel comfortable when I went to see Richard, the new shrink. There was so much to tell him since I had last seen him: about the operation and the pain and the nightmares and the bad news at the hospital and the feeling I had all the time that I was being stretched on a rack. But I could also tell him the good news, which was that the FISH test had been wrong. When I had gone back to the hospital, this time with my mother, the oncologist had told me that my cancer wasn't HER2 + and that I didn't need chemotherapy after all. I was just taking this in when the registrar looked at my reconstructed breast, which was pink and burning hot. 'That's an infection,' he said. 'We don't want you to lose the flap.' He sent me straight back to the ward, pumped me full of antibiotics and released me after three days. The plastic surgeon told me that we wouldn't know if the reconstruction was safe for another three months.

So now I was waiting to know if I could keep 'the flap'. I was back in my flat, waiting for the scars to heal, waiting for the woody lump where my breast had been to soften, waiting for the muscle on my stomach to stretch so I could stand up straight again. Winston had brought Michele and Daniel round to see me. Michele had put her arm on Daniel's shoulder, pushed him forward and said: 'Go on, ask.' Daniel looked at Michele and then down at the floor, and then Michele said: 'He wants to see the scar.' I asked if they meant the scar on my stomach and they both nodded. Daniel tiptoed towards me as I lifted my T-shirt. 'I'm scared,' he said. When he saw the scar, he screamed and ran away.

I told Richard I was frightened that men would also scream and run away. I told him this while I was lying on the couch, which he had suggested I do and which proved to be marginally less embarrassing than telling him these things face to face. The first time I lay on the couch, he asked me why I had my hands over my eyes. 'Are you,' he said, 'trying to protect yourself?' I didn't realise I was covering my eyes, but then said I probably was. Of course I needed to protect myself. My body felt as if it had been run over and now I felt as if I was being asked to rip open my heart.

I never usually remember my dreams, but now, every morning, I was waking up exhausted from the strange, hectic adventures that had taken over my nights. Richard loved them, of course. Shrinks always love dreams. Everyone else wants to yawn as soon as you mention one, but Richard is a Jungian, and dreams, for him, are a precious glimpse into a psyche or soul.

My dreams were full of rejection and embarrassment

and impossible circumstances and difficult men. I dreamt that the man who dumped me had arrived uninvited at my parents' home with a girlfriend and a big bunch of people in tow, and had taken over the loft my parents had converted into a spare room. In my dream, my father said that his behaviour had been 'very shabby'. He agreed to write him a letter saying so. When I woke up, my heart was thumping. I was touched that someone had stood up for me, and that it was my father, though in real life no one had.

In one dream, I was with a group of people by a river and I was showing them my reconstructed breast and my stomach, which were both red and bleeding. Then I tried swimming in the river, but I was swept downstream and had to fight against the current to make my way back. Suddenly, I was with Martin Amis. We were both swimming across the river. When I woke up, I thought it was hard enough to have to swim against a current, and hard enough to have to show your mutilated body to a bunch of strangers, but that it really was too much to have to do all, or any of this, with Martin Amis.

I told Richard I had a 'stupid little crush' on the plastic surgeon. Richard asked me why I called it 'stupid'. I said it was because he was clearly quite a bit younger than me, and married with a young family, and that he would think it ludicrous that a middle-aged woman whose breast he had replaced should tangle these things up with teenage feelings of romance.

I told him about the friend I'd seen, for the first time for months, who had asked me what it was like to be thinking about death, and that I had told her it wasn't dying so much that I was afraid of, but dying a failure. I told him, but felt embarrassed to say it, that she had said she didn't see me as a failure, but as a successful woman. She didn't, I added, see me as a sad spinster! She didn't see me as damaged goods.

I thought Richard might smile at my self-deprecating charm, but he didn't. He said that the cruel part of me that I used to attack myself was relentless. We didn't know where it came from, or why it had been necessary to develop it, but it was 'all-pervasive and ruthlessly efficient'.

I was so shocked I couldn't say anything at all. I wanted to say that I had been joking, or half-joking, but then I realised I hadn't. And there, on the couch, in front of the man who felt like a headmaster who had told me off, a headmaster who thought I was vicious and cruel, even if largely to myself, and that I attracted vicious, cruel, charming men, I howled.

I saw Richard for three years. In that time, my stock on the paper rose before the change of regime that led to its fall. When I recovered from my operation, I was asked to write the lead column once a week and given a full-page column in the news pages on a Saturday. That summer, I was asked to do the first interview with Gordon Brown after he left office and spent a day with him in his freezing constituency in Fife. I liked him. He was serious. He was modest. He had a burning sense of justice and of wanting to fight for the underdog. He was also a little bit awkward. That night, when I was transcribing the tape of my interview, Tom phoned. He asked me what Gordon Brown was like, and then he said something that took me by surprise. He said: 'Did he remind you of Dad?'

Oh yes. Clever Tom. Of course he reminded me of Dad.

I started being invited to do lots of radio and TV. I was introduced on BBC 2's *Review Show* as a 'star columnist'. I nearly laughed when I heard the word 'star' next to my name, but even I had to admit that the 'failure' riff wasn't wearing well.

I started looking forward to seeing Richard. I still sometimes cried on his couch, but I also often laughed. Once, after I'd had a migraine for a week, I just lay in silence on the couch. I felt as if I was drinking in something, though I couldn't say what it was. Once I had a dream about Bristol and Richard pointed out that 'bristol' was a slang word for a breast. I wanted to run screaming from the room. I hated the thought of all those Freudian clichés about babies and mothers' breasts. But by the end of that silent session, the migraine had gone.

Friends who saw the change in me often asked what happened in those sessions and how the therapy had worked. I couldn't tell them and I still can't. Yes, of course we talked about my family and Caroline's breakdown and my discovery of a vicious, cruel God. We talked about how that God seemed to be alive and well long after I told him to 'fuck off'. It was, I realised, as if I had swallowed him. Jonah and the whale, perhaps, but I had swallowed the whale.

I don't know if it was God or just a nervous teenager who dreamt up the list of things I wasn't allowed. I didn't realise it existed until I wrote it down, after seeing a counsellor for a couple of sessions a few years before. The list was, with other miscellaneous bits of paper, in the inbox on my desk: I am not allowed to be healthy, I am not allowed to be successful, I am not allowed to have a successful relationship, I am not allowed to find love.

Accounts of therapy nearly always sound banal. *And how did that make you feel?* Even the question makes my skin crawl. I can only describe what happened in that room as alchemy. It changed me. My atoms felt different. By the end of it, I felt strong. And I felt as if that list of things I wasn't allowed could finally be torn up.

Chapter 26
Lucky

'Lovely man seeks lovely woman.' When he popped up in my inbox, I thought he looked, well, lovely. I have always used the word 'lovely' far too much. Almost every time I take a sip of coffee or wine, or a bite of cake or a crunch of a crisp, I'll say 'lovely', sometimes in my head, but quite often out loud. I think I got the habit from my mother. Yes, thank you, I had a lovely time. Delightful, pleasant, nice or enjoyable, according to the *Oxford English Dictionary*. Not the sun, the moon, the stars, but you can't live on the sun, the moon or the stars, so let's stick with what you can get on Earth.

Thanks to Richard, and the three years on that couch, I felt I could use the word about myself. 'Lovely woman seeks lovely bloke' was the strapline I chose for my dating profile. And here he was, or here was a man describing himself as lovely, and using the same strapline as me! He had, I thought, a lovely face. Handsome, yes, with sculpted cheeks and a James Bond jaw, but also thoughtful and kind. And when I met him, he was.

He spoke in a quiet voice. He had a gentle manner. Over lobster linguine and Chilean Sauvignon, he talked about his work and I talked about mine. It was five years since my big operation and two years since the regime change at the *Independent* that had led to a dramatic final meeting with the editor. He had told me that he was 'freshening up' the pages, I had shouted at him and he had threatened to call security. And I had walked out into Kensington High Street feeling that I had lost the thing I'd spent my whole adult life building up.

I gave Anthony the edited version, and had to dash off after a couple of hours because I had a deadline. I always had a deadline. At 6.30 the next morning, he sent me an email. 'Your website,' he said, 'says "let me know what you think". I always try to rise to a challenge . . .' And so, in a ten-point list, he did. His first point was about my writing style. He had clearly spent hours reading my work online. His second was about my former employer. 'I think the *Independent* are TWATS. I refuse to buy the rag – and I was a loyal supporter when it first started.' It was his sixth point that touched me most. 'I think you have had hardship in your life, and are brave in the way that you have dealt with it.' His seventh point made me feel as if I had just sunk into a warm bath after a long, long walk. 'I think,' he wrote, 'I can offer you a lot of unconditional support.'

We met again that night. We kissed at the bus stop and

his lips were so soft I was reminded of my first ever kiss, and of the electric jolt when skin first meets skin. In the bus on the way home, I looked out of the window and had a feeling that felt like a fact: I will never meet anyone who is capable of loving me as much as this man.

We met two days later, at a party for a project I was helping to launch. Afterwards, we went out to dinner and I felt his arm round my waist and couldn't believe it felt so natural to have fingers resting on the curve of my hip as I walked. That weekend, we took a train out to a village in Hertfordshire. After a burger in a pub garden, we set off through the village and down a footpath winding through woods full of wild garlic and a first sprinkling of bluebells. At one point, in a clearing, we passed a child's trampoline and I could not stop myself from climbing on it. As I bounced up and down, in the fresh, clear air, my heart was bouncing, too.

In a sunlit field, we lay on the grass and kissed. That night, we danced in my sitting room to Madeleine Peyroux singing 'Dance Me to the End of Love'.

Later, he told me that he wasn't sure what he would find. He had steeled himself, but what he found was soft flesh, my soft flesh, with a nipple made out of my soft flesh and a faint, silvery scar. That plastic surgeon had wrought a miracle, or something like one. No wonder I'd had a crush on the man who, as Carole King sang, on the record Tom always used to play at top volume, had made me feel 'like a natural woman'.

We went for a weekend in the Cotswolds, and held

hands in a courtyard as we listened out for the blackbird's song. We went for a day trip to Whitstable and ate fish and chips on the beach. Since childhood, I had only ever been able to do these things with friends. That summer, we went to Italy, to the tiny flat in Tuscany I had remortgaged my own flat to buy. I had made an offer on the flat without even seeing it, in a fit of what Italians call *folla di proprieta*. I had done it because Italy has always felt to me like a kind of home, but also because my friends were nearly all paired off and I wanted somewhere lovely – that word again – to go to on my own. My tiny Tuscan flat *is* lovely. It cost less than an extra bedroom, but it's one of my favourite places in the world. For eight years, I had rented it out to couples, sometimes honeymooning couples. I had, I realised, created a love nest, but I was the only one who was in it alone.

On our first evening there, we sat on the bench by the well and gazed out at the olive groves and the cypresses, that landscape that always made me think of the Renaissance paintings in my father's *History of Italian Art*. In the soft, pink light, I felt something wash over me. It was a feeling of joy, but also of deep, deep calm. It is the birthday of my life, I thought, because my love is come to me.

When my mother met Anthony for the first time, I thought she was actually going to clap. Her standards had dropped. She had originally hoped for a doctor, or a diplomat, or a professor, a man with a brilliant brain and a brilliant career she could smuggle into conversations with friends. Over the years, that had changed to a man with a job, or perhaps just a pulse. 'My son-in-law' would have been lovely, but 'Christina's boyfriend' would have been a start. That phrase had rarely been tested, since it suggested something that lasted more than a few weeks.

So when I arrived at Nelson Gardens with a tall, handsome man, in a nice shirt and a nice pair of trousers, my mother looked as if she'd just been told she'd won a Nobel Prize. Not just a man, but an architect! With a first from Cambridge! Like Dad! And he had grown-up children, which was good, because I, sadly, wouldn't be able to give him children, and we wouldn't want him to be disappointed. Let's hope, in fact, that I didn't wreck things, as I nearly always did.

We had tea and cake in the garden, outside the tiny summer house that replaced the Wendy house, where Monique and I cast Halloween spells and drank Cherryade blood. My mother was entranced by my new man's manners. 'Isn't he lovely?' she hissed when we passed each other in the kitchen, as she was topping up the teapot and I was getting another fork. Yes, Mum, he's lovely. I was tempted to ask her if she could lower the enthusiasm level just a notch because it might make a man wary. But I couldn't bear to dim her joy. And he wasn't wary. He isn't wary. One of the many lovely things about my 'lovely bloke' is that he's confident enough to know what he wants and he doesn't play games.

My mother sent photos, of course. She still took photos of almost every meeting with her children, or with any of her friends. Here we are, eating Victoria sponge in the sunshine, Anthony in a short-sleeved white shirt, me in a red and white spotty dress. Here we are again, during a weekend in Guildford, having lamb shanks in a pub in Shere. The photos aren't in an album, because I never get round to putting my photos in albums. They're in a pile of photos on one of the bookshelves above my desk. From the size of the pile, it looks as if my mother took a photo of every coffee she had with us, and every meal.

'It's so nice he's practical!' she said, after he had mended a leaking tap. It was not a word anyone ever used to describe my father. IKEA furniture triggered some of his darkest moods. Thump, thump, long, long sigh, oh hang. Anthony can knock up an IKEA wardrobe in the time it takes to whip up a meal. If he sees something broken, he'll mend it. When my car windows stopped working, he sent away for some missing widget and hey presto, I had windows that went up and down. When my car hood was ripped beyond repair, he fitted a new one. It took hours, but he stuck with it. He sticks with things. He sticks with things more than I do, and so far he has stuck with me.

Perhaps it's because he was married for so long that he has learnt what makes a relationship work and what doesn't. He knows the mistakes he made and doesn't want to make them again. He has taught me that love is like a garden. You have to tend it, in good weather and bad.

It isn't always about how you feel, which is just as well, because sometimes when we argue what I feel is that I'd like to run away. That's what I've always done. I thought a row meant something was broken. Now I see that it's just a thunderstorm and if you let it pass, the sun comes out again.

Eighteen months after I met Anthony, my mother tripped on the stairs. It was several hours before she managed to crawl to the phone to call a neighbour. Even when she was lying in screaming agony on the floor, she wouldn't call an ambulance. It was the neighbour who called for one and it was Tom who called me to say she was in hospital and had broken her hip.

They operated on the morning of her 82nd birthday. I brought coffee and little cakes and a card and a book, but at first I didn't recognise the frail old woman with wild white hair. Every day of her life, my mother coiled her hair into an elegant bun. She backcombed it at the top to 'add some volume'. She wore foundation and powder and mascara and lipstick, even when she didn't leave the house. She wore earrings and brooches and neat white blouses and navy jackets and navy skirts. My mother always looked as if she was off to a meeting or a party.

She didn't now.

Tom and I made sure that one of us went to see her every day. Sometimes, I stayed at Nelson Gardens for a couple of nights. Most of the time, I drove down from Stoke Newington, which sometimes took three hours. The machines in the car park kept swallowing my money. I queued up at a cubicle to get change and it swallowed that, too. Once, when I was turning into the car park, my car skidded on black ice and I just missed an approaching car.

I took my mother little treats, but she didn't want to eat them. Once, I brought her gin and tonic, with glasses and ice from Nelson Gardens, but she just pushed it away. I tried to think of things that would cheer her up. She loved the Queen and always cried over her speech on Christmas Day, so I subscribed to Netflix, so we could watch *The Crown*. I showed her how to get it on her iPad. She was good at tech. She had done more computer training than I had. She wasn't good at tech now.

When the physiotherapist came round, I tried to help her walk. She clutched on to the Zimmer frame as if it was a ledge above a pool of crocodiles. When I asked her to move her feet, she looked as if I'd just asked her to swim in that pool. She tried, but I could tell that she was only trying for me.

One Sunday morning, two weeks after her operation, Tom called to say she was in a bad way. I felt sick as I set off. In the car, I texted a friend. 'I think my mother might be dying.' I stared at the words, but couldn't let them sink in. No, I thought. You can't. You can't leave me. I can't let you. I was ready to summon an army, kill a lion, fly over a moon to get her well.

Her eyes were half open and the curtains around her bed were closed. I held her hand and told her that having her as my mother had been the biggest blessing of my life. I saw something ripple across her face and asked her what had been the best thing in hers. Suddenly, her eyes snapped open and her mouth split into a smile. 'My children,' she said.

I still thought she would get better. We managed to get her moved to a community hospital where she had her own room. Every time I went to see her, I tried to get her to do her exercises. When Anthony was there, we all did them together. I got her to put on her lipstick. I bought her some tracksuit trousers. Navy blue, of course. My mother had never, ever worn tracksuit trousers, but she agreed to let the nurse help her get them on. She tried to smile, but her eyes had lost their glint. When Anthony was out of the room, she turned to me. 'Darling,' she whispered, 'I've had enough.'

I prayed. For the first time since I had told God to fuck off, I begged him to let her die. I could not imagine a world without my mother, but if she wanted to go, I didn't want to stop her. Let her go, I mouthed, as I ran round my local park. OK, Mum, I said. You can go now. I don't want you to go, but if you want to go then I want you to go.

'Your mother is very, very poorly,' said the nurse who rang. 'Please come now.' I was stuck in traffic in Green Lanes when Tom called. I pulled in to call him back. I wanted to stop the cars, stop the clocks, stop everything and write it in the sky. Help me, please. Please, please, please. The person I love most in the world is dead.

My mother had left detailed instructions, of course. She had picked the funeral director. She had picked the music, the readings and the hymns. 'For John's funeral,' she had written, 'I asked for double time at the crematorium but I don't think that will be necessary for me.' She had picked a choice of venues for the wake: two pubs and then the Tithe Barn at Loseley Park, but she had crossed that out and written '(too big)'.

When I rang the funeral director, I didn't like his tone. No, I thought, you're not touching my mum. I spoke to another one who was kind and sounded as though she meant it. When I went round to see her, to fill out the forms and pick up leaflets about coffins, I wanted to throw myself into her arms.

I booked one of the pubs and paid a deposit, but as the letters and messages poured in, it became clear that it would be far too small. I booked the Tithe Barn at Loseley, where we used to pick raspberries and eat honey and ginger ice cream.

Tom was happy for me to arrange the funeral while he worked his way through the list of friends. My mother had written one that ran to several pages: 'People to contact when I die'. She had written another one, with circles and lines hanging off them, each like a Portuguese man-of-war. In each circle was a category: 'school', 'university',

'Bangkok', 'Guildford neighbours', 'Lanesborough colleagues', 'Stoughton Infants: lots of colleagues', 'Rome'. I've never met anyone with so many friends. At eighty-two, my mother had lost quite a few, but there were still so, so many left. Some had had Christmas cards from her after she died. Even on her deathbed, she was churning them out.

We had pink roses on the coffin, like the ones she had in her wedding bouquet. My heart did something like a somersault when I saw it. I looked at Tom and he looked at me and I knew we were both thinking we couldn't do this thing, we couldn't sing those hymns, we couldn't speak the words we had written, we couldn't do any of it, but we also knew we had to. We followed the vicar behind the coffin, the vicar who had buried Caroline and Dad.

We sang 'Now Thank We All Our God'. The vicar prayed and then Tom read his eulogy. I wasn't sure whether he would be able to read it, but he did and it was funny and sweet and true. After the next hymn, I read mine. I said that my mother often said she was lucky. She said that thirteen was her lucky number because she was born on the thirteenth. She was lucky, she would say, to get the last free parking space when she went shopping and lucky to snap up the last half-price navy dress. She was lucky, she told us after the first *Star Wars* film at Guildford Odeon, to have found pine kitchen cupboards at Debenhams with 33 per cent off.

I talked about her meeting with my father, on that

hill in Heidelberg, and the glamorous life that followed, in Bangkok and Rome. I talked about her teaching, and her Open University degrees, and the five languages she spoke, and her endless entertaining, and her energy, and her *joie de vivre*, and her zest. I said that her philosophy was to work hard – unbelievably hard – and then have a tiny little treat. I talked about how she brought me up to love coffee and cake, and how she'd take a tiny sip of coffee and then a tiny nibble of cake while I wolfed down mine.

I talked about the candles at Christmas, and the Swedish songs and the *pepparkakor*, and the sparkle and the fun. I talked about how, in spite of everything, she had kept her sense of humour. I mentioned the card she bought me, after years of despairing that I would always be single. 'Looking for Mr Right?' it said on the outside. Inside, it said: 'Look in fiction!'

I talked about how shocked she was, when she first came to Britain, by the British class system, and how she was, and always had been, a social democrat who believed everyone should be given an equal chance. I said that we were the lucky ones to have had her as our mother and that she had shown us all the meaning of class.

Chapter 27

Outsiders and Underdogs

'I am a Carer.' That's what it says on the card I find in my mother's navy handbag, in the wardrobe in Tom's spare room. I find her purse in it, too, and the lipstick she always wore, and her hairbrush, and her glasses, and a little packet of Läkerol, the Swedish liquorice pastilles she always carried and used whenever she lost her voice. With her, it was always the first sign of stress. She would forge on in the face of migraines, colds, pulled muscles, marking SATs, guests, Christmas cards and, of course, the demands of her own family, fuelled by coffee and, when necessary, paracetamol. But when her voice started fading, we knew that some inner Rubicon had been crossed. My mother would fish out her Läkerol, suck as if she was trying to extract some life-saving marrow and resume her hectic schedule with a whisper that was sometimes more like a hiss.

I don't know why that card was still in my mother's

handbag, sixteen years after Caroline died. Perhaps it just got stuck in the archaeological layers. I don't know why Tom kept the handbag. I suppose he just couldn't bear to throw it out. I do know that that card, issued by Carers National Association in partnership with Panadol, is a good way of summing up a big chunk of my mother's life. On it, she has had to name two contacts, in case of an emergency. She has put Mrs Behard, her next-door-neighbour-but-one for forty years, and Tom. In the section under her own name and address, she has inserted my sister's name. 'I care for [Caroline Patterson] who is disabled and relies on me to look after him/her.'

You can say that again.

In the red lever arch 'MENTAL HEALTH' file, there's a copy of an article from the *British Medical Journal* in 1974, the year after Caroline's trip to Norway. It's called 'Burden of Schizophrenia'. It is, the article says, 'predominantly the parents who are responsible for the primary care' of people with the illness, 'and on whom the burden of that care falls'. It mentions the National Schizophrenia Fellowship, 'a middle-class organisation' that has 'taken upon itself the task of asking questions and so letting some of the deficiencies of community care be known'. For many years, my mother ran and hosted the local branch. 'I am writing to reassure you that the Carers' Support meetings on June 13 and July 11 are still going to be held here,' my mother has written in a letter to all the members. My father was just out of hospital after his first big operation.

Caroline's heart condition had just been diagnosed. Only death turned out to be a good enough excuse to stop.

In that file, there are leaflets with titles like 'The shock of diagnosis', 'Schizophrenia: whose problem?' and 'Strategies for coping with psychotic symptoms'. There's a flyer for a one-day seminar at the University of Surrey on 'Understanding Schizophrenia'. And there's a review by my mother, in the *National Schizophrenia Fellowship Magazine*, of a leaflet called 'About Schizophrenia', which she 'cannot praise highly enough'. It is, she explains, full of 'practical and sensible advice'. At the end of the booklet, she adds, 'there is a moving article called ACCEPTANCE, from which I take the liberty of quoting some passages: "Even when we accept in our minds that this is an illness, how can we accept it in our hearts and not react with exasperation, frustration, anger, hostility, self-pity and resentment at the limitations that are being imposed on our own lives? . . . The heart of the problem is to be aware of the need for acceptance, and if we have achieved that we can hope to make progress."'

A few pages on from that review, there's the typed script for a talk my mother gave, with the title 'A Mental Health Carer's Perspective'. There are also index cards in the plastic sleeve, with her neatly written prompts. 'What does it feel like to care for someone who has a mental illness, in our case schizophrenia?' my mother begins. 'My first answer,' she says, 'would be that your life is never the same again.'

She describes the feelings of 'shock, horror, fear, incredulity' when Caroline got back from Norway and announced that she had been responsible for the recent IRA bombs. She talks about the support group she now runs. 'I think the prevailing feeling that we have all experienced,' she says, 'is one of total isolation. You just don't know what has happened to your loved one, you don't know where to turn, nobody tells you anything. After all, you are just the relative. Nobody tells you the truth about the illness, you don't know how to manage it and you are totally on your own and only learn by trial and error. You are bursting with questions you want to ask the psychiatrist. But you hardly ever see him or her alone. In any case, it may take years to get the diagnosis because the psychiatrist is usually unwilling to label the patient. It is only after you have read up on schizophrenia that you realise that this must be what it is.

'You have to learn how to manage this illness,' she continues, 'and this is not easy. It is like walking a tightrope all the time and you are under almost constant emotional pressure. There are so many emotions involved and the whole process is very much like a bereavement, at least in its early stages. There is a great feeling of loss. Obviously, the person suffering from schizophrenia has lost most, but for us there was the loss of our daughter as she would have been, had she not been struck by this terrible illness. You gradually have to give up any thoughts of a normal life for her with independence, marriage, children, a career or even a job of any kind, and just be grateful if she stays on an even keel.'

I hardly ever heard my mother talk as honestly as this. She was so polite to everyone that I once yelled at her, as a teenager, that she'd be making cups of tea for Hitler. When Caroline lost her washing-up job, she wrote to her psychiatrist. She mentions that Tom is off work with anxiety and 'a relapse of a post-viral condition' and that he's now being treated with 'antidepressants and beta-blockers'. She mentions my recent diagnosis of lupus. 'Christina still can't walk,' she says, and 'all the children have been home with us since before Christmas.' She tells the psychiatrist about Caroline's sacking and how she has had to increase her dose of Largactil 'to make her sleep and calm her down'. At the end of the letter, she says she is 'sorry to burden' him 'with all this background information' and thanks him for looking after Caroline. 'Best wishes to your wife,' she ends. 'I hope she is still enjoying her singing.'

What strikes me most, flicking through these files, is the sheer, exhausting effort. It's the hundreds of job applications my mother helped Caroline fill in. It's the letters to psychiatrists. It's the letters about benefits applied for, but not yet received, and to community psychiatric nurses who made appointments and didn't turn up. It's the lists of medication that get longer and longer. It's the letters begging employers to take, or keep, Caroline on. She rarely flagged and she rarely lost her temper. Even in her diary, she usually kept things cheerful. But when my father was recovering from his cancer operation and Caroline was having panic attacks, she didn't. 'Good Friday,' she has written. 'Not a very good Friday. Rang Caroline and she sounded as bad as ever. Hardly able to talk and she had slept in her clothes. After breakfast with John, I cleaned the house and thought and thought. I suddenly felt so angry – that I have spent twenty-seven years of my life looking after my daughter with schizophrenia, with all the humiliation and sorrows and lost opportunities and now that my husband needs me and I want to nurture him, I shall be prevented by schizophrenia again.'

In the file, there's a letter from a Carers Support Worker to social services. She talks about Caroline's schizophrenia and the fact that she is now 'extremely incapacitated, very breathless and weak and needs help with all care'. She mentions my father's operation for cancer and the fact that he's now 'having daily chemotherapy injections and coping with a colostomy'. She says she is 'very concerned about the effect that these two caring situations are having on Mrs Patterson'. My father was 'very concerned', too. He was usually patient with Caroline, but on that Good Friday, he snapped. 'John rang Caroline and told her that I needed a bit of rest today,' my mother's diary entry continues. 'Perhaps she could use a bit of her excellent willpower to get herself better.'

He wasn't being sarcastic. He knew, everyone knew,

how much effort Caroline made. In a 'CAROLINE CARDS AND LETTERS' file there are birthday cards to her from both my parents. For her 31st birthday, my father gave her a card with pink roses. 'I hope you have a very happy day, dearest Caroline,' he has written inside it. 'I am so proud that you have your job at the University of Surrey. I am so glad that you have so many friends – like your mother, you are very good at making friends.' In another card, he had written, 'You are a wonderful and thoughtful friend to so many people, and so sympathetic to those with problems.'

There's a card, with a bunch of pink flowers on the cover and a gold-embossed message: 'For a Daughter Who's Loved So Much'. Inside it, he has written: 'To our very dear daughter and oldest of our three children. We are so glad that you have built such an active life of your own, Caroline. It is wonderful that you have so many good friends and enjoyable activities. We do so wish you a very happy and healthy 35th year.' Under the rather sentimental gold verse inside, he has inserted the words 'lots and lots and lots' between the word 'With' and the word 'Love'.

For her 40th birthday, he gave her a card with a birthday cake and balloons. The official message is 'Happy 40th Birthday to a truly remarkable person!' Underneath it, he has written 'I liked the words on this card! You are very friendly, very kind and very brave – a truly remarkable person.' The last card in the file has yellow sunflowers. 'Lots of love on your last birthday of this Millennium!'

he has written. It was, in fact, her last birthday because willpower has its limits.

When Caroline lost her last ever job, her employers managed to lose her birth certificate. My mother wrote to complain about this and the personnel officer wrote to say he had requested a replacement. 'I must correct one point in your letter,' he said. 'We did not dismiss Caroline, she decided to leave us.' My father was so angry when he saw the letter, he wrote back. 'It may be that you did not actually dismiss Caroline,' he wrote. 'But despite her medical condition and vulnerability, she was summoned to the personnel people and given such a poor picture of her performance and prospects that she concluded that if she did not decide to leave she would be dismissed . . . We shall go on thinking that this was very shabby treatment of a vulnerable member of society. Morally speaking, she was dismissed.'

I would not like to have been that personnel officer. I could tell him that 'shabby' from my father is about as bad as it gets.

My father rarely talked about religion, but he always kept his prayer book on his bedside table and only an emergency would keep him away from a Sunday trip to church. In one of his files, I've found something in his handwriting that looks like a sermon. 'HOLY TRINITY, SUNDAY 5 NOVEMBER, ALL SAINTS' it says at the top. 'On the day we celebrate All Saints I decided to talk to you about my favourite saint,' he starts. 'He wrote a gospel. Paul tells us that he was a doctor, and he was the only non-Jew in the New Testament. So he writes as an outsider to explain the life of Jesus to other outsiders. Matthew writes to explain the Old Testament prophecy with Jesus as Messiah. Mark gives us a wonderful plain account – the Daily Mirror school of gospel writing. John soars to philosophical heights. Luke gives us the gospel for OUTSIDERS and UNDERDOGS. This is the gospel I would take to my Desert Island.'

The rest of the sermon, which runs to four pages, is a passionate, erudite and, yes, compelling account of Luke's gospel. In his careful arguments and analysis, I'm reminded that my father taught himself New Testament Greek. The themes of Luke's gospel, he argues, are 'women, the poor, sinners, outsiders'. I'm particularly touched by a reference in his section on sinners. 'If you want to know what the love of God looks like,' he says, 'go to the Hermitage Museum in St Petersburg. Seek out the Rembrandt Room and stand before his painting of the Prodigal Son.'

St Petersburg. The place where he and my mother helped Caroline fulfil her dream.

In the section on outsiders, he says: 'It seems to be human nature to define the rules of clubs so that we are in and others are out. But this is not Luke's way and I would like to think that it is not God's way.' It was the Samaritan, he says, 'the racial outsider – the underdog – who showed mercy' when others walked by. 'To me,' he says, 'Luke is the world's greatest writer for outsiders and underdogs. The author of *Crime and Punishment* would rank a close second. And the sting in the tail of the Good Samaritan story is the clearest possible bit of down-to-earth advice – GO AND DO LIKEWISE.'

I don't know if my father always had this passion for 'the underdog'. I think he probably did. But I do know that nothing made it burn more brightly than Caroline. He loved her the moment he gazed into her blue eyes. He loved her when he kissed her for the last time, in the Royal Surrey Hospital's chapel of rest. ('John touched her and was shocked to find she was cold,' my mother wrote in her diary. 'We said our last farewell to our beloved daughter. Eric said he would ask Dr Foley to sign the death certificate.') He loved Caroline, and he loved spending time with her. 'I do so hope that the year ahead will be a good one for us both,' he has written in the first birthday card after she lost that washing-up job and when he was due to retire. 'More time for us to be together.'

It's certainly true that he had less of the work. It was my mother who took on the chief burden, of letter-writing, driving, organising, begging, phoning and orchestrating that forms a big part of any parent/carer's life. But my father had another advantage. You could call it stiff upper lip. You could call it stoicism. You could even call it resignation. My father accepted Caroline's illness in a way my mother couldn't. It was like the weather forecast. 'Well, that's it, then,' he would say if the man on the TV announced a weekend of 'steady rain'. Not what you wanted, but you couldn't fight it. You just had to get on with it. It was my mother who wrote, in that review of that pamphlet, about the need for acceptance, but for her it was like trying to grasp a ledge on a cliff that was always just out of reach.

In one of my father's files, I've found a church magazine from 1984. 'John Patterson discusses "Why do bad things happen to good people?"' is the heading. My father is reviewing a book of the same title by a Jewish rabbi called Harold Kushner. 'His key point,' says my father, 'is that we have a loving God and a fair God. It is not God who brings disease and suffering on the undeserving. We should not blame God for the suffering. Instead of demanding explanations, we should look to God for strength to carry on.

'Do buy this book and give it to your friends, particularly those to whom life has been very cruel. Accept that pain and sorrow are often undeserved. Whenever we feel that we did not deserve our own suffering, we can think of the Son of God who volunteered to endure the most undeserved suffering. And if we can endure our own problems without bitterness, we can help others to carry on too.'

My father, clearly, did not tell God to fuck off. He did not tell Satan that he'd won. He tried to support Caroline and then, when he retired, he tried to support other vulnerable people through the local Citizens Advice Bureau. Auntie Bell told me recently that he meant it when he said that he found this more fulfilling than anything else in his career.

When my father died, we found a tiny card in his wallet. I've found it in one of his files. On one side, there's an extract from the magazine of the school my mother taught at, which he had carefully copied out: 'The school and parents alike have come to be grateful that she chose to complete her distinguished teaching career at Lanesborough. Mrs Patterson's tenure was characterised by her eminent professionalism, dedication, grace and charm.'

On the other side of the card, he has written this: 'Jane Austen's character sketch of our dear Caroline: "Open, candid, artless, guileless, with affections strong but simple, forming no pretensions and knowing no disguise." [*Northanger Abbey*, page 207, Penguin English Library Edition]'.

Towards the back of the 'MENTAL HEALTH' file, there's 'A brief history of theories as to the causes of schizophrenia'. It starts with a section on 'early theories'. It says that 'until as recently as the 1970s, many people believed that this was because some parents somehow brought up their children wrongly, and this led to the development of mental illness in their children. We now know, of course, that this is not true.'

My mother wanted to believe this, but she didn't. She had done a sociology A level and had read about R. D. Laing. On her bedside table, for quite a while, there was a book called *Maternal Deprivation*. She was haunted by her memory of leaving Bangkok with a smiling toddler and landing at Tilbury with one who screamed for hours and wouldn't stop.

Also in the file, there's a letter from my mother to a distant relative on my father's side called Dr Murray. 'You won't know me,' she begins. She explains that my father's sister, Bell, had told her that she had met her, and said that she had a sister with schizophrenia. 'I have been planning to write to you ever since I heard this,' she says, 'to ask if you know of anyone else in the family who suffers from this illness. Our own lives,' she continues, 'have been rather dominated and affected by schizophrenia.' She explains how Caroline's illness hit 'like a bolt from a blue sky'. She outlines some of the family history, and says that Caroline 'has accepted the illness and its limitations and leads quite a happy life'. But my mother says that she has 'been so puzzled by this illness as there seemed to be no precedent in either of our families.' She would, she says, be 'extremely grateful' if Dr Murray would tell her a bit about her sister's schizophrenia. 'Having blamed myself for Caroline's illness for eighteen years,' she says, 'I would find it such a relief to know that there may be genetic predisposition after all.'

I can't find the reply. What I have found in the file is a scrawled note by my mother, clipped to a letter to one of Caroline's psychiatrists. I think it must be from a meeting with him, one where she jotted down his words. 'You are innocent,' it says. 'If you have erred, you have probably been too kind.'

Chapter 28

Enigmatic Cycles

When Caroline was ten, my mother took her to the Child Guidance clinic. She typed up a list of questions, in Swedish, just in case any of us found it. When I wanted to find out more about Caroline's illness, my mother translated it for me.

The heading was 'Neurotiska symptom' and the list includes the following questions:

'Reaction against certain words that I use: shall I consciously try to avoid all words that irritate her? How can I get the other children to avoid such words? Negative reaction against almost any suggestion: shall we always let her decide, or shall we not consider her, even if it causes a scene? Shall I let her eat by herself? Can I demand the same things from her as I think I ought to do from my five-year-old daughter, make her own bed, and remove her own plate? Or should I make an exception for her, because she almost always causes a scene? What stand shall I take, faced with her obsessional interests? Shall I encourage or discourage? Should we ever force her to have her hair cut against her will? What do we do when she cuts off her dolls' hair or her friends' hair? Should she have any discipline at all? Any punishments? Can the whole thing go back to her experience on the ship?'

Thirteen years later, when she took Caroline for an independent assessment from a psychiatrist, she mentioned the visit in some detailed notes she wrote for him. The Child Guidance psychiatrist was, she told him, a 'hopeless man' who said that Caroline was 'perfectly OK and put it all down to worry about the 11+'. Which, my mother added, 'her pro-comprehensive, anti 11+ parents had never mentioned'. My mother said she was 'taught behaviourist techniques, mostly of the stick variety'. They were told, she said, 'not to let her get away with any strange or uncontrolled behaviour'. So, she added, 'my husband frightened her into conformity and the symptoms gradually disappeared'.

This certainly explains some of my father's strictness, and I didn't even know about some of the 'neurotic symptoms', so 'the stick' must have worked. The 'scenes' didn't disappear, but perhaps there were fewer than there had been. Happiness, as the French novelist Henry de Montherlant once said, writes white, and memory does something similar, so of course what I remember is the bad days. What I also remember is the feeling that I was always waiting for them, always holding my breath.

Caroline's psychiatrists, my mother explains in her notes for the new one, 'have given a diagnosis of schizo-affective illness', but the GP 'usually writes schizophrenia on certificates'. She is desperate, she doesn't quite say but strongly implies, to know for sure.

In the file, on the same cream paper and in the same typed script, there's an account of the meeting with the independent psychiatrist. 'He gave us two and a half hours of his time!' my mother writes. 'Caroline was a bit overwhelmed by all the talking, but said she liked him very much indeed. He treated her with great respect and dignity.'

In the follow-up letter, also in the file, he certainly does. 'I was delighted to meet Caroline on Thursday,' he begins. 'I can truthfully say that I have not met anyone before who has been able to talk about their illness so sensibly and objectively. For that reason, I feel it is quite in order for Caroline to read this report if she wishes. This objectivity, too, augurs well for her future.

'First of all, then, what is my opinion re Caroline's diagnosis? I am sure she is schizophrenic. Thus she gave a classical account of – when the illness was florid years ago – intense feelings of shyness (you also gave a history of withdrawal from other children when she was very young), derealisation ("trees didn't belong to today", "living in a different age"), positive and negative misidentification ("wasn't the real psychiatrist"), grandiose delusions ("felt I was being filmed", "felt there was a grand-duchess in the family"), paranoid ideation ("everyone talking about me"), passivity feelings ("mind being read"), delusions of influence ("bombs being planned because of me"). Caroline seemed particularly sensitive when you mentioned the feeling she has had at times of knives/sharp things cutting through her, so I did not press her on this, but it's possible this was a manifestation of what is termed a "somatic delusional perception", another so-called "first rank" or Schneiderian symptom of schizophrenia, any one of which in itself is sufficient to make the diagnosis.'

The psychiatrist says that 'the fact that Caroline shows spontaneity, motivation (e.g. loves watching TV) and a reasonable degree of normal emotional response in the interview situation are very hopeful signs.' He says that she 'will always be a rather shy, sensitive girl, and should not be pushed into social or occupational contacts that are too stressful'. He says that 'feelings of pathological jealousy' may 'respond to neuroleptic therapy'. Which, apparently, means antipsychotic drugs. 'Caroline, as you well know, admits to strong feelings of jealousy in respect of her "bright, well" younger sister. I noticed during our talk a slight degree of regressive emotionality which suggests her present medication is not quite "holding" her.'

My mother's summary, in her notes to him, is more punchy. 'She hates her sister, whom she is very jealous of. She loves her brother, who is very good to her.'

I'm shocked that those words can still make me cry. They feel, to quote the psychiatrist's report, like 'knives/

sharp things cutting through' me. It's twenty years since Caroline died, and those words still cut me to the quick. But they don't cut as deep as the words I read when I slit the Sellotape in Caroline's diary. Perhaps it was my punishment for reading it. When my mother said I could, it felt like a benediction, but perhaps I shouldn't even have looked at it. My own relationship with God has hardly been straightforward, but 'Dear God, my only wish on earth is to be rid of Christina' is a whole lot further than I've ever gone. It was the next sentence that made me feel that someone was slicing through the chambers of my heart. 'Let Christina die this year of cancer.'

Afterwards, I didn't stop shaking for days. I felt like a ghost. I know that sounds ridiculous, but I felt as if I'd had my blood sucked out. If I hadn't spent a year thinking about knives and drugs and wounds and shadows and rogue cells, perhaps I would have laughed it off. I don't think I would, but it's possible. But I had. I had lain awake, night after night after night, feeling as if I had been dipped in an ice-cold liquid I couldn't wipe off. When I did finally fall asleep, my dreams were full of hairless heads and severed breasts and jagged scars. I sometimes woke up in a cold sweat and felt, like a spasm running through me, a sense of something so urgent I wanted to scream it: I don't want to die. Please, please, please don't let me die.

But my sister had been praying for the opposite.

These curses will be a sign and a wonder against you and your descendants for ever. It's amazing the words of the Bible that still come back to me, after all these years. This is from Deuteronomy and it's one of the verses I went through, with the two women who prayed with me, as I tried to repent of any sin my family might have committed and break the curse they told me was hanging over us all. I was twenty-six. Still young enough to have children. I was forty when I read the Sellotaped words in Caroline's diary. Probably too old, but you can never be sure. And now it's clear that the signs and wonders stop with me.

Even when I read those words in her diary, I knew it was the illness speaking. Caroline was twenty when she wrote them and I was just fifteen. Of course she resented me. Of course she envied her 'bright, well' younger sister. Of course, at times, she hated me. At times, the feeling was mutual.

I just didn't expect her to want me to die.

I know the power of envy. I have allowed it to poison too much. As a child, I envied my friends with 'normal' families. I envied my friends who went to Oxford when Jesus turned me down. I envied my friends with boyfriends. I envied my friends with children. I envied my friends with pain-free joints and clear skin. When my friend Lisa told me she was pregnant, I burst into tears and then howled. I had just been diagnosed with cancer. I thought it wasn't fair that my friends went into hospital to have babies and I went into hospital to have tumours cut out. I thought it wasn't fair that in my family we only had funerals.

It isn't fair, but what also isn't fair is to come back

from a holiday when you're fourteen and believe that you have planted bombs. It isn't fair to be stuck in a hospital where old men tell you that they want to 'make love to you' when you're not even sure what that means, and when the people on the TV suddenly start talking to you but you're not sure what they're saying, and when your mother comes to visit you but you're not sure she's your real mother, and when you have to be careful because the people in the beds around you are planning to cut you up and turn you into sausage meat, and when even your own parents, who you love more than anyone in the world, are trying to poison you, which is why you have to run away. It isn't fair to be stuffed full of drugs that make you fat and spotty and dry-mouthed and slow, and which make your hands shake and your speech slurred, and discover that you have to take them for the rest of your life.

Every day of her life, from the age of fourteen, my sister had to climb a mountain with boulders in her pockets. She had to take exams when she was so drugged she could hardly stay awake. She had to hear that she had failed them while her siblings clocked up straight As. She had to watch us both go off to university. She had to watch us both get jobs and buy flats. And most of the time, she did this with extraordinary grace. I don't think she ever resented Tom. He could have done anything and she would have forgiven him, but she didn't need to forgive Tom because he treated her like the person, for him, she was: his beloved, kind, gentle, adoring older sister. Every time he saw her, he wrapped her in a bear hug. He prodded her tummy. He teased her about her weight. 'And how,' he would say, 'is the Crow?' He always called her 'the Crow'. Every time she saw him, her face burst into a smile that was like the Hallelujah chorus on a face.

I did not get the Hallelujah chorus, but then I didn't give it. As the years passed, I did get warmer hugs and sweeter smiles. Sometimes, the resentment burst out. Sometimes, resentment does. It was not her fault. I want to say that again. It was not her fault. It was not her fault that she felt envy. It was not my fault that I inspired it, but it took me a long, long, long time to feel this in my bones.

As my calamities piled up, the envy faded. By the time I was twenty-six, and unemployed and disabled and with a diagnosis of an incurable disease, I suppose you could say that we were as near as we could get to being neck and neck. I suppose you could say that my strategy – unconscious, of course, unintended and profoundly upsetting for everyone – had worked.

When I started having therapy, at twenty-six, I didn't know anything about Freud or the connections between the body and mind. I know a lot more now. I know, for example, that Freud wrote in 1905 that 'all mental states, including those we usually regard as "processes of thought", are to some degree "affective" and not one of them is without its physical manifestation or is incapable of modifying somatic process.'

I know Freud is out of fashion. I don't know if he was right about 'mental states' and 'somatic processes', but I do know that my body has often said the things I feel I can't say. When my skin burst out, my anger and pain were written on my face. I felt ugly and I made myself ugly. I felt unloved and I felt I didn't deserve love.

I wanted to move forward and I wanted to walk away from the pain at home. I wanted to walk away from the shame and the guilt, but the pain that wracked my joints, and made me feel as if my knees were being twisted, wouldn't let me go.

'It has been established,' says the psychoanalyst Darian Leader, 'that between 25 and 50 per cent of GP visits are for medically inexplicable complaints.' He says this in a book he co-wrote called *Why Do People Get Ill?* 'I had a lot of patients with autoimmune disorders,' he told me when I went to interview him for the *Independent*. 'It wasn't just the correlation between the emergence of the illness and an episode in their life that seemed charged. It was also the fact that talking about different things would generate improvements in their symptomology which were completely real . . . I thought if words and thought processes can actually have such a real effect on the tissue of the body, couldn't they have an effect on the illness in the first place?'

He says in the book that 'if one family member is afflicted with an illness linked to genetic inheritance, it is quite common to witness the sense of debilitating guilt in those sharing the same genetic inheritance, but who escape the disease.' Physical symptoms, he says, 'are frequently a sign that something is being communicated, and this is perhaps clearest in skin and gastrointestinal disorders'. But 'symptom shifts' from one part of the body to another are 'very frequent'. The 'famously enigmatic cycles of exacerbation and remission in autoimmune disorders' have been 'linked to psychological factors in countless studies' and particularly in lupus and other diseases 'in which the immune system reacts against the body's own tissue'.

When I read this, I felt as if I had finally managed to complete a crossword I had spent years trying to fill in. Those 'enigmatic cycles' had been far too enigmatic for me.

It took me quite a while to realise that my body's breakdowns, like Caroline's psychotic breakdowns, happened about every three years. It took me quite a while, too, to realise that she was fourteen when she had her first one, and I was fourteen when I found, or thought I'd found, God. It was, I realised, a good way to make sure that a 'sunshine girl' wasn't a 'sunshine girl' any more.

'My character is one of terrible shyness and being very hysterical and unbalanced at the most embarrassing times.' It's Caroline's handwriting, in blue fountain pen, on lined foolscap. It looks like a school assignment. In later years, her handwriting shrunk to a tiny scrawl, but this is neat, so I think she must have been about fourteen. 'I tend to be too interested in people,' she writes, 'and too uninterested in possessions and to think too much about books. The things that make me most angry are having to look around furniture shops sometimes with my mother or shopping for clothes. Looking at clothes for more than five minutes makes me very angry and extremely bored. Superficial talk annoys me if I hear too much of it. Being told to do my homework by my mother makes me very irritable even though I know I should be doing it and also being urged to come out of my room in which I am told I spend too much of my time.'

It makes me want to give her one of Tom's bear hugs. As the psychiatrist says, she's remarkably objective, particularly for an adolescent. It never occurred to me, when Caroline had her 'scenes', that she knew she was being 'hysterical and unbalanced'. I'm touched that she thinks it's a bad thing to care too little about possessions and too much about books. I'm touched that she thinks it's a bad thing to hate clothes shopping. I'm with her. I find it extremely boring. I'm not with her on furniture shops. There is a corner of my heart that will be forever IKEA. But the thing that strikes me most is that she can't be bothered with the nonsense. What she cares about is people.

And she certainly did care about people. I'm not sure how she managed it, but she forced herself to overcome her natural shyness and was, as my father said, 'very friendly'. She made, and kept up with, friends from the

Boxgrove estate, friends from school, friends from her typing course, friends from church, friends from 'the bookshop', even friends from my parents' time in the diplomatic service, which they left when she was five. There were times, particularly at school after her first breakdown, when her friends made an effort to support her, because they had been asked to, and because they were kind. This was the time when I didn't even want to be seen with her. That girl, with the pink skin and the spotty face and the pot belly who's walking like a zombie? No, no, she's not my sister!

Many people were kind to her, but they were her friends because they liked her. They liked her passion, for books and writing and historical drama and taking photos and, of course, the Romanovs. They liked her enthusiasm. They liked her curiosity. They liked her interest in their lives. Everyone was amazed by Caroline's memory. She remembered every birthday and almost every conversation. She could quote chapter and verse on other people's lives. 'How are you?' she would say as soon as she saw someone she knew. There was an eagerness and urgency in her voice. She wasn't being polite. She really wanted to know. And if you weren't 'fine', she wanted to know that, too. If you weren't fine, a look of sorrow would flicker across her face. If you suffered, she felt it and wanted to lighten your burden, because she knew what suffering was like.

Oh my God, she knew what suffering was like.

When she died, my mother got about 200 cards.

She typed up some of the messages and put them in a file. 'She was very kind and gentle, always interested in me,' said one, 'while also sharing her own struggles and joys.' Another said they 'always felt encouraged as a person when we met together and talked things over'. Others highlighted her 'huge gift of friendship' and 'the exceptional cheerfulness and philosophy with which she put up with her ongoing disability'. Her 'kindness and enthusiasm and interest,' said one, 'were so much part of our family meetings, memories of which are much treasured'. Another remembered her with a song. 'I think of Neil Diamond's song "Sweet Caroline",' they wrote, 'because she was such a sweet person who saw good in everybody.'

It's the kind of thing people say in funeral messages, but it's also true. Aside from her outbursts, which were rare as an adult, I never heard her say anything unkind. And when I was wracked with pain, and wanted witnesses to that pain, I sometimes felt that she was the only one who would look.

My mother found a poem she had written when she was clearing out her flat. It wouldn't win any poetry prizes, but it taught me more about what she struggled with every day. In it, she talks about the feelings of 'unreality' that strike when her illness flares up, and of the 'fiendish goblin smile' that 'descends' on her 'spirit'. She talks about some days feeling 'like a famous queen' and others feeling that she is 'the worst person ever seen'. She talks about the fear that strikes that she 'might be killed'. The illness, she says is 'too much to bear'. But she had to bear it anyway.

Sweet Caroline? Yes, but that's only part of the story. Boadicea Caroline feels more apt to me.

When my mother cleared Caroline's flat, she found a blank birthday card among her papers. On the front, there was a picture of a girl reading and above it, in gold letters: 'Happy birthday to a wonderful sister'. Sweet Caroline, Boadicea Caroline, had bought it more than five months in advance.

Chapter 29

Cut Off

I couldn't wait to show Tom the house. I really couldn't wait to show him the garden. I haven't had a garden since leaving Nelson Gardens, apart from that spell off the Walworth Road when I had a patch of lawn so far from my attic flat that it felt like an allotment. When I look out of my bedroom window in Stoke Newington, I see shop-fronts, some with broken or missing signs, rooftops with a motley array of plywood erections like some secret shanty town, PVC mock-Georgian windows on Victorian buildings and the top decks of double-decker buses. My adult life, it's safe to say, has been extremely urban. I wake to the sound of police sirens, motorbikes and the thrum of traffic. My idea of a life, in fact, that wakes you up and keeps you on your toes. Tom's idea of hell.

Tom liked peace and quiet and plants and trees and fields and woodland and mountains. He liked birds and hedgehogs. He had four or five bird feeders in his garden and binoculars for spotting birds on walks. He had a 'hog house' for the hedgehogs and used to go out, at the same time every evening, to check on them. He would interrupt phone calls to say, 'It's time to check the hogs!' He loved walking. He climbed the Munros, with my father and Uncle George and our cousin, David. He loved driving through the Highlands and the Lake District and gazing out at hills and rugged moors.

When Tom bought his first flat, it was on the edge of Ranmore Common, deep in the Surrey Hills. It's an 'area of outstanding natural beauty' and it *is* beautiful, a gentle, undulating landscape of hills and fields, dotted with hazel, hornbeam, sweet chestnut trees and oaks. Just a few minutes' drive away, it rises up to Box Hill, where Emma Woodhouse was unkind to Miss Bates and Mr Knightley told her it was 'badly done'. Jane Austen describes the view as 'sweet to the eye and the mind. English verdure, English culture, English comfort, seen under a sun bright, without being oppressive.' That's what Tom liked: English verdure, English culture and English comfort. He loved France, too, but after he lived there, he mostly loved it from afar. His bookshelves are full of French literature in French: Zola, Camus, Victor Hugo, François Mauriac, Flaubert, Stendhal, Gide. At the end of a long day, he'd relax with a glass of good red wine and one of the French masters, or one of his French thrillers, or Jane Austen, or one of his Scandi-noirs. It was what he needed after a day of hard, physical work.

It was after Tom bought his house, in a village near Dorking, that he decided to become a gardener. The stresses at work had boiled over, and he had had enough of office life. He was meticulous and efficient, but what he wasn't good at was office politics. When people didn't pull their weight, or spent hours chatting on the phone to friends, it unleashed a sense of injustice that turned into silent fury. When one colleague showed no signs of reforming, Tom stormed out.

It triggered a bout of depression and, in my mother, a weary sense of déjà vu. It was nearly three years since my father had died, eighteen months since I'd had finished my first bout of cancer treatment, and since my mother could, perhaps, have swapped that 'I am a Carer' card for one saying 'I am free!' My mother made the most of her freedom. She went on more courses, more holidays, more weekends away, sometimes with friends, sometimes with Tom, sometimes with me. She had hoped for a longer stretch unsullied by the physical or mental breakdowns of her adult offspring. When Tom walked out of his job, her heart started leaping and bucking. She was diagnosed with atrial fibrillation, which meant more trips to hospitals and more pills.

In time, my mother's heart calmed down and so did Tom. He started working as a freelance gardener, at first for my mother's friends and neighbours, and then for friends and neighbours of theirs. He loved the work, he loved not having a boss and his clients seemed to love him.

Like Caroline, he started almost every conversation with what he called 'the three magic words': How are you? It would irritate him when other people didn't.

We'd meet, with my mother, for Sunday roasts, at his house or my flat. We'd take it in turns to host Christmas. Sometimes, I did other things on Christmas Day and they'd both come up to mine on Boxing Day. All our trees looked the same. We all had white lights, straw stars and the little red woollen *tomtar*. We all had the Swedish straw goat under the tree. My mother hadn't expected to spend every Christmas with her single grown-up children, but when she walked in, with a big bag of presents for us both, she still managed to look as if her Christmas was complete.

Sometimes, Tom and I clashed. At a Mother's Day lunch at his house, we had a huge row about something in the news and Tom accused me of being a member of a sneering metropolitan elite. On that occasion, my mother backed him up and I had that feeling I'd often had as a child, of being the odd one out. We were, my mother always said, 'chalk and cheese', but we mostly rubbed along.

When she died, we stumbled over our tenses as we sat at the kitchen table in Nelson Gardens, eating pizza and drinking red wine. 'Mum has, I mean had . . . Mum does, I mean did.' It was like the collapse of the Roman Empire, this loss of our rock, our Empress, our scrupulously polite, diamond-strong tiger mum. I sorted out the funeral. Tom sorted out the house. He wanted to sort out the house. He said it was part of the process of letting her go. And then one day, in Rome, as I was standing outside Tom's first home and mine, or the house I think was our first home, he called to tell me it was done. The house was empty. The door had shut.

I had met my 'lovely bloke' in the nick of time. It didn't stop the pain, of course, but it helped. Tom was on his own. His grief was a cold, dark winter with blasts of sleet and sudden fog. He carried on gardening through that cold winter. He carried on seeing friends, and choosing wines for his wine group, and reading his French literature, and checking on his hedgehogs, and the storms started to abate and winter started to turn to spring.

It was spring when Anthony picked up the keys to his cottage. It didn't feel like spring. It felt like the apocalypse with squalls of driving rain. The previous owners took away four removal-van-fulls of stuff. We turned up in my Mazda MX-5 with an airbed, a duvet and a kettle. Once we had dumped them, we drove to IKEA in Milton Keynes, and bought some mugs and plates and pots and pans and had meatballs. I can't go to IKEA and not have meatballs. I have to raise a meatball to my mum. When we got back to the cottage, I managed to leave the keys on the kitchen table and then shut the front door. We had to smash a window to break back in.

Anthony had been living with me for nine months. I had been worried about sharing my space, after living on my own for more than twenty-five years, but we had both been surprised by how well it had gone. When his family home went on the market, we decided it would be fun to do that thing so many people dream of, and move between a cottage in the country that he would buy and my flat in town. We'd found something that looked perfect: a thatched house in a tiny village in Northamptonshire, with an inglenook and beams. The garden is full of ox-eye daisies, hollyhocks and roses. There are apple, pear and plum trees. There's a willow tree and a pond. We gaze out at fields dotted with sheep.

By the time Tom was due to visit, we had furniture and pictures on the walls. We were still spending most of our weekdays in London, but the house was beginning to feel like a home. It was early July and the garden was ablaze with colour. I couldn't wait to uncork the good wine I knew he would bring and for us to raise a glass, in sunshine, by the pond.

We were just about to eat, on the Friday night, when Auntie Rosemary rang. She had been talking to Tom on the phone, and the line had suddenly gone silent. It was, she said, probably nothing to worry about, but she thought she should let me know. I called Tom's landline. I called Tom's mobile. I sent him an email. I tried to find the number of some friends of my parents who didn't live all that far away. I tried to find the number of Stuart, Tom's best friend from the age of eleven. Stuart has lived in Wales for more than thirty years, but he and Tom are still best friends. I have never seen a friendship like it.

I didn't have Stuart's number, but sent him a message on Twitter. I called Auntie Rosemary and asked her if she thought I should call an ambulance. She used to be a nurse, so when she said yes, my stomach lurched. I called 999. I explained the situation, but the operator said they wouldn't send an ambulance. I called the police and begged them to send someone round. Anthony called a local cab company and asked them to go to Tom's house. My phone rang. It was Stuart. By incredible coincidence, he was in Guildford, having dinner with his son. Mathew is also Tom's godson. Stuart said they would get straight into a cab.

The cab driver Anthony had called, called back. He had got to the house and had no response. He told us that a neighbour had got a ladder and was climbing in through a window. Another neighbour called to say an ambulance had just pulled up.

I was shaking as Anthony reversed the car out of his drive. We were on the M1 when Stuart called to say he and Mathew had arrived at Tom's house. He said the paramedics were inside, and they were 'working on' Tom. Twenty minutes later, he called back. 'I'm sorry,' he said. 'I'm so, so sorry.'

It took two hours to get to Tom's house. There was a paramedic waiting in a van at the end of his road. He told me that he was leaving now, but the police would be there soon.

The front door was open. Tom was lying on the floor. I

lay down next to him and wrapped my arms around him, and thought I would die of grief.

No one tells you about the admin. When you just want to crawl under a rock and sleep for a hundred years, you can't because there's so much admin. First, you have to tell everyone. I searched the house, but I couldn't find Tom's address book. I found his phone, which wasn't a smartphone and didn't have any of his contacts locked in it. I found a card index box of gardening clients but didn't know which of them were current. I wrote to all of them. I asked his friends to help me track down other friends. Tom didn't use social media. He scorned these scourges of decline. It didn't help. I used all my journalistic skills, and Facebook and LinkedIn, to try to find the people who needed to know. Every time I heard the fresh anguish in a fresh voice, it felt like an electric shock. Yes, it has happened, it's true.

You can't organise a funeral without a post-mortem, or at least not when someone dies out of the blue. So you wait. You try to conduct a symphony – of friends, and relatives, and caterers, and funeral directors, and order of service sheets, and flowers, and a crematorium that is, unfortunately, currently being renovated – but without the score that will let the orchestra play. When the score, or rather email, came, it said that Tom had died of a heart attack. His blood flow, his life flow, had been suddenly cut off.

The night before I registered his death, I drove down to his house. I had been there so many times, but I couldn't find it. I drove up and down the roads near his cul-de-sac and when I finally opened the front door, I discovered a pile of cards addressed to me. I read them on the bed in his spare room and that night I didn't sleep at all. In the morning, as I waited for my appointment at the registry office, I stared at the notices on the wall. There was a photo of Britt Ekland and Peter Sellers, who got married there in 1964. It was the year we moved to Guildford, the year of the grinning baby in the cine films, plopped in the middle of the lawn. When my name was called, I got ten copies of the death certificate and walked back to my car down steps strewn with confetti.

When I went to the bank to close Tom's account, I found I had lost my glasses. I had to borrow the bank clerk's glasses to try to read the forms. On the drop-down menu, under 'relationship to customer', it offered 'children, grandchildren or great-grandchildren'. There was no option for a sibling. The clerk went off to check and came back with a senior manager who went through the process again. The system was clear. It did not allow for the death of a childless, spouse-less sibling. It was a breach of the norm.

I spent a week at Tom's house, going through his papers and fixing the final details of his funeral. Stuart drove from Wales one day with boxes of wine for the wake. We went to a pub opposite Box Hill and sat in the garden and talked about Tom. Stuart told me that Tom's sitting room was his 'sanctuary'. When he turned up, Tom would open the front door, raise his arms high like a saint about to give a blessing, and yell, 'Fantastic to see you!' He would pour Stuart a glass of wine, show him to the black leather armchair they both called 'the pilot's chair' and say, 'Let's plug you in.' Stuart reminded me about some of Tom's quirks: how he called our father 'the Big Chief' and used to salute when he saw a white Nissan (he called his own white Nissan 'White Knight') and, in tribute to my mother's car, when he saw a blue Nissan Note. He reminded me that Tom always cheered when he saw an Eddie Stobart lorry, which explains the Eddie Stobart models on the windowsill in his spare room. He reminded me that Tom was always thrilled when it was 21 degrees because that was our father's favourite temperature.

When Stuart left, to drive back to Wales, I looked through more photos. The next thing I knew, I was lying on the kitchen floor. It was only when I had crawled up to bed that I realised I had fainted. I woke with a pounding headache and a sore back. I wasn't sure I could move. I phoned my doctor's surgery and a locum called back and told me that I had probably concussed myself. If I started vomiting, he said, I should go to A & E. But I couldn't go to A & E. I couldn't even get to the car to drive to get some painkillers. In the end, I got some from Tom's next-door neighbours. I knew I had to keep going for six more days. There could be knocks, there could be floods, there could be storms, there could be plagues, but there was one day in the whole of my life that nothing in the world would make me miss.

The night before Tom's funeral, I walked across the fields from Anthony's house and howled like a dog. I howled at the sheep. I howled at the trees. I howled at the clouds in the sky. I thought my howls would be too much for a human to hear. I thought that once I started howling I might not be able to stop.

I managed not to howl when I saw the hearse draw up, and when I caught my first glimpse of the coffin. I had wanted it to be beech, like Mum's, like Dad's, like Caroline's, but the funeral director had called me to say that seven-foot coffins only came in rosewood. And so it was dark red, the colour of the cottage in Sweden, and covered, or partially covered, with roses, lisianthus, alstroemeria, eryngium and veronica, a mix of pink, lilac, cream and woody blue flowers the florists called a 'woodland spray'. I followed the coffin and the vicar into the chapel as the choir, in the recording of the St John Passion I had picked, sang the words that are meant to soothe: 'Sleep well, and rest in God's safekeeping, who makes an end of all our weeping.' Well, it's a nice thought.

The vicar, Robert Cotton, who had buried Caroline, Dad and Mum, welcomed us with the gentle warmth he had brought to his pastoral care of both my parents through so many of their woes. When I arranged my mother's funeral, he told me that he and my father often talked about novels they had read. He said that my father was the only other person he had met who had read a book called *The Decipherment of Linear B*.

We sang 'The Lord's My Shepherd' and then I went up to the lectern to speak. My voice sounded strange, but I managed to read out what I had written. I talked about Tom's love of sport, and birds, and nature, and mountains. I mentioned that I'd found a list among his papers of all the Munros he had climbed. Fifty-nine. More than one for every year of his life. I talked about how much he loved his house in Dukes Ride, but how he never came to terms with the lack of an apostrophe. I said that Stuart had told me, over our pub supper facing Box Hill, that Tom would have been shocked by my incorrect use of the word 'decimate'. And that he loved correcting Dad, with his Cambridge double first.

I talked about the pleasure he took in golf, in fine wine, in Dickens, in soul, in classical music, in collecting stamps, in killer sudoku and in putting money on the horses. I said that when Caroline was at her lowest, he was the only one who could make her laugh. I said that when my book had come out, the year before, he had arrived at the launch before me. He had been outside in his anorak, waiting for the door to be unlocked.

Mathew read from I Corinthians 13. 'Love is patient, love is kind. It does not envy. It does not boast, it is not proud.'

Stuart spoke, without notes. He told touching, funny

stories about Tom, including the time he was with Stuart in an Indian restaurant in Stuart's home town. A bunch of drunk squaddies were doing press-ups by the bar and ignoring the proprietor's polite requests to stop. Tom strode over, clapped his hands and said, 'Right, lads, time to go home.' It was the only time, Stuart said, that he ever saw Tom use his height to intimidate. They looked up at the giant looming over them, saluted Tom and left.

Stuart said that Tom couldn't care less about job titles or the conventional marks of success. He said he referred to himself as 'a jobbing gardener', and called me 'the big hitter'. I had no idea. But I was more shocked by the next thing he said. 'Christina,' he said, and he looked right at me. 'Tom was very proud of you.'

At the wake, back at the Tithe Barn at Loseley, people kept coming up to me: friends of Tom from golf, from his wine group, from his pension jobs, from university, from his gardening jobs, from school. They said the things they had said in the cards they had sent me: that he was admired for his decency, loved for his kindness and adored for his wit. One man told me about something that had happened when they worked together. A 'big cheese' had come down from head office and given them all a 'dressing-down'. Afterwards, there had been silence and then Tom had spoken up. Tom told the man that that was 'no way to speak to his staff'. The man had apologised and blushed. When the 'big cheese' left, his colleagues cheered.

Tom hated confrontation. He would walk away from a job in order to avoid an argument. He wrote 'Dear John' letters to gardening clients when he didn't like their tone. I was so pleased that he had stood up for his colleagues. I wanted to tell him that. I wanted to tell him that so many people had turned up to say goodbye to him, and the sun was shining, and the grounds of Loseley looked 'sweet to the eye and the mind'. I wanted to tell him that it was 24 degrees centigrade. Not the perfect 21, but not far off.

Chapter 30

Paradiso

I still can't listen to Tom's music. He had a magnificent collection of LPs. I look at them from time to time, those cardboard sleeves with their seventies typefaces, smiling faces and satin suits. He had CDs, too, which was about as modern as he was going to get, but it was the LPs he loved: the Commodores, Earth, Wind & Fire, Joan Armatrading, Marvin Gaye. From his early teens, Tom was our own king of soul, blasting out the heart-kicking rhythms of Motown and the spine-tingling strains of the blues. He became my soul consultant, and for Christmas he'd often give me a selection of CDs: Barry White, in top walrus-of-lurve form, Randy Crawford gloating about her 'secret combination', Aretha Franklin, in long, sparkly earrings, letting the world know she was 'So Damn Happy'.

When Tom came to stay with me, after leaving his last pensions job, he said he'd still like to have a family. He had a Pied Piper's gift with children. They would gaze in awe at the giant in their midst and soon they'd be clambering on him or tugging his hand. The trouble was that to get a family, you had to find someone to help you produce one. Tom, like me, was keen on the idea, but bad at the practice. Like me, he had been burned. Like me, he got into the habit of being on his own. And he liked it. He liked getting back from work, having 'a tub' – he didn't see the need for futuristic quirks like showers – stretching out on his sofa, pouring a glass of wine, lighting a cigarette (the first of the four he would allow himself a day) and letting Barry, Randy, Marvin or Aretha soothe his soul.

The LPs are now in Anthony's dining room, next to the music system Tom had only recently bought. I found the receipt in his study. It was his present to himself when he sold our mother's house. As a gardener, Tom earned way below the average salary. He rarely bought new clothes. He hardly ever went out for meals. He bought good wine, but would rarely drink more than a couple of glasses. Like my mother, like my father, he savoured his pleasures. In his British Birds calendar, on his study wall, I found an entry that reminded me of my parents' delight on that Thomas Cook coach tour of Italy when I was nineteen. 'Marvellous holiday,' he has written of a solo minibreak, just a few weeks before he was due to come and see us. 'Coffee in sun at Membury, walk at Ross. Drive to Merthyr. Premier Inn great. Drive to Brecon. Super McDonald's.'

* * *

I haven't taken all that much from his house. I don't have the space for it. I've taken some of the old pictures, from Bangkok and Rome. I've taken some of the ornaments: the ebony elephants from Sri Lanka, the silver bowls and trinkets from Bangkok, some of my mother's blue and white china vases, a couple of rugs. I've taken the silver coffee pot, sugar bowl and milk jug that belonged to my Swedish great-aunt Agnes. She never had hot water in the house she shared with her brother, Arthur, but the silver was polished for her coffee parties, and the tablecloths were crisp and clean. And I've taken Tom's Christmas decorations, which are now mixed with my mother's. I could practically start a Swedish Christmas market.

Anthony helped me with Tom's house. He scrubbed and cleaned and tidied up the garden and painted the front door. He helped me carry box after box into the garage. I've left the furniture and just enough personal stuff for it to look lived in. You want a house to look lived in even when it isn't. When a couple of offers fell through, we spent a weekend painting. Tom had spent weeks choosing paint colours to brighten the place up: lilac for the kitchen, electric blue for the bathroom, maroon for the downstairs loo and terracotta for the hall. Bright, certainly, but too bright for most tastes, and so we tried to calm it down. When the house is sold, I'll need to get someone to clear it, and the garage. The garage is full of pictures, ornaments, framed photos, files, CDs, videos and books belonging to my parents and Caroline as well as Tom. I don't want to think about what it will be like to throw it all out.

What I can't throw out are the photo albums, literally scores of photo albums, and the letters and diaries and box files and cards. Anthony has let me store some on his bookshelves and in his garage. I've got piles stuffed under the bookshelves in my study in my flat. It's the archive of my family, but I feel as though curating it would be a lifetime's work.

Tom didn't have a will. We both confessed to each other last year that we had been meaning to do one for years. When I went into hospital for my big operation ten years ago, I took one into hospital that I'd bought online. I asked the ward manager if she would sign it, but she said she couldn't, so the will wasn't valid. I'd put it off for the reasons I've always put it off. I don't know who to leave my stuff to. I don't mean my actual stuff: my books and diaries and papers and files and furniture and crockery and clothes. I'm pretty sure no one will want that. I mean my 'assets', my flat, my tiny flat in Italy, what there is of my pension. When I did that will, I left almost everything to a charity that was later found to be corrupt. Should I leave it all to a charity whose CEO earns more than anyone I know? Should I leave it to my friends? I need a deadline, I suppose, but deadlines, as I've learnt, can come too late.

In one of the boxes I dumped in Anthony's garage, I found a pile of very old photos. There's one of Mormor, my mother's mother, with her mother, Alida, her father,

Alfred, and her three sisters and two brothers. Mormor, who was christened Ingeborg Hildegard but usually called Bojan, is wearing a dark dress with a huge lacy collar. Her hair is in bunches and she looks about four. The photo must have been taken in about 1906. It makes me think of Caroline's photos of the Romanovs. My great-uncle Arthur even looks a bit like the Tsarevich in his little sailor suit. Their father, Alfred, looks fierce. There's no ghost of a smile as they all stare out at the camera. It makes me wonder what hopes and dreams lie behind those glassy eyes.

I have Alida's engagement brooch. It looks to me like two ornamental daggers joined with a ribbon studded with tiny pearls. Alida sailed out to America to join Alfred when she was eighteen. He had gone in search of work. They married in Pennsylvania and had three children before deciding to go back to Halmstad. Agnes was just three weeks old when she sailed back. She was given the middle name Sjöflora, which means Seaflower. Seven years later, Alfred died of kidney failure. He was dead by the time the photo was taken, but my great-grandmother had his portrait pasted in. She kept the family going by running a small grocery shop and letting out rooms.

Three of Mormor's siblings never married. Arthur, a cobbler, lived in the family home with Agnes until he died. Meri became a teacher. When Arthur died, they found a stash of brand-new clothes in a storeroom. His secret dream had been to open a shop. Ingeborg did work in a shop, but her dream was to find love, and she did. She and Folke, my mother's father, were in love until he died. There's a photo of them at the Berlin Olympics in 1936. They're standing in front of a giant swastika, smiling and holding hands. History is what we live through and often don't notice. On my last trip to Sweden with my mother, one of her childhood friends showed me a book about Nazis who had lovely holidays on the beach near our cottage.

As I gaze at the photo of Alida and her children, I can't help wondering what she wanted for them, and if they made her proud. Did she mind that three of them didn't have children? Was that a mark of failure or success? My mother once told me that her other grandmother, Anna, had wrapped her arms around one of the silver birches in her garden and wept because at forty-four, and after eight children, she was pregnant and didn't want to have another child. She and her husband, Ivar, rented a farm at Söndrum, by the church where my parents got married.

There are old photos of my father's family, too, though some of the oldest are photocopies. Here's Mama May, a glamorous flapper in the twenties. Here's Dada William, dashing in tweed plus fours. May was thrilled to be marrying a doctor. Her father was a joiner, from a line of farm labourers. William's father was a headmaster, from a line of factory workers and miners. Two of his relatives died in the Motherwell poorhouse. Many of them were Christian Brethren and the ones in the photos look grim. But Agnes and Arthur look grim in those early photos, and they were as sweet as the cakes they laid out for us and the goody bags they spent all year saving up for. If they were in any way dissatisfied with their lot, they certainly didn't show it.

On Tom's birthday, I had planned to go to Tom's wine group. Stuart had bought some of the wines Tom had selected for a tasting he'd hosted at Stuart's law firm, which had, Stuart said, 'gone down a storm'. We were going to make it a celebration. We had both done far too much weeping in the months since Tom died and we wanted, we needed, a celebration. Two nights before, I swallowed a fish bone that stuck in my throat and wondered if I'd need to go to A & E. I decided not to, but in the night I got up to get some water, bent over to pick something up, bashed my eye on a chair and thought I had blinded myself. I spent seven hours yelping in pain at two different hospitals and had to cancel everything for a week.

I'd planned to have a party for my birthday two months earlier, but got a vomiting virus and had to cancel that too. I still have the salmon in the freezer. I was disappointed, not just because I love parties, but because parties, for me, are a sacred rite. I had a party the year I got cancer. I had a party the second time I got cancer. I had a party for my fiftieth, which was the year I lost my job. Parties, for me, are a way of saying: you can knock me down, but you can't knock me out. Parties, for me, are a way of saying: I choose life.

And then the pandemic hit and no one was having parties, or at least not if they weren't sociopaths with a secret urge to kill. Once, on a Zoom call, someone said, 'If your number's up, your number's up.' I had to fight the urge to scream: NO, YOU FUCKING MORON! You play Russian roulette if you want to, I'll stay at home, thanks. I'll lock myself up, I'll lock Anthony up, I'll lock everyone I love up until there's a vaccine, because death is not a fucking game.

I had to delay Tom's interment. Then a second lockdown was announced, and I wasn't sure if I'd be able to go ahead. The first reports said 'close family only', which would have meant Stuart and Mathew couldn't come. When the rules were published, it was clear that they could, but that we wouldn't be able to have lunch together afterwards, since all pubs and restaurants would be closed. It was November. The weather forecast was bad. I thought we'd be standing by the grave in icy rain. The night before, I barely slept.

It was a shock to see the grave with a gaping hole. At first, I was worried that it wasn't big enough, but Anthony measured the casket and the hole and it – just – was. I put red roses in the vase on the headstone. They covered the gap where Tom's name will go. There won't be enough space for mine.

When I was going through some papers, I found the tribute Tom wrote for our mother's interment. 'Mum and Dad bought this plot on my 24th birthday,' he said, 'but it only came with a fifty-year lease. So if I manage to survive to age seventy-four, I hope I will have sufficient savings left to buy an extension.' He managed another eighteen months, and I have to admit I'm torn. Tom often went to put flowers on the grave. He went on birthdays and anniversaries, and when he just wanted to feel close to the people he loved most. On his desk, I found a letter he'd recently sent to the management of Brookwood Cemetery complaining that someone had disturbed his peace by chatting on their mobile phone.

I hardly ever go to the grave. I probably should, but I don't. For me, the grave screams: these people you loved are dead. I know it sounds ridiculous, but I don't want to be reminded. In my head, I like to keep them alive. And who will visit it after I've gone? I don't even know whether to get myself put in it. Someone would have to get a bigger headstone and start all over again.

The whole thing makes me feel exhausted. I know what the admin's like and don't want to inflict it on anyone else. But I think I know what my family would have wanted and so I'll extend the lease.

When I looked up, and saw Stuart and Mathew strolling from their car, I wanted to hug them, but I couldn't. A few minutes later, Robert, the vicar, turned up. His smile was so warm I wanted to hug him, too. The ceremony was short and sweet. I had been dreading it, but it really was sweet. I spoke briefly, Stuart spoke briefly and Mathew spoke after him. We all blinked away tears, but we all smiled as Robert talked about Tom's sense of humour and the funeral he said he would never forget. Anthony read from 1 Corinthians 13. We sang a hymn, said the Lord's Prayer and each put a rose on the casket in the hole. I told Tom, or perhaps the casket, that the hedgehogs in his garden had had babies, and his next-door neighbours were giving them milk.

And then, sitting at a table among the silver birches, we had the most wonderful picnic of my life. Anthony had made smoked salmon sandwiches. He had been up till 1 a.m. making millionaire's shortbread. We drank Sancerre, which was one of Tom's favourite wines. We had coffee and cake, because my mother thought you should always have coffee and cake, and because millionaire's shortbread was her morning-coffee nibble of choice. The sun came out. On a November day in England, during a pandemic, in a section of a cemetery that really does feel like Sweden, the sun shone and the sky was blue.

Six weeks later, and a week before Christmas, we got married. We had planned to do it on my mother's birthday, three days after I buried Tom. I really wanted to get married on her birthday. It felt like a way of telling her that one of her children had finally done one of the things she desperately wanted us to do. But all weddings were cancelled during lockdown, even weddings with only two guests.

Anthony had been married for thirty years and didn't want to get married again. I had thought I was too much of a commitment-phobe to marry anyone, and anyway marriage wasn't on offer. But then we hatched a dream and hit a hitch. We were in Italy, the summer of the pandemic. We had driven through France, to avoid getting on a plane. As soon as I got to my flat, I felt I could breathe out again. Italy makes me happy. Even when the world seems to be ending, even when my sky has fallen, Italy makes me happy. When I'm there, I want to share this joy with everyone I care about. That's a challenge in a one-bedroom flat.

Anthony loves Italy, too. Two days before we left, he suggested we join forces to get something bigger, a place we could invite people to, a place where we could sip delicious wine and eat delicious food and drink in the beauty and soak up the sunshine with people who make life better.

He was the one who spotted the ad for part of an Umbrian farmhouse, with spectacular views and a rock-bottom price. The proceeds of my Tuscan flat should just about cover my half of it, though clearly it would be better if I had sold it first. Perhaps it's an umbilical thing, perhaps it's *nostalgia* for the land of my birth, but Italy sweeps me off my feet and out of my senses. I made an offer on my Tuscan flat without seeing it. We made an offer on the Umbrian farmhouse on the way home. It's called Paradiso. It's actually called Paradiso. How can you not want a place called Paradiso? And it's twenty-five minutes from Arezzo, the golden city on a hill where God, or perhaps Bev, told me I wasn't allowed to live.

It was when we got back that we realised that owning a

property jointly in Italy, and more particularly owning just half of it when your co-owner is not immortal, can risk turning your little slice of paradise into an Italian version of *Bleak House*. The solution was clear, but unromantic, and I didn't want to be the one to say it. We sat on the sofa. We stared at our iPads. 'So,' said Anthony after an awkward pause, 'how would you feel about marrying me?'

Until he said it, I wasn't sure. I thought I should be wanting to do somersaults, but felt strangely calm. 'I think,' I said, 'I would feel fine.' I heard the word and thought it sounded wrong. Then I felt a ripple of something running through me and realised it was pure, piercing, piquant joy. 'Yes,' I said and I wanted to shout it. 'Yes, the answer's yes!'

It's not the wedding my mother would have planned for me: a fifteen-minute ceremony in an ugly council building, with two guests who arrived in masks. A 'socially distanced' lunch for four in an empty hotel restaurant after a mad dash through the rain. But who cares about the building or the weather or the masks? Val and Jon had brought us a perfect, tiny wedding cake, decorated with chocolate dividers and a chocolate pen. And I told my darling that I took him as my wedded husband and he told me that he took me as his wedded wife. We didn't promise to honour, obey or stick with each other through sickness, misery or passive aggression. I can't promise anyone that, and nor can he, but I do know that I can't imagine finding anyone I want to be with more.

When I got cancer, I thought I'd die without finding love. I've had five and a half years of love I never thought I'd have. I've had ten years of life I never thought I'd have. I've had eighteen, in fact, since I first had cancer at thirty-nine. I've just turned fifty-seven. The age Tom was when he died. I hope I last a lot longer, but I've already won the lottery. My cup runneth over. I mean it. My cup runneth over. When the time comes, someone will have to wrest it out of my hands.

And did you get what you wanted from this life? That's the question Raymond Carver asks in his poem 'Late Fragment', the one I read at Caroline's funeral and standing by Tom's casket at the grave. I can't answer for anyone else, but I can make some guesses. My parents both wanted to find someone wonderful to share their life with. My father's last card to my mother was addressed to 'my dearest wife and heartbreakingly lovely Valentine'. In one of her last cards to him, she thanks her 'wonderful, kind, much-loved and best companion'. In another, she says simply: 'I adore you.' They had this for nearly fifty years.

They wanted children who would value what they valued, who would call a friend in trouble, help a neighbour with their shopping, and understand the power of the 'three magic words'. They wanted children who could find joy in a crocus or a candle or a cup of coffee or a caramel slice. They wanted children who understood that problems come and problems go, but there are always new things to see and learn and taste and smell in our big, bright, beautiful world.

I think my parents got what they wanted. There were other things they wanted, of course, but none of us gets everything we want. They got plenty. We got plenty. And most of all, what we got was love.

If I speak in the tongues of men or of angels, but do not have love, I am only a resounding gong. I can't quite believe now that I once spoke in tongues. What a waste of time and adolescence and breath. But it's the rest of the verse that matters. Love is patient, love is kind. It does not envy, it does not boast, it is not proud. It is not self-seeking. It always perseveres.

That's my family. The sweet, kind, modest, witty, slightly eccentric, ever-persevering Pattersons. Mum, Dad, Caroline, Tom, I am so damn proud of you. I hope I can live up to you. And I am so damn happy to tell you that I got married in a cut-price navy dress.

Acknowledgements

Anyone close to me knows that I've wanted to write a version of this story for many years. When I finally did, it was a sprint, but that was after quite a few false starts. This time round, my friends were spared the agonised conversations and the sheaves of A4 with requests for feedback. They had certainly earned the break.

It was Sophie Lambert, my wonderful agent, who held my hand when my heart was broken and led me through the fog to the version of the story I finally told. I cannot thank her enough for her rigour, nous and faith.

I will never forget my first meeting by Zoom (which was still quite a novelty) with Imogen Taylor from Tinder Press. I was so overwhelmed by her kind words that I went for a celebratory run, something I've never done before or since. Imogen has been the perfect editor, sensitive, thoughtful and wise. I would also like to thank her colleagues, Amy Perkins, Rosie Margesson and Yeti Lambregts.

I would like to thank my dear friends Helen Chaloner, Ian Cowmeadow, Maura Dooley, Jane Feaver, Jo Minogue and Louise Murray for ploughing through a prehistoric version of this story and saving me from the ignominy of trying to get it published.

I would like to thank David Hunter for the title.

I would like to thank Arifa Akbar, Rachel Alexander, Nick Bowering, Katherine Butler, Ros Cary, Patsy Collman, Anne Elletson, Heather and Iain Fairbairn, Lavinia Greenlaw, Rob Jackson, Emma Joseph, Richard Kelly, Mimi Khalvati, Jon and Val Mahoney, Tony Mason, Rosamund McCarthy, Stefano Nappo, Tina Radziszewicz, Lisa Roberts, Norbert and Josephine Schembri, Julia Stuart, Randall Wright and Robin Wilson for love, laughter, company, conversation, cooking and crisps.

I would like to thank Louise Bissell, Stacey Cartwright, Caroline Kinsey, Caroline Liberson, Sarah Newman, Monique Pulsford, Karen Walker and Linda Walz for friendship in childhood – and now.

I would like to thank Stuart and Mathew Brothers for rock-solid support when my sky (and a big part of theirs) had fallen.

I would like to thank Anthony Charnley for being my pot of gold.